A Brief History of the Spanish L

A Brief History of the
Spanish Language *Second Edition*

DAVID A. PHARIES

The University of Chicago Press ∗ CHICAGO AND LONDON

DAVID A. PHARIES is associate dean for humanities and professor
of Spanish at the University of Florida. He is editor in chief of the
sixth edition of the *University of Chicago Spanish–English Dictionary /
Diccionario Universidad de Chicago inglés–español.*

The University of Chicago Press, Chicago 60637
The University of Chicago Press, Ltd., London
© 2007, 2015 by David A. Pharies
All rights reserved. Published 2015.
Printed in the United States of America

24 23 22 21 20 19 18 17 16 15   1 2 3 4 5

ISBN-13: 978-0-226-13394-2 (paper)
ISBN-13: 978-0-226-13413-0 (e-book)
DOI: 10.7208/chicago/9780226134130.001.0001

Library of Congress Cataloging-in-Publication Data

Pharies, David A., author.
    A brief history of the Spanish language / David A. Pharies. — Second
edition.
        pages ; cm
    Includes bibliographical references and index.
    Simultaneously published in Spanish under title: Breve historia de la
lengua española.
    ISBN 978-0-226-13394-2 (pbk. : alk. paper) —
ISBN 978-0-226-13413-0 (e-book) 1. Spanish language—History.
I. Title.
PC4075.P48 2015
460'.9—dc23

                                                        2015022546

♾ This paper meets the requirements of ANSI/NISO Z39.48-1992
(Permanence of Paper).

Contents

Author's Note

The following typographical conventions are used in this book.

- **Boldface** type is used to mark the first significant use of terms included in the Glossary of Linguistic Terms: "**anthroponyms** or personal names."
- *Italic* type indicates a linguistic element cited as such: "Why do some people say *tú* and others *vos*?"
- Single quotes (' ') indicate the meanings (or English equivalents) of words: "*falda* 'skirt.'"
- A single asterisk (*) marks a reconstructed form, i.e., a form that must have existed but is not documented: "Late Lat. *palumba* > */pa 'lom ma/ > paloma*."
- A double asterisk (**) marks an alternative form that never existed: "*cēdunt* > **cedon*."
- A triple asterisk (***) marks forms that are considered incorrect: "****le lo doy* 'se lo doy.'"
- "*x > y*" means that *x* changes to *y* over time; "*x < y*" means that *x* is a descendant of *y*.
- "*x → y*" means that *x* changes its meaning to *y* or adds an additional meaning *y*; also, *x* produces a derivative *y*.

Preface

The history of a language can be understood as the combination of its internal history and external history.

The internal history of a language includes all events of a linguistic nature, such as phonological, grammatical, and **lexical** changes. Among the questions it addresses are these: What changes have occurred in the language's inventory of sounds over time? What grammatical structures have been lost, and what other structures have arisen to replace them? What are the most important sources of new words, and to what extent have other words become obsolete?

External history is the history of the people or peoples who speak the language, though naturally a language history focuses principally on the events that have had linguistic repercussions. Thus external history addresses questions such as the following: What peoples spoke the language originally? What other peoples adopted the language and under what circumstances? What invasions, migrations, and other events have contributed to the current geographic and demographic distribution of the language? What cultural developments have affected the evolution of the language?

Ideally we would like to find one-to-one correspondences between these two perspectives—the internal and the external—and in fact we recognize three different types of correspondences, however general in nature. First, it is unquestionable that events such as the Roman and Muslim invasions of the Iberian Peninsula are crucial in its linguistic history. Second, it is also undeniable that cultural movements such as the Renaissance and the technological revolution of the twentieth and twenty-first centuries have fostered the acceptance of large numbers of **neologisms** into Castilian, mostly learned Latin words during the Renaissance and **Anglicisms**

in recent decades. Finally, it seems probable that times of accelerated change correspond with the many periods of accommodation
among linguistic varieties (also called periods of **koineization**) that
characterize the history of Spanish.

The language whose story is being told in this book is Spanish—
also called Castilian—which evolved from the **spoken Latin** brought
by the invading Roman forces, beginning in 218 BC, to the Iberian
Peninsula, where it established itself as the language of the land before the beginning of the Christian era. With the disintegration of
the Roman Empire, this linguistic community experienced a series
of foreign invasions that put the future of its language in jeopardy.
However, it eventually recovered its vitality, and its descendants, the
Ibero-**Romance languages**, achieved dominance on the Peninsula.
One of these, Spanish, is now an official language in twenty-one
countries, with a total of more than four hundred million speakers
worldwide.

As its title indicates, this work's account of the history of Spanish
is meant to be brief, a quality that is desirable for several reasons.
First, an accessible presentation with a minimum of technical jargon
will appeal to the many people who, although sincerely interested
in Spanish and its history, have been intimidated by traditional histories such as Rafael Lapesa's 1981 *Historia de la lengua española*,
with its 690 pages. Second, specialists in the field have long felt the
need for a work that is appropriate to the conditions and needs of a
one-semester college course on the history of Spanish. Finally, in se-
lecting the materials and themes for this *Brief History* I have striven
to limit the scope of the work to topics of greatest importance and
interest, so that the text fulfills the goal of answering the most basic
questions that Spanish speakers tend to ask, such as these: How did
the *th* sound develop in Castilian, and why is it not found in the
other varieties of the language? Why does the singular of *el agua*
'the water' appear to be masculine, while the plural, *las aguas*, is
clearly feminine? Why does Spanish grammar require *se lo mandé*
'I sent it to him' instead of ***le lo mandé*, as one would suppose?
Why do some speakers of Spanish say *le veo* 'I see him' while others
say *lo veo*? How do the principal varieties of Spanish differ among
themselves, and to what causes are these differences attributable? In

other words, the work is brief because an effort has been made to concentrate attention on the most intriguing aspects of the history of Spanish. This strategy avoids the mistake that has been made by the authors of many comparable works, which is to overwhelm beginners with details and technical explanations that are inappropriate for an introductory work. The goal of *Brief History* is to awaken readers' interest in this material and to offer them background material sufficient to enable them, should they wish, to delve deeper into the subject through further study.

At the same time, readers will see that despite being introductory and brief, this book is not lacking in academic rigor. Regarding the level of difficulty of the presentation, it should be pointed out that the nucleus formed by chapters 5, 6, and 7—which trace the principal changes through which spoken Latin is transformed first into Medieval Castilian and finally into Modern Spanish—presupposes a knowledge of basic linguistic concepts. In order to attenuate this difficulty, the text has been supplemented through the inclusion of explanatory notes, a glossary of linguistic terms, an appendix in which the basic concepts of Spanish phonetics and **phonology** are outlined, and a general index of subjects. Still, it is inevitable that readers who already have a broad acquaintance with linguistic concepts will derive the greatest value from this book.

Brief History is notable for the diversity of its content. Among the topics treated here that are often omitted from similar works are the nature of linguistic change, a complete linguistic genealogy of Spanish, a description of the linguistic components of Classical Latin, the basic principles of etymology, and the history of the Spanish language outside the Iberian Peninsula. The work is also unusual for the balance that has been achieved between aspects of internal and external history, and for the importance that has been accorded to **syntactic** evolution, an aspect that is often given short shrift in comparable works.

Why Study the History of Spanish?

The history of the Spanish language is a part of the history of Spain and Spanish America. The events that make up the history of the

Iberian Peninsula—settlements, migrations, invasions, wars, and political upheaval—have shaped the history of the Spanish language. The Roman invasion together with the Muslim invasion and the subsequent Reconquest of the Peninsula are most fundamental in this respect, but other events have also been decisive, such as the cultural movements called Renaissance and Enlightenment and the "discovery" of America. All of these events are reflected in the Spanish language: Without the Roman invasion, the language of Iberia might still be Iberian, or perhaps Visigothic or Arabic. Without the Muslim invasion and the Reconquest, it is doubtful that Modern Spanish would be based on the Castilian **variety** or **dialect**, and without Spanish colonial activity, Spanish would be spoken today on the Iberian Peninsula only.

The history of Spanish is a laboratory for historical linguistics. Modern Spanish, like the other Romance languages, offers the possibility of comparing its current parameters with those of its two-thousand-year-old ancestor. In this respect, it represents a valuable object of study for historical linguists, whose goal is precisely to discover the principles that govern language change.

The history of Spanish provides explanations for some of the language's most interesting eccentricities. Several of these were mentioned above, but others can be added. Why, for example, do some people use *tú* as a form of familiar address while others use *vos*? Why do some use *vosotros* as a second-person plural pronoun while others use *ustedes*? Why does Spanish have two forms for the imperfect subjunctive, as exemplified in *hablara* and *hablase* (both forms of *hablar* 'to speak')? What verb forms are used in the proverb *adonde fueres, haz como vieres* ('when in Rome, do as the Romans do')? When did authors stop writing *miráronse en el espejo* and begin writing *se miraron en el espejo* 'they looked at themselves in the mirror'? What is the historical relation between the passive constructions *fueron eliminados* and *se eliminaron*?

The many people who truly love the Spanish language do not ask themselves why it is worthwhile to study its history. They want to know the origins of its words and what languages have contributed to its vocabulary. They are interested in the processes through which new words have been formed and continue to be formed in the language. They are curious about how the Castilians at the court of Alfonso X expressed themselves, as well as those of the Golden Age. They want to be able to read and truly understand the immortal works of Spanish literature, such as the *Poema del Cid*, *La Celestina*, and *El ingenioso hidalgo don Quijote de la Mancha*. Finally, they want to understand the linguistic processes that contributed to the formation of the American varieties of Spanish. Hopefully this book will serve these people as a faithful guide on this grand journey of discovery.

What's New in the Second Edition

Readers who are familiar with the first edition will notice a series of additions and enhancements in this second edition. Most significantly, the content of the book has been updated to reflect the theoretical and philological achievements of the last decade of scholarship. This is most evident in the introduction or revision of subsections referring to koineization, the concept of linguistic change, the re-Latinization of the Spanish vocabulary, grammaticalization, and the transition between Latin and Romance vernacular. The presentation of phonological changes has been enhanced both by combining the discussions of vocalic and consonantal changes and by following more closely the norms of the International Phonetic Alphabet. This new edition also reflects much more than the first the rich and abundant resources offered by the Internet, perhaps most clearly in the geographic, demographic, and dialectal data provided. Finally, an effort has been made to enhance chapter questions by making them more practical, hence more useful for review and self-evaluation.

Acknowledgments

Needless to say, this is not a work of original research but rather of compilation and dissemination. The goal has been to produce a clear and precise synthesis of the material, making it accessible not only to students of Spanish but also to the many people who love the Spanish language and want to know more about it. In this respect, I would like to acknowledge the many scholars whose names appear in the notes and the list of works cited, as the task of writing this book would not have been possible without their contributions. I am pleased also to express my gratitude to the many people who helped me directly in the preparation of this second edition of *Brief History*. A crucial role was played by Prof. Julián Méndez Dosuna of the University of Salamanca, who accepted the challenge of editing the original Spanish-language manuscript, and in doing so provided innumerable suggestions for improving its content. Likewise, I profited considerably from the suggestions contained in four reviews of the first edition of this work, namely those of Javier Rodríguez Molina (2008), José Andrés Alonso de la Fuente (2008), Diana Ranson (2009), and Viola Miglio (2009). Each one of these collaborators and scholars deserves a large amount of credit for any merits the book may have. At the same time, I assume responsibility for the deficiencies that remain.

Abbreviations

abl.	ablative	Gr.	Greek
ac.	accusative	irreg.	irregular
act.	active	It.	Italian
adj.	adjective	Lat.	Latin
And.	Andalusian	Leon.	Leonese
Ar.	Arabic	lit.	literally
ca.	circa (approximately)	m.	masculine
Cast.	Castilian	Med.	Medieval
Cat.	Catalan	Mod.	Modern
cf.	*confer* (compare)	n.	neuter
conj.	conjugation	nom.	nominative
Cub.	Cuban	Occ.	Occitan
dat.	dative	p.	person, page
decl.	declension	pas.	passive
Dom. Repub.	Dominican Republic	pl.	plural
ed(s).	edition, editor(s)	Port.	Portuguese
Eng.	English	sg.	singular
Equat. Guin.	Equatorial Guinea	Sp.	Spanish
et al.	and others	var.	variant
ex.	example	viz.	*videlicet* (namely)
f.	feminine	voc.	vocative
Fr.	French	vols.	volumes
gen.	genitive		

Timeline

7000 BC Appearance of Proto-Indo-European in Anatolia

1000 BC Arrival of proto-Italic in the Italian Peninsula

Before 8th century BC Arrival of Basques and Iberians in the Iberian Peninsula

8th century BC Arrival of Phoenicians in the Iberian Peninsula

6th century BC Arrival of Celts in the Iberian Peninsula

218–202 BC Second Punic War

202–19 BC Roman conquest of the Iberian Peninsula

5th–6th centuries AD Set point of the popular vocabulary of Iberian Latin

507 Beginning of Visigothic dominance of the Iberian Peninsula

711 Muslim invasion of the Iberian Peninsula; origins of Mozarabic

8th century Beginning of the Reconquest

1004 Establishment of the Kingdom of Castile

1085 Liberation of Toledo

12th century First documents written entirely in Castilian

1212 Battle of Las Navas de Tolosa

1230–1252 Reign of Fernando III; Castilian as de facto official language

1252–1284 Reign of Alfonso X el Sabio; incipient standardization of Medieval Castilian

1492 End of Reconquest; expulsion of Sephardic Jews; arrival of Columbus in America; publication of Nebrija's Latin-Castilian dictionary

15th century Beginning of Spanish Renaissance

1516–1665 Golden Age of Spanish literature

1611 Publication of first monolingual Spanish dictionary (Covarrubias)

1713–1714 Establishment of Royal Spanish Academy

1726–1737 Publication of the first edition of the Academy dictionary

19th–21st centuries Adaptation of Spanish vocabulary to technological and scientific advances

Language Change

Inexorability of Language Change

The one constant in our world and our universe is change. Some things change so slowly as to be hardly perceptible, as in the case of geologic change, whereby over the course of millions of years a mountain may be reduced to a plain. Other changes are imperceptible because of their rapidity, like the movements of subatomic particles. In contrast, changes in human culture occur at a pace that makes them susceptible to detailed observation.

These observations reveal that all aspects of human culture are engaged in an implacable process of change, including fashion, politics, media, technology, and human relations. This explains, for example, why today's grandparents dress differently from their grandchildren, have different political opinions, are slow in accepting modern digital technology and new means of communication, and are baffled by modern-day sexual mores and child-rearing practices. Inevitably, by the time today's children are grandparents, they will be similarly out of step with their grandchildren's world.

Language, as a central aspect of human culture, is equally susceptible to this inexorable process of change. Some language change—especially the coining of new words—is in response to changes in other cultural spheres, but even the most abstract and fundamental components of a language such as its sounds, grammatical forms, and syntactic rules are involved in a process that will eventually render the current form of today's languages all but unintelligible to future speakers.

Nature of Language Change

In order to characterize the nature of language change, it is necessary to distinguish between the initiation of a change and its diffusion through the language.

A language change is initiated with the introduction of an innovation—that is, a new way of expressing something. For example, the possibility might arise to say *coach* for *entrenador* (lexical innovation), *freído* for *frito* 'fried' (**morphological** innovation), or *el hombre que su casa se vendió* for *el hombre cuya casa se vendió* 'the man whose house was sold' (syntactic innovation). It is possible to understand *canguro* 'kangaroo' to mean 'babysitter' (**semantic** change) or to pronounce *presidente* 'president' as *prehidente* (phonetic change called **jejeo**).

The innovations that arise in this way come into competition with established forms. For this reason, as Florentino Paredes and Pedro Sánchez-Prieto Borja (2008:22) explain, what speakers perceive is not "change" but "variation". Old and new **variants** alternate among themselves and are statistically distributed in a specific way according to social, regional, and stylistic factors. In time, this distribution evolves, with some variants becoming more dominant and others less so, in a process that can be represented as follows, where the introduction of an innovative variant (V_2) results in the eventual wholesale replacement of the original variant (V_1).

$$V_1 \rightarrow V_1 \, _{V_2} \rightarrow _{V_1} V_2 \rightarrow V_2$$

What we call "change", then, is the long-term difference between the two ends of this process. During the period of competition among variants, this process can be termed a **change in progress**.

The characterization of change as a competition among variants brings up two questions: Where do the new variants come from? And what principles determine the success or failure of any one of them?

Factors That Produce Innovative Variants

Probably the majority of innovative variants are due to the heterogeneous nature of language—that is, the uncountable variants that are arbitrarily introduced into human speech by chance. Occasionally more specific causes can be identified. In phonology, for example, many innovations are due to the physical nature of sounds and the human organs that produce and perceive them. These factors are outlined in chapter 5, which is dedicated to this aspect of the language's evolution. Focusing on the other language components, which are by nature more purely cognitive, we can identify some of the more general sources of innovations.

- **Economy of effort.** In language, as in any human activity, there is a general tendency to use the least effort necessary in order to achieve communicative goals. In morphology, the economy factor is expressed in a phenomenon called **analogy**, that is, the modification of certain words in order to accommodate them to a more frequent or regular model in the language. This process explains the **reanalysis** and subsequent regularization of morphemes such as the past participles *frito > freído* and *preso > prendido* and the names of female agents *presidente > presidenta* and *juez > jueza*.
- **Influence of other languages or varieties.** In derivational morphology, it is not unusual for languages to absorb foreign **affixes** (Visigothic *-ingôs* > Cast. *-engo*), and in the **lexicon** there are various types of influence such as those that English is currently exerting upon Spanish, most obviously in the case of lexical borrowings (*escáner < scanner*) but also in **calques**, both lexical (*año luz*, on the model of *light year*) and phraseological (*tener en mente*, on *to have in mind*), as well as in semantic borrowings (*educado* 'well-bred' → 'well-schooled', influenced by *educated*). Also, in situations where a new variety arises through massive contact among speakers of related varieties or languages, the resulting process of koineization can generate new variants.
- **Grammaticalization**. This is a process through which a word is bleached of its lexical meaning and becomes purely grammatical. In Spanish the grammaticalized word that is most often cited is Med. Cast. *auer* 'to have', which in the course of the Middle Ages cedes to its rival *tener* the lexical function of

designating possession and becomes a purely auxiliary verb, the only function of its modern descendant, *haber*. As we will see in chapters 6 and 7, grammaticalization is also involved in the creation of the Spanish articles, third-person pronouns, and **personal *a***, among other elements.

- **Reaction to a change in another linguistic component.** Language is a system in which everything is connected, such that a change in one component is likely to prompt a change in others. One example of this principle is the loss of **case endings** in Latin, which obliges later forms of the language to impose a more rigid word order and to instrumentalize prepositions to signal grammatical functions that were previously indicated by case endings.

Factors in the Selection of Variants

Once such new variants or innovations have been introduced, it is clear that there must be a process or mechanism that determines the selection among them and their diffusion through the language. Thanks to the findings of modern **sociolinguistics**, we now recognize that this mechanism is driven by social factors. In this respect the studies of the American sociolinguist William Labov (1927–) have been most fundamental. Thanks to methodological innovations, he was able to show that, contrary to what had been claimed before, language change is susceptible to being observed in a **synchronic** context he terms "apparent time". Studies of this type systematically compare the speech of the oldest members of a linguistic community with that of its young adults, interpreting the linguistic differences between the two groups as representative of a half-century of language change. Once the validity of this method is accepted—including the implied supposition that the way a person speaks does not change substantially after the attainment of adulthood—it becomes possible to study change empirically in a scientifically selected and controlled population.

The basic principles of the mechanism of language change postulated by Labov (described most fully in his two-volume *Principles of Linguistic Change* [1994, 2001]) are as follows:

SOCIOLINGUISTICS

Linguistics is defined as the scientific study of language. As such, it is concerned fundamentally with the description, analysis, and explanation of phonological, morphological, syntactic, semantic, and lexical structures of human languages. These are the goals of descriptive and theoretical linguistics.

It is, however, possible to study language from other points of view. Psycholinguistics, for example, focuses on the cognitive processes that make the learning, use, and interpretation of language possible. Applied linguistics focuses primarily on the learning of foreign languages, but other disciplines, such as translation and lexicography, can also be considered to be applied. One group of linguistic disciplines focuses on the intrinsic variability of languages, whether in time (the object of study of historical or **diachronic** linguistics), in space (the sphere of geographic linguistics, also called **dialectology**), or in society (the focus of sociolinguistics). Often both spatial and societal variation are considered to be within the scope of sociolinguistics. In European linguistics, regional variation is often termed **diatopic**, social variation **diastratic**, and situational variation **diaphasic**. The above-mentioned term for temporal variation—*diachronic*—is used on both sides of the Atlantic.

Sociolinguists have discovered that language varies according to social criteria. That is, they have observed that the way people express themselves within a speech community depends on social variables such as gender, age, socioeconomic status, level of educational attainment, ethnic status, and context or situation. Thus they study the differences between the speech of women and men, the young and the old, the rich and the poor, and they study the effects that different situations have on the way people talk.

- *Variation is an intrinsic characteristic of language.* Paradoxically, linguists have often affirmed the reality of linguistic heterogeneity while at the same time denying its relevance for the theory of language change. For Labov, on the contrary, variation—that is, the possibility of saying the same thing in many different ways—is an essential aspect of language, with-

out which it would not be able to perform the many functions
that speakers ask of it.

- *Social groups use linguistic variants to mark their identity within
  a speech community.* According to Labov, a language change
  is initiated when a variant acquires a specific social value for
  a social group that for some reason regards its place in the
  community as being threatened. In other words, members of
  the group use the variant as a way of differentiating themselves
  from outsiders. Once the variant has been adopted by the
  most prestigious members of the group, it spreads rapidly to
  the others. In this way the group uses a linguistic difference to
  highlight a social difference.

  Changes of this type sometimes become generalized
  throughout an entire speech community, but it is also possible
  that a community may reject a change by stigmatizing it. The
  decisive factor is the perceived prestige, both that of the group
  members who introduce the change and that of the group itself
  within the larger community. Labov distinguishes between
  changes "from above", that is, usually conscious changes based
  on innovations introduced by members of high-prestige
  groups, and changes "from below", often unconscious changes
  that are initiated by high-status members of groups that do
  not enjoy universal acceptance. In these cases it is common to
  speak of "covert" prestige (Caravedo 2003:49). Ralph J. Penny
  (2000:69) believes that the **aspiration** of /s/ in syllable-final
  position (as in *estos tíos* ['eh toh 'ti oh]) exemplifies this type of
  change in contemporary Spanish. Another possible example is
  the replacement of the (often unvoiced) alveolar trill /r̝/ by the
  unvoiced **uvular** fricative /χ/ in Puerto Rican Spanish, where it
  may be becoming a symbol of national pride (Lipski 1996:140).

- *Variants spread gradually through the lexicon and the speech
  community.* Linguistic innovations do not spread instanta-
  neously but instead gradually through both the lexicon and the
  speech community. In the case of phonological and morphological changes, a select group of words is affected first, after
  which the innnovation spreads gradually through the rest of

the vocabulary. All innovations, regardless of the component involved, become generalized as they are adopted by a growing number of social groups, a phenomenon that is amplified by the fact that a single individual may be a member of several social groups.

It seems clear that in our exploration of the nature of linguistic change, we have also discovered its root cause. In view of the above, it seems accurate to say that we, the speakers of languages, are the cause of language change. Labov's studies have made it clear that we want—even need—our languages to change so that they can perform certain social functions. Seen from this perspective, human language represents a balance between conservative forces, necessary for language to function as an instrument of communication, and opposing innovative forces, which enable us to show, through our use of language, who we are and the groups to which we belong.

....

Questions

1. Make a list of changes in progress that you have noticed in the languages you speak.
2. For the following innovations, first identify first the linguistic component to which they belong (phonological, morphological, etc.), and then speculate on the factor or factors that might have generated them (language contact, economy of effort, etc.).

   mismo [ˈmis mo] > [ˈmiz mo]
   la sastre > *la sastra* '(female) tailor'; *el modista* > *el modisto* '(male) dressmaker'
   es la niña cuyo (→ *que su*) *papá ganó el premio* 'it's the girl whose father won the prize'
   han impreso (→ *imprimido*) *las hojas del folleto* 'they have printed the pages of the pamphlet'
   belleza [be ˈje θa] > [be ˈʤe θa] 'beauty'

subir 'to go up' → 'to upload'

estos [ˈes tos] > And. Sp. [ˈeh toh] 'these'

satisfaré > *satisfaceré* 'I will satisfy'

tengo un hambre canina → *tengo un hambre canino* 'I'm starving'

perro [ˈpe ro] > And. Sp. [ˈpe řo] 'dog'

retirarse 'to step back', 'to recede' → 'to retire'

que → *porque* (*apresúrate, que no hay mucho tiempo* 'hurry, there's not much time')

registrar 'to search' → 'to enroll'

The Genealogy of Spanish

2

Language Families

It is customary to apply terms such as *family*, *genetic relationship*, *mother*, and *daughter* to both linguistic and human relations. In one sense this identification appears to be appropriate. Even as the existence of each human being presupposes an uninterrupted chain of ancestors who managed to reproduce before dying, every language presupposes an uninterrupted chain of speakers, almost always native speakers, who as a speech community were able to maintain the vitality of their form of communicating.[1]

However, a closer examination of the question forces us to the conclusion that human and linguistic relationships are qualitatively different. First, human lineage proceeds by generations, as new generations are born and older generations die. Conversely, in linguistic "lineage" there are no generations, births, or deaths, because the successive linguistic stages evolve gradually from earlier to later. Second, since human reproduction is sexual, each father and each mother transmits only 50 percent of their genetic material to their children, while the "genetic material" of languages—their sounds, grammatical structures, and words—remains intact from one historical period the next. For these reasons it is more reasonable to say that the linguistic organism that we now call Spanish is the *continuation* of earlier stages of the language and that therefore it is several millennia old. For the same reasons it is clear that the life of a language is more comparable to that of an individual than to

---

1. In the case of **creole** languages, the chain of speakers begins with the first native speakers that emerge from the corresponding **pidgin** community. In the case of Hebrew, there was a gap in the chain, as it was remade into a living language after having existed for several centuries as only a liturgical language.

that of a family. A language undergoes many changes during its long existence, just as a person experiences numerous transformations during a long life, and in both cases one and the same organism is involved.

Another difference between linguistic and human evolution is the fact that languages are capable of dividing themselves into two or more different varieties. These bifurcations in the family or **genealogical tree**[2] of a language are not due to reproduction, as they are in the case of individual human beings, but to the inexorable process of linguistic change combined with the movements and migrations of speakers. When subpopulations of a linguistic community become isolated from each other through migration, a process is initiated by which the original language may transform itself into two or more different linguistic entities through the gradual accumulation of different linguistic innovations in each subpopulation. Normally this process is repeated over and over in the history of a given language, thus producing highly complex linguistic genealogies, that is, family trees with complex systems of branches. Given the pace of linguistic change, it may eventually become difficult to detect the relatedness between two languages whose ancestors became isolated from each other in the remote past.

Linguists employ a set of tools in order to trace genetic relatedness among languages, the most important of which is the **comparative method**, which involves the systematic comparison of languages in search of linguistic similarities—sounds, words, syntactic structures—indicative of a common ancestry. Such shared features are called **cognates**, a term whose origin suggests linguistic consanguinity or kinship; it derives from Lat. *cognātus* 'blood relative', which in turn can be analyzed as the prefix *co-*, 'with', and *gnātus* (variant of *nātus*) 'born'.

Let us consider some examples of the comparative method. Spanish, French, and Italian all belong to the same **language family**—the Romance languages—which is the same as saying that if we follow their respective uninterrupted chains of speakers back

---

2. Penny 2000:20–28 discusses the theoretical limitations of the "genealogical tree" model.

in time, we will ultimately arrive at a point where they are speaking the same language, Latin. In order to verify this through the comparative method, we study lists of cognates such as the following, where we will concentrate mainly on the initial consonant:

	PENINSULAR SPANISH	ITALIAN	FRENCH
'to know'	/sa ˈbeɾ/	/sa ˈpe ɾe/	/sa vwaʀ/
'sack'	/ˈsa ko/	/ˈsak ko/	/sak/
'wise'	/ˈsa bjo/	/ˈsad dʒo/	/saʒ/
'blood'	/ˈsan gɾe/	/ˈsan gwe/	/sã/

All the words cited here begin with /s/, and though they differ in other aspects, it is not hard to believe that they could be cognates, that is, outcomes of the same Latin words. And indeed, upon consulting our Latin dictionary we find some credible candidates: *sapere* /ˈsa pe ɾe/ 'to taste (of)', *saccus* /ˈsak kus/ 'sack', *sapidus* /ˈsa pi dus/ 'delicious' (→ 'judicious, prudent'), and *sanguis* /ˈsan gʷis/ 'blood'.

Unfortunately, cognates are not always so easy to identify. Consider the following table of equivalents:

	PENINSULAR SPANISH	ITALIAN	FRENCH
'wax'	/ˈθe ɾa/	/ˈʧe ɾa/	/siʀ/
'center'	/ˈθen tro/	/ˈʧen tro/	/sãtʀ/
'sky'	/ˈθje lo/	/ˈʧɛ lo/	/sjɛl/
'one hundred'	/θjen/, /ˈθjen to/	/ˈʧɛn to/	/sã/

If we were to judge exclusively by the initial consonants of these examples, we would say that they are unlikely to be cognates, because where the Spanish examples begin with /θ/, the Italian examples begin with /ʧ/ and the French examples with /s/. However, the fact that the examples—with the exception of their initial consonants—seem to be quite similar obliges us to rethink the issue. Now we notice that though the initial consonants are different in the three languages, there is a regular correspondence among them. In other words, it occurs to us that /θ/, /ʧ/, and /s/ could be outcomes of a single Latin sound and that the discrepancy could be due to differences in the phonological evolution of the three languages. As a matter of fact, this seems to be the case, because the Latin equivalents of the examples cited all have the same initial consonant. Contrary to what one might expect, this consonant is /k/: *cēra* /'ke: ɾa/ 'wax', *centrum* /'ken trum/ 'center', *caelum* /'kae lum/ 'sky', and *centum* /'ken tum/ 'one hundred'. The different outcomes are due to variances in the palatalization of the velar consonant before a front vowel.

Let us return to the equivalents with initial /s/ in order to address one more important point. Consider the following table:

	PENINSULAR SPANISH	ITALIAN	FRENCH
'tennis set'	/set/	/set/	/sɛt/
'sexy'	/'sek si/	/'sek si/	/sek si/
'soda water'	/'so da/	/'sɔ da/	/sɔ da/

Here the striking similarity among the examples would seem to place their kinship beyond doubt. However, in this case the kinship is an illusion, because in all three languages the words cited are recent borrowings of the English words *set*, *sexy*, and *soda*. The similarity, in other words, is due to the late incorporation of these three English words into the vocabularies of all three Romance languages rather than the existence of common lexical ancestors in a single language of origin (there are no antecedents of *set*, *sexy*, and *soda* in Latin).

This example serves as a warning that when one is compiling examples for comparative analysis, care should be taken to choose elements that are unlikely to be borrowed, such as those that refer to the human body (*cabeza* 'head', *pelo* 'hair'), the numbers one to ten, names of blood relatives (*hija* 'daughter', *padre* 'father'), natural phenomena (*viento* 'wind', *fuego* 'fire'), basic qualities (*grande* 'large', *duro* 'hard'), et cetera. Conversely, other types of words should be avoided, such as names of abstract qualities (*sexy*, *estrafalario* 'gaudy') and terms relating to spheres of activity such as science (*clima* 'climate', *astronomía* 'astronomy'), art (*soprano, madrigal*), commerce (*bancarrota* 'bankruptcy', *mercancía* 'merchandise'), sports (*fútbol* 'soccer', *set*), and the military (*bayoneta* 'bayonet', *coronel* 'colonel').

Some Important Language Families

The task of trying to genetically classify the world's approximately six thousand languages has been ongoing for more than two centuries. Here I present a list of some of the most important families, as determined by number of speakers and cultural impact. The family to which Spanish belongs is presented last.[3]

- Sino-Tibetan, with more than a billion speakers of Chinese and 37 million of Burmese
- Dravidian (e.g., Tamil), with 25 languages and 175 million speakers in southern India
- Afroasiatic, whose Semitic subgroup includes Arabic, with more than 150 million speakers, and Hebrew, with 6 million
- Niger-Kordofanian, whose Bantu subgroup has 150 million speakers, 50 million of whom speak Swahili
- Turkic, with 125 million speakers in Azerbaijan, China, Russia, and Turkey (where 56 million speak Turkish)
- Uralic, whose Finno-Ugric subgroup includes Hungarian (14 million speakers), Finnish (5 million), and Estonian (1.5 million)
- Indo-European (more than 1 billion speakers; see below)

Indo-European Language Family

From the perspective of Western civilization, the most important language family, given that it is the family to which the languages of almost all European countries and many of their former colonies belong, is the Indo-European language family. According to R. D. Gray and Q. D. Atkinson (2003), it seems likely that the ancestor language from which the entire family descends was spoken in Anatolia (today Turkey) about nine thousand years ago (i.e., in 7000 BC). From there, it must have spread in successive migratory waves toward both the East—where it continues to exist in the form

3. For more information on language families, see Comrie 1990. Note that some families consist of a single language, as in the cases of Japanese, Korean, and Basque, which are therefore termed **language isolates**.

of the Indic, Iranian, and Armenian languages—and the West and
the European continent. Since in linguistic terminology the initial
element *proto-* is used to refer to ancestral languages for which we
have no direct documentation, this language is called **Proto-Indo-
European**. The term **Indo-European** is used in this sense as well, and
also as an adjective, that is, to refer to the Indo-European languages.

During the many millennia since the appearance of Proto-Indo-
European, the combination of the factors of demographic disper-
sion and language change has produced a very complex family tree.
Some of the best-known Indo-European branches are listed below.

- Germanic (440 million current native speakers): German, En-
  glish, Dutch, Frisian, Danish, Norwegian, Swedish, Icelandic
- Indic (900 million): Hindi, Urdu, Bengali, Romany
- Slavic (485 million): Russian, Czech, Slovak, Slovene, Serbo-
  Croatian, Macedonian, Bulgarian, Belarusian, Polish
- Iranian (73 million): Farsi, Kurdish
- Celtic (12 million): Welsh, Irish, Breton
- Hellenic (10 million): Greek
- Italic (750 million; see below)

Italic Branch of Indo-European

The first speakers of the Italic branch of the Indo-European language family arrive on the Italian Peninsula around 1000 BC, when
ancestors of the Latins and Faliscans settle in the center of the
Peninsula around the site of their future capital, Rome. Later on,
speakers of other Italic varieties arrive: the Oscans, who settle in
the south, and the Umbrians, who establish themselves northeast of
Rome. With the increasing importance of Rome, Latin establishes a
linguistic monopoly on the Peninsula by the year AD 100.

At a certain point in its history, a special type of **bilingualism**
called **diglossia** develops in Latin. This means that the language develops two varieties—one "high" and the other "low"—to be employed in different situations. The high form of the language (called
sermō urbānus 'urban speech') is taught in the schools and used in
the most formal **registers**, especially writing. In time this variety

BILINGUALISM AND DIGLOSSIA

Traditionally, it was thought that the only truly bilingual people are those who speak two languages at the level of a native speaker, in all contexts. When linguists discovered that this definition eliminates the great majority of people who use two languages on a regular basis, they opted to relax this requirement. Now it is recognized that in most bilinguals one language is dominant and the other subordinate, and that the degree of competence in each language can vary greatly. Bilingualism arises wherever there is contact between language groups, for example, on both sides of a political boundary (like the border between Mexico and the United States) or where there has been an influx of immigrants or invaders.

Originally, diglossia was conceptualized as a variant of bilingualism in which a linguistic community uses *two variants of a single language*: the high variant for the most formal contexts of public life, such as education and literature, and the low variant for more informal contexts, such as conversation with family and friends. There are many examples of this kind of diglossia in linguistic history, including the one I have described here between written and vernacular Latin. Situations of this type can be found today, for example, between classical Arabic and the national Arabic "dialects", and between **standard** German and local Swiss dialects.

Nowadays, the use of the term *diglossia* has undergone an important modification, eliminating the requirement that the two varieties pertain to the same language while retaining the requirement that they be functionally differentiated. From this modified perspective, it can be claimed that Spanish participates in diglossic relationships with languages in many parts of the world, such as Spanish America—where it plays the role of high language vis-à-vis the indigenous languages—and the United States, where in many communities it is the low language with respect to English.

becomes what María Teresa Echenique Elizondo calls a "father language", that is, "a semi-living language, the spoken and written form of communication of an elite group."[4] The low form (*sermō rusticus,*

4. Una "lengua paterna . . . una lengua semiviva, un medio de comunicación hablado y escrito de una élite."

plēbēius, quotidiānus, vulgāris 'rustic, popular, daily, vulgar speech'),
conversely, is neither taught nor written but is used by everyone in
the course of daily life. It is this popular form of Latin—usually
called spoken or Vulgar Latin—that evolved into the Romance languages,[5] currently spoken by 750 million people. Among the members of this family are Spanish, French, Italian, Portuguese, Galician,
Catalan, Occitan, Romanian, Sardinian, and Romansch.

Latin and Romance

Scholars have not been able to agree on the relationship between
the two forms of the language—Latin and Romance—during the
postimperial period. Francisco Beltrán Lloris (2004:86) and José
Jesús de Bustos Tovar (2004:68) believe, for example, that it is unlikely that the difference between literary and spoken Latin would
have been very great before the Muslim invasion of 711, while for
Manuel Ariza (2004b:310) it seems certain that "in the eighth century the uneducated inhabitants—who were a majority—no longer
understood Latin because what they spoke was something very dis-
tant from the phonetic and morphological norms of the language
of Rome".[6] There are also radical differences in the characterization
of ninth- to eleventh-century legal and notarial documents that
were written in a Latin clearly influenced by Romance. For Roger
Wright (2010:36), "what we call Latin was nothing more, at least for
some of the medieval scribes, than a writing system". In other words,
Wright thinks that an apparently Latin text such as "dicouos quomo
uiderunt homines de Uilla Uela quod pascebant in suos términos",
written in Burgos around the year 1100,[7] should be considered a Ro-

5. The word *romance* derives from the Latin adverbial expression *fābulāre
rōmānicē* 'to speak in the manner of the Roman world' (as opposed to the barbarian
world). *Romance* eventually becomes the designation of all vernacular languages deriving from Latin.

6. "en el siglo VIII los habitantes no cultos–que eran la mayoría–ya no entendían
el latín porque lo que ellos hablaban era algo ya muy alejado de las normas fonéticas
y morfológicas de la lengua de Roma"

7. Text from Gifford and Hodcroft 1966:26–27: "*Leuaronse homines de Bonille
cum suo ganato & trocieron Aslanzon, & pascebant erbas de terminos que non debe-*

mance text that would have been read aloud as follows: "dígovos como vieron hombres de Villavieja que pacían en sus términos". For Ariza (2004b:318–19) and Bustos Tovar (2004:280), by contrast, this would be a Latin text whose characteristics are determined by the scribe's (low) level of knowledge and the expectations of the uneducated audience to which it is addressed.

Setting aside these differences of opinion, there is one point on which everyone can agree. As Bustos Tovar (2004:85) states: "The separation between Latin and Romance was consummated when legal and notarial texts fully adopted Romance as a form of expression. This occurred during the course of the 12th century and was complete by the beginning of the 13th century."[8] After this period, texts in Romance and Latin are clearly distinguishable, and in time written Romance deprives written Latin of more and more functions, to the point that it begins to be considered a "dead language".

Genealogy of Spanish

Having reviewed the key concepts of genetic linguistics (language families, cognates, and the comparative method) and seen a description of the different branches of the Indo-European family (in particular the Italic branch with its Romance descendants), we are finally ready to consider the genealogy of Spanish. Figure 1 shows the family of languages to which Castilian belongs and its place in this family, as well as the path of evolution by which Proto-Indo-European is gradually transformed into Spanish. Note the large number of **proto-languages** that must be posited. At some point after the disintegration of the Roman Empire, a linguistic entity that we call **Proto-Ibero-Romance** must have arisen on the Iberian Pen-

---

bant pascere de Uilla Uela. Dicouos quomo uiderunt homines de Uilla Uela quod pascebant in suos terminos, & irati sunt." Translation: Some men from Buniel went with their cattle and crossed the Arlanzón, and they grazed on grasses in areas belonging to Villa Vela where they should not have grazed. I'm telling you how men from Villa Vela saw that they were grazing on their lands, and they got angry.

8. "La separación entre latín y romance se consumó en la lengua escrita cuando los textos jurídicos y notariales adoptaron plenamente el romance como forma de expresión. Ello ocurrió a lo largo del siglo XII y culminó a principios del XIII."

Genealogy of Spanish

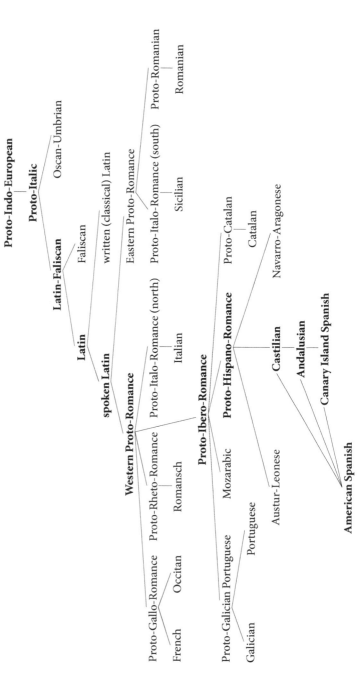

insula, a variant of the same Western **Proto-Romance** from which both Proto-Gallo-Romance and Proto-Italo-Romance arose. Later on, Proto-Ibero-Romance would have undergone incipient dialectal differentiation, with Proto-Catalan in the east, **Proto-Hispano-Romance**[9] in the middle, and Proto-Galician-Portuguese in the west. Finally, the differentiation of the Hispano-Romance dialects begins, though naturally they resemble Galician in the west (e.g., Asturian) and Catalan in the east (e.g., Aragonese). In the center arises the dialect known as **Castilian**, which need not be called a proto-language, because we have a considerable amount of written evidence of this language beginning in the twelfth century, with first glimpses as early as the tenth century. Later on, Andalusian and Canary Island Spanish develop from Castilian, after which all three of these varieties contribute to the genesis of American Spanish.

....

Questions

1. Why is it customary to say that Latin is a dead language? In what respect is this statement correct? In what respect is it incorrect?
2. Why is it important to identify Spanish as a "continuation" rather than a "daughter" of Latin?
3. Explain the concept of "genealogical tree". What factor determines whether or not such a tree will have complex "branching"?
4. Which of the following words would be appropriate for a list of possible cognates? Explain your answer in each case: *banana*, *ojo* 'eye', *piel* 'skin', *aerosol*, *chimpancé* 'chimpanzee', *esquí* 'ski', *agua* 'water', *tierra* 'land', *jefe* 'boss', *etiqueta* 'label', *cuatro* 'four', *chacal* 'jackal', *suegra* 'mother-in-law', *sobrina* 'niece', *diente* 'tooth', *garaje* 'garage', *vitrina* 'showcase', *frío* 'cold', *tomate* 'tomato', *canoa* 'canoe', *oreja* '(outer) ear', *dedo* 'finger', 'toe', *digital*

---

9. Some scholars (for example, Harris 1988:6) employ the term *Hispano-Romance* to designate all Ibero-Romance languages except Catalan. Mozarabic arises in the south beginning in the eighth century.

'digital', *rinoplastia* 'rhinoplasty', *brazo* 'arm', *auricular* '(tele-
phone) receiver', *óptico* 'optical', *padre* 'father', *calor* 'heat', *toro*
'bull', *meteorológico* 'meterological', *globalización* 'globalization',
veinte 'twenty', *verde* 'green', *uña* 'fingernail', 'toenail', *unión*
'union', *tigre* 'tiger'.

5. What is the genetic relationship between Castilian and the
    following languages and dialects: Hungarian, Basque, Catalan,
    English, Greek, Romanian, Mozarabic, Chinese, Asturian,
    Arabic, Finnish, Tamil, Dutch, Polish, Hindi, Bulgarian, Farsi,
    Osco-Umbrian, Sicilian, Occitan, Canary Island Spanish,
    Proto-Indo-European?

6. Characterize the two possible interpretations (and readings) of
    the following notarial text, written in Castile in 940:[10]

Et tradidi . . . ipsas kasas que laborabi in Villa Merosa cum regulan-
tes de Sancte Marie et cum pane et uino et carne de regula Sancte
Marie et leuabimus matera de IIII casas et I orreo et tectus de III
ecclesias de Valle Posita et composuimus de ipsa matera casas de
ecclesias in Villa Merosa, et restaurabimus eas.

10. Text from Gifford and Hodcroft 1966:24. Spanish translation: Y entregué esas casas que edifiqué en Villambrosa con los monjes de Santa María y con pan y vino y carne del monasterio de Santa María y llevamos [la] madera de cuatro casas y un hórreo y la techumbre de tres iglesias de Valpuesta y arreglamos/construimos con esa madera [las] casas e iglesias en Villambrosa y las restauramos. English translation: And I handed over . . . those houses that I built in Villambrosa with the monks of the Monastery of St. Mary, and with the bread, wine, and meat of the Monastery of Santa María, and we brought wood for four houses and one granary and the roofing of three churches in Valpuesta, and we built the houses and churches in Villambrosa with that wood and we restored them.

External History of the Iberian Peninsula through the Thirteenth Century

3

This chapter examines the sociopolitical and cultural events that were crucial in shaping the linguistic configuration of the Iberian Peninsula. We will see that the Romans were not the first group to establish themselves in this region, and that they were also not the last. However, the arrival of the Romans and the subsequent Romanization of the Peninsula are undoubtedly dominant factors in its linguistic history, since the language that the Romans introduced more than two millennia ago is still spoken today in almost every part of the Peninsula. Almost a thousand years after the Roman incursion, the Peninsula witnesses another invasion—that of the Muslims—whose effects in the linguistic configuration of the region are almost equally profound. If indeed the Roman invasion explains the fact that Romance languages are spoken today on the Peninsula, it is the second of the incursions that set in motion the events that eventually made Castilian, rather than one of the other Ibero-Romance varieties, the national language of Spain.

Iberian Peninsula before the Arrival of the Romans

The following is a partial list of paleo-Hispanic populations—groups that inhabited the Iberian Peninsula before the arrival of the Romans. Various factors are identified, including their probable origins, when they arrived, where they settled (see map 1), and their linguistic contributions to Modern Spanish.

- **Iberians.** This group inhabited a wide area from southeast France (Languedoc, Rosellón) along the Mediterranean coast to Murcia, as well as the valley of the Ebro (originally called the

Íber, whence *ibero* 'Iberian'). These settlements date from the beginning of recorded history in the region. Since it is has not been possible to translate Iberian inscriptions, the language's genetic affiliation is not known, though phonological analysis of the inscriptions seems to indicate that it is neither Indo-European nor Basque. For the same reason it has not been possible to identify any definite Iberian relics in the Spanish vocabulary. However, certain words pertaining to domestic and rural life could possibly be of Iberian origin: *barro* 'mud', *charco* 'puddle', *boñiga* 'dung', *perro* 'dog', *álamo* 'poplar tree'.

- **Celts.** Archaeological evidence shows that by the sixth century BC, groups of Celts—an Indo-European people whose settlements are spread over practically the entire continent—were living in Galicia and Portugal. Later they moved into the central plateau and parts of Navarre and Aragon, where they adopted cultural elements from the Iberians, although not their language. These so-called Celtiberians continued to speak Celtic, as proved by documents found in the area (Botorrita plaques). Two Celtic words for 'fort', *briga* and *dunum*, still survive as elements of **toponyms** or place-names: The former figures in *Coimbra* (formerly *Conimbriga*), the name of an important Portuguese city, the latter in *Navardún*, the name of a town in the province of Zaragoza. Also of Celtic origin are a number of words that refer to concrete aspects of nature—like the name of the narcotic plant *beleño* 'henbane'—and of material life: *carro* 'cart', *cerveza* 'beer', *camino* 'road', and, notably, *braga* 'breeches', from Celtic *braca*, the characteristic clothing of this people, which differs markedly from the Roman tunic.

- **Phoenicians.** The Semitic people known by this name settle on the Iberian Peninsula as early as the eighth century BC, one century after founding, in North Africa, their most important city, Carthage, whence the other name by which they are known, Carthaginians. From the Latin name of the inhabitants of this city—*Poeni*, from Gr. *Phoinikes*—derives *púnico* 'Punic', an adjective used to refer to the Carthaginians. To their language can be attributed several place-names, such as *Cádiz* (< *Gádir* 'walled area'), *Málaga* (< *málaka* 'trading post'),

Cartagena 'New Carthage' (Phoenician *Qart Hadasht* 'new city', Lat. *Carthago Noua* 'new Carthage'), and even *Hispania*, possibly based on a Phoenician root meaning 'land of rabbits' (Lapesa 1981:15).

- **Greeks.** From the beginning of recorded history, this nation of sailors and traders of Indo-European origin competed with the Carthaginians over commercial trade rights on the south and east of the Peninsula. The sphere of their influence can be seen most clearly in the toponyms they left, undoubtedly names of trading posts or port installations, such as *Ampurias* (Gr. *empórion* 'center of maritime trade') and *Alicante* (from Gr. *Akra Leuké* 'white promontory').

- **Basques.** As in the case of the Iberians, the date of arrival of this group on the Iberian Peninsula is unknown. Unlike the others, they continue to inhabit the region today and preserve their language and separate identity. The language of the Basques (called, in Spanish, *vasco*, *vascuence*, or *euskera*) is of unknown affiliation; it is certainly not Indo-European. Nowadays it is spoken in the Spanish autonomous regions of the Basque Country and Navarre and in the French department of Pyrénées-Atlantiques, though the presence of numerous toponyms of indisputable Basque origin indicates that the Basque-speaking territory was formerly much larger. Aside from toponyms, the Basque contribution to the Spanish lexicon has been slight. Among the most notable loanwords are *boina*, the name of the typical Basque beret; *izquierdo* 'left', which replaces *siniestro* (Lat. *sinister* 'left') when the latter acquires pejorative connotations; *cencerro* 'cowbell', the Spanish version of a Basque onomatopoeia; and *pizarra* 'slate', from Basque *lapitz-arri* 'slate stone'.

Romanization of the Iberian Peninsula

In the middle of the third century BC, Roman power extends over the entire Italian Peninsula but not beyond its boundaries. The Roman domination of the Mediterranean basin begins with the First Punic War, which breaks out in 264 when the Carthaginians occupy the Sicilian city of Massana (Mesina) and ends with a Roman victory in 241 after a land war around this city. As a result, Rome annexes Sicily, Sardinia, and Corsica, and the Carthaginians are forced to indemnify the Romans with a large amount of gold.

The need to pay this indemnization indirectly brings about the Second Punic War, when, in an attempt to compensate for their losses, the Carthaginians decide to conquer and exploit Hispania, where they had formerly limited their activities to pursuing commercial interests. The Carthaginian general Hannibal undertakes a systematic military conquest of the Peninsula, beginning with the central plateau and continuing, in 219, with an attack on the city of Sagunto, whose inhabitants happen to be Roman allies. Because of this alliance, when the city falls after eight months of siege, the Romans are obliged to respond, and this marks the beginning of the second war between these two great powers. Hannibal crosses the Pyrenees and the Alps with his army and engages the Roman forces with some success, but in vain, as the Romans capture Cartagena and Cadiz in 206, and in 202 take the Punic capital, Cartago. As indemnization for this war, the Carthaginians are forced to pay even more gold, hand over their fleet of ships, and allow the Romans to annex all their foreign territories in Hispania and the coast of Africa. Half a century later, seeing that the Carthaginians are once again beginning to recover their commercial and military power, Rome again wages war on Carthage (the Third Punic War, 149–146 BC), which ends with the total destruction of the city and Rome's absolute supremacy in the Mediterranean basin.

The defeat of the Carthaginians means that the Romans' domination of Hispania is no longer contested by any other colonizing power. It does not mean, however, that they are able to take political control of the Peninsula without opposition. The Roman conquest of the territory begins in 218 with the arrival of Roman forces at Ampurias, but it is not completed until 199 years later, in 19 BC.

Resistance in Hispania to the imposition of Roman civilization—that is, **Romanization**—varies from region to region (see map 2). On the Mediterranean and Andalusian coasts and in the valley of the Baetis River (now known as the Guadalquivir), Romanization is intense and early (197 BC). Shortly thereafter, control over the Ebro

Valley is achieved as well. Most of the interior of the Peninsula is conquered in a military campaign that lasts from 155 to 133 BC, ending with the fall of the principal Celtiberian city, Numancia. The Romans finally conquer the peoples of the Cantabrian Mountains in a campaign that lasts from 29 to 19 BC, under the command of Agrippa (Fear 2000:31). Even so, Roman domination is never particularly strong in the northern part of the Peninsula, where peoples such as the Asturians, the Cantabrians, and the Vascones resist the imposition of Roman customs—including the language—for a long time.

On the rest of the Peninsula, however, the process of Romanization, while sometimes slow and difficult, is complete. The Romans impose their language—through a process called **Latinization**—as well as civil and military organization, law, education, agricultural and industrial techniques, roads, and even to a certain extent their religion (Lapesa 1981:55; Dietrich and Geckeler 1990:124).

Once all regions and all peoples are conquered, Romanization and Latinization proceed without coercion or even any systematic efforts on the part of the Romans (Kulikowski 2004:8–9). The social and political structures they establish are sufficient to ensure the displacement of local customs and languages. The principal factor in this process is the prestige of Latin as the language of the empire. The shift to Latin is encouraged by the indigenous populations' need to communicate with the agents of the new dominant power and by the economic advantages that accrue to those who can deal with them directly. Other factors that contribute to the imposition of Latin include education and obligatory military service, which have the effect of intensifying contact with Latin and establishing it as a lingua franca among peoples from all over the Peninsula. Still, as Rafael Lapesa (1981:56) points out, the imposition of Latin is gradual and follows a long period of bilingualism.

It may be assumed that the **language shift** that takes place on the Iberian Peninsula at this point is comparable to parallel cases that may be observed in today's world, products of the clash of dominant and subaltern languages, notably in the Americas, where there is contact between Spanish and indigenous languages in the south and between Spanish and English in the north. The pace of the process of language shift depends on the intensity of contact, but in general one observes an evolution from **monolingualism** in the traditional language to a bilingualism that ends in another state of monolingualism in the new language. The process normally operates by generations: The young adjust quickly to the new circumstances, using the prestige language in more contexts and the traditional language in fewer. When the last monolingual speakers of the traditional language die, the need to maintain a bilingualism that is less and less useful dies with them.

End of the Roman Empire

Beginning in the third century AD, the Roman Empire begins to disintegrate, for several interrelated reasons. First of all, a series of measures taken by the Roman administration has the effect of destroying the agricultural middle class in Italy. Among these measures are the establishment of mandatory military service, which obliges farmers to abandon their farms for several years, and the imposition of high taxes to finance the maintenance of up to four hundred thousand soldiers in the provinces. As a result, Roman citizens are often forced to sell or hand over their land to a small group of rich families, who prefer to employ slaves brought from the conquered territories rather than provide work to their free countrymen. Second, a tradition of corruption in government and bureaucracy develops in Rome, leading to the accumulation of public funds in the hands of politicians and bureaucrats. Finally, since the Romans fail to establish a mechanism for the election of new emperors, a series of civil wars breaks out. In the midst of the resulting political instability, power is transferred to the army, which ends up electing as emperor the candidate who offers the biggest bribe. The obligation to maintain public order and welfare is neglected, resulting in an upsurge in violence and crime in the streets.

Weakened by so many internal problems, the empire loses the will and the dynamism needed to continue resisting external pressures, especially those applied with ever greater vigor by Germanic tribes beginning in the third century. The strategy of trying to diminish this pressure by recruiting Germanic warriors as mercenaries turns out to be misguided, as it has the concomitant effect of diminishing military allegiance to Rome. The weakness of the empire is made plain for all to see when, in AD 410, the Visigoths, under their chieftain Alaric, invade and sack the city of Rome. The date that is usually given for the fall of the empire is 476, when a general named Odoacer (also called Odovacar) deposes the last emperor. The refusal of the Roman forces stationed outside the Italian Peninsula to recognize the authority of Odoacer marks the end of an empire that had lasted almost five centuries.

Visigothic Invasion

The Iberian Peninsula, an important region for the empire in spite of its distance from the center, also undergoes incursions by Germanic barbarians. In 409, for example, several Germanic tribes, among them the Swabians and the Vandals, penetrate Roman defenses and spread terror in parts of Galicia and Andalusia[1] for several years. The Roman authorities deftly handle this problem by enlisting their old adversaries the Visigoths to chase off the invaders with the promise of lands in the south of Gaul (now called France) around Toulouse. The Visigoths achieve this objective in 416, and by 419 they are already enjoying their new territory, from whence in 451 they help the Romans defeat the Hun army under the command of Attila.

What the Romans cannot foresee is the arrival in Gaul of the Franks, who, under Clovis, proceed to drive out the Visigoths in 507. The Visigoths' immediate impulse is to flee to the Iberian Peninsula, an area they had never fully abandoned after their incursions there on behalf of the Romans (Barton 2004:13). According to W. D. Elcock (1975:233), the Visigoths settle first in Barcelona and then defin-

1. José Mondéjar Cumpián (2008) contradicts the traditional conjecture that the toponym *Andalucía* might derive from the name of the Vandals. He argues (p. 251) that since the Vandals were on the Peninsula for a period of only 18 years (411–29) and since the Arabs did not arrive for another 282 years (711), it is unlikely that the Arabs would use the name of the Germanic tribe to designate the newly conquered lands. Mondéjar (p. 255) proposes a new etymology, the toponym *Andalos*, from Celtic *Andévalo* < *ande* 'large' + *valun* 'wall', perhaps reflecting the mountainous barrier that separates Andalusia from the rest of Hispania.

itively in Toledo (see map 3). From here they manage to neutralize their political rivals—the Swabians in Galicia, the Basques in the north, and the Roman nobility in the south—by the year 629.

Despite their political domination of the region, the Visigoths exercise very little influence on the essentially Roman culture of the Peninsula, first because there are few of them (probably about 200,000, according to Antonio Alatorre 1989:66, as against several million Ibero-Romans), and second because their culture is so different. It is true that the Visigoths had been Romanized to a certain degree after centuries of contact with the empire (which began in 268 BC on the Balkan Peninsula)—to the point of adopting the Latin language for their official documents—but the Roman population continues to view them as barbarous and uncultured. Even more important is the religious difference: While the Hispano-Romans adopt the Catholicism of the Roman Church, the Visigoths persist in their fidelity to the precepts of Arianism, a doctrine that denies the divinity of Jesus. Due to this difference, the Visigothic authorities prohibit intermarriage between the two groups. The Visigothic king Recaredo finally takes a first step toward uniting the two peoples when, in 589, he abandons Arianism in favor of Catholicism, and by the middle of the seventh century the two nations are also united by a common set of laws, the Forum Judicum, which later on, under the name Fuero Juzgo, will serve as the basis for many medieval charters or *fueros*.

Considering the brevity of the Visigothic reign (507–711), the lack of intensity of the contacts between the Visigothic people and the Roman inhabitants of Hispania, and the Visigoths' already advanced state of Romanization (it is estimated that the Visigothic language was already extinct by the seventh century), it is not surprising that the influence of their language on the spoken Latin of the region should have been slight and exclusively lexical in nature. In this respect several **anthroponyms** or personal names are worth mentioning, such as *Fernando, Ramiro, Alfonso*, and *Elvira*, besides toponyms like *Godos, Revillagodos, Gudillos*, and *Godones*. Borrowed common nouns include *ganso* 'goose', *aya* 'governess', *ropa* 'clothes', alongside verbs such as *ganar* 'to win', *brotar* 'to sprout', and *agasajar* 'to regale' (Elcock 1975:234–35). To Gothic can also be attributed the introduction of the suffix *-engo* (< *-ingôs*), originally **patronymic**, that is, appended to the first name of the father to produce a family name.[2]

Actually, the majority of Spanish words of Germanic origin do not date from the period of contact with the Visigoths but to other periods, both before and after. Especially important is the group of Germanisms that percolate into the spoken Latin of the fourth and fifth centuries through intense contact between Romans and the Germanic tribes that live all along the northwestern border of the empire. The introduction of a series of words into almost all the western Romance languages can be attributed to these contacts. From Germanic *suppa* 'soup', we have Fr. *soupe*, Occ., Cat., Sp., Port. *sopa*, and It. *zuppa*; from *bank* 'bench', we have Fr., Occ., Cat. *banc*, Sp., Port., It. *banco*. Other Spanish words of this origin: *harpa* 'harp', *fango* 'mud', *tregua* 'truce', *guerra* 'war', *blanco* 'white'. Another source of Germanisms is Old French, which in the twelfth and thirteenth centuries indirectly conveys a large number of originally Frankish words into Spanish, such as *barón* 'baron', *varón* 'male', *blandir* 'to brandish', *bruñir* 'to burnish', *buque* 'ship', *estandarte* 'banner', *flecha* 'arrow', and *guante* 'glove' (Penny 2002:264).[3]

Muslim Invasion

It is ironic that shortly after the approval of marriage between Visigoths and Ibero-Romans toward the middle of the seventh century the Visigothic kingdom should end, when a Muslim army invades from the south in 711 and, encountering little resistance among the Hispano-Gothic population, manages to conquer almost the entire Peninsula in just seven years. The name of the invading Muslim general, Tariq, has been immortalized in the name of the place from which he began the invasion, the rock of Gibraltar (<Ar. *ǧabal* 'mountain' + *Tariq*), previously called Calpe (Elcock 1975:288). The Muslims ac-

2. For the history of *-engo*, see Pharies 1990:87–126.

3. See "The Germanic Invasions of the Roman Empire 378–479 AD," 2014, http://mapas.owje.com/maps/11202_the-germanic-invasions-of-the-roman-empire-378-439-ad.html, for a map of the Germanic invasions of this period of history.

tually penetrate into European territory as far as Tours, in France, but here they suffer a crushing defeat at the hands of the Franks in 732. Seeing their dream of Islamicizing all of Europe frustrated, they retire to Spain, where they establish a brilliant civilization that for centuries eclipses European civilization in almost every respect.

The presence of so many speakers of Arabic during such a long period transforms the linguistic physiognomy of the Peninsula and profoundly affects the future of the Spanish language. The influence is of a bipartite nature. From a purely linguistic point of view, it is notable for the contribution of several thousand words to the Hispano-Romance vocabulary. From a historical and political perspective, it sets in motion the events through which finally, among all the Ibero-Romance varieties that are concentrated in the north of the Peninsula, it is Castilian that manages to establish itself as the dominant linguistic form in a region that one day will call itself Spain.

It is likely that despite the official status of Arabic in the conquered territories—which are called *Al-Ándalus* by the Muslims—a form of Ibero-Romance continues to be the dominant language in daily life. This is due to several factors. First, the number of invaders, and later of Muslim colonists, is small in comparison with the Latin-speaking population that has been inhabiting the territory for centuries. Rafael Cano Aguilar (1992:44) calculates that in the year 756 about sixty thousand Muslims might be living among the approximately four million **Ibero-Latin** speakers. Second, since the invading forces arrive without women, it is to be expected that the children born from the inevitable mixed marriages will have learned Ibero-Latin at home with their mothers. Third, during the early centuries of their domination, the Muslims prove to be tolerant of their non-Muslim subjects, demanding only the payment of a personal tax.

The existence of the *jarchas* (see sidebar), shows that as late as the tenth century a variety of Romance is still being spoken in Muslim Iberia and that this language is considered appropriate in Arabic literary circles for the lyrical expression of feelings of love. For all these reasons, the bilingualism that inevitably develops in the region does not lead, as might be expected, to Arabic monolingualism but stabilizes as such and becomes a fundamental feature of Hispano-Arabic society. The eventual extinction of this southern variety of

AN EXTINCT VARIETY OF IBERO-ROMANCE: MOZARABIC

As is pointed out by the genealogical table of Spanish, Mozarabic is one of the Romance varieties that evolve directly from Proto-Ibero-Romance, on the same level as Galician-Portuguese, Hispano-Romance, and Catalan. This is a variety spoken by the Hispano-Latin population under Muslim rule which, given the political conditions imposed by the invaders, is obliged to engage in a more or less intense diglossia, over time, with Hispano-Arabic. Since the Christian Mozarabs, like the Christians of the north, continue to regard Latin as the language of culture and writing, we have very little evidence of this oral variety. The principal source of evidence is the *jarchas*, refrains of two to four verses written in Romance and appended to poems belonging to an Arabic lyric form called the *moaxaja*. Generally, the *jarchas* are written in the voice of a young woman who laments the absence of her lover. Since the *moaxaja* is an Arabic genre, the Mozarabic words of the *jarchas* are written using the Arabic alphabet, whose lack of letters corresponding to vowels complicates reading and comprehension. Let us consider, for example, the following *jarcha*, written toward the end of the eleventh century. It appears below in three versions: transcribed with the Roman alphabet, written in Mozarabic, and translated into Modern Spanish[†] (taken from García Gómez 1975:86–87):

TRANSCRIPTION	MOZARABIC	MODERN SPANISH
mw sīdī 'ibrāhīm	*mew sidi 'Ibrahim*	Dueño mío Ibrahim,
y' nw'mn dlŷ	*ya nuemne dolže*	oh nombre dulce,
f'nt myb	*fen-te mib*	vente a mí
dy njt.	*de nojte.*	de noche.
In nwn š nwn k'rš	*In non, si non keríš*	Si no, si no quieres,
yrym tyb	*yire-me tib*	ireme a ti
grmy 'wb	*gar-me 'a 'ob*	dime adónde
'frt.	*a fer-te.*	a verte.

Notable features here include the Arabism *sidi* 'lord' and the Mozarabism *garir* 'to say'. Grammatically, we notice the pronominal forms *tib* and *mib*, which reflect, respectively, Lat. *tibi* and *mihi* (the latter analogically influenced by *tibi*) and the future verb form *yire* 'I shall go', already completely grammaticalized. For more information on Mozarabic see Galmés de Fuentes 1983, and for more on the *jarchas* see, in addition to García Gómez, Corriente 1997 and 2004.

[†] English translation: My lord Ibrahim, oh sweet name, come to me at night. If you do not, if you don't want to, I will come to you—tell me where [to go]—to see you.

Ibero-Romance—called **Mozarabic**[4]—is due both to the policy of linguistic repression instituted by the fundamentalist Muslims who in the eleventh century gain power in Al-Ándalus and to the assimilation of **Mozarabs** by the peoples of the north once the Reconquest is set into motion.[5]

The most obvious result of the centuries of contact with Arabic is the presence in the Spanish vocabulary of many **Arabisms** or borrowings from Arabic. Federico Corriente Córdoba (2004:188) maintains that Arabisms are transferred to the Romance lexicon both directly and indirectly. They are conveyed directly by the Mozarabs moving north into Castile and by the occasional contacts between Muslims and Christians. Indirect sources include Arabic words without Romance or Latin equivalents that are used in translations, as well as those brought by non-Castilian merchants, travelers, and soldiers who have had contact with Arabic.

The Arabisms absorbed into the Spanish vocabulary are concentrated in several semantic fields, such as the following:

- administration   *alcalde* 'mayor', *alguacil* 'bailiff', *barrio* 'neighborhood'
- military   *alcázar* 'fortress', *almirante* 'admiral', *arsenal* 'arsenal', *jinete* 'horse rider', *hazaña* 'heroic deed', *rehén* 'hostage'
- housing   *albañil* 'bricklayer', *alcoba* 'bedroom', *alfombra* 'carpet', *andamio* 'scaffold', *azotea* 'terrace roof', *diván* 'divan', *zaguán* 'hallway'
- agriculture   *aceituna* 'olive', *acequia* 'ditch', *algodón* 'cotton', *arroz* 'rice', *azúcar* 'sugar', *naranja* 'orange', *zanahoria* 'carrot'

4. The word *Mozarabic* comes from an Arabic word meaning 'one who imitates Arabs'. Corriente Córdoba (2004:186) believes that the term *Mozarabic* was used originally to designate the people but not their language, and for this reason he suggests the term *romanandalusí* or *romance andalusí* for this variety.

5. According to Ariza (2004a), the exodus of the Mozarabs begins in the tenth and is finalized by the twelfth century. Two factors contribute to the pressure to emigrate: the religious intolerance of the increasingly radical Muslims and the suspicion among Muslims that the Mozarabs are serving as a fifth column in the Reconquest.

- crafts   *alfarero* 'potter', *alfiler* 'needle', *badana* 'poor-quality leather'
- commerce   *aduana* 'customs', *almacén* 'storehouse', *alquiler* 'rent', *arancel* 'tariff', *fanega* 'unit of capacity', *maravedí* 'ancient coin', *tarifa* 'tariff', 'fare'
- toponyms   *Guadalquivir, Guadarrama, Madrid*
- music and games   *ajedrez* 'chess', *dado* 'die', *guitarra* 'guitar', *laúd* 'lute', *tahúr* 'gambler', *tambor* 'drum'
- science   *álgebra* 'algebra', *alquimia* 'alchemy', *cero* 'zero', *cifra* 'digit', 'cipher'

It is interesting to ponder what might have been the linguistic destiny of the Iberian Peninsula if the Muslims had not intervened in its history in such a decisive way. We know that—unless there had been other invasions—one or more Romance languages would be spoken there, continuations of the Ibero-Latin spoken in 711 under the Visigoths. Since the Visigoths had their capital in Toledo, it is possible that peripheral regions might have differentiated themselves linguistically, perhaps in the northwest (the region isolated under the Swabians) and in the northeast (a region exposed to the influence of Gallo-Romance). Under the most probable scenario, the central dialect of the Visigothic court would have formed the nucleus of the national language after the formation of a modern nation-state.

Reconquest

It has been remarked that the Muslims conquered *almost* the entire Peninsula (see map 4), and this was their big mistake (Collins 1999:314), because although the great majority of the Hispano-Goths resign themselves to Muslim domination, a few members of the Visigothic court find refuge in Asturias, beyond the Cantabrian Mountains. From this small and isolated redoubt, under the command of the Asturian king Pelayo (who dies in 737), they undertake a defensive campaign against the Muslim forces that gradually turns into a systematic reconquest of the usurped lands.[6] Pelayo's successors, known as the kings of Leon, retake ever more territory in their expansion toward the south. In the tenth century we find mention for the first time of a region in the upper Ebro Valley whose many fortresses constructed to protect Leon against Muslim incursions lend it the name *Castilla*,[7] that is, 'land of fortified castles'.

It is believed that early Castilian shows the effects of a process of koineization that comes about when the kings of Leon expel the Muslim inhabitants of the conquered territories and repopulate them with Christian settlers. Donald N. Tuten (2003:143) states that as part of the **repopulation** efforts between the ninth and eleventh centuries, Christian settlers moved into the area from Cantabria, Asturias, the Basque territory, Navarre, La Rioja, Leon, Galicia, and Al-Ándalus. With the exception of the Basques, all these groups speak mutually intelligible Ibero-Romance varieties. The resulting meeting of varieties has the effect of accelerating language change because it represents, from the perspective of each of the speakers in this very heterogeneous new linguistic situation, the introduction of a great number of innovations among which they are obliged to choose. As Penny (2009:47) points out, koineization occurs when speakers accommodate their speech to that of others: "It is normal for speakers to cooperate with their interlocutors. . . . Each speaker selects those variants that come nearest to those used by the others."[8]

6. According to José Ángel García de Cortázar (2004:240), "The Muslim control of the Peninsula had two modalities: the direct and absolute dominance of most of the Peninsula, and the control of the mountainous zones of the territory through the levying of tribute and the threat of punitive expeditions against pockets of resistance. . . . This second modality . . . facilitated the actual autonomy of the population of the northern valleys." ('El control musulmán de la Península incluyó dos modalidades. El dominio directo y absoluto de la mayor parte de aquélla y el control, mediante el cobro de tributos y la amenaza de expediciones de castigo contra los insolentes, de aquellas zonas montañosas del territorio. . . . Esta segunda modalidad . . . facilitó la autonomía de hecho de la población de los valles norteños.')

7. *Castilla* derives from Lat. *castella*, plural of *castellum* 'barracks', 'military camp', which in turn is a diminutive of *castrum* 'fort'.

8. "Es normal la cooperación del hablante con el interlocutor . . . cada hablante selecciona aquellas variantes que se acercan a las empleadas por el otro."

We will see that this process of koineization of varieties is repeated several times in the history of Spanish.

Already in 981[9] Castile becomes an independent county under Count Fernán González, and only twenty-three years later, in 1004, it achieves the rank of kingdom (see map 5). During this period the pace of the Reconquest reaches its peak, in part because of the political dissolution of the Caliphate of Al-Ándalus, which disintegrates into small kingdoms called *taifas* that are hard pressed to defend themselves against the aggressors from the north. By 1085 the Christian incursions manage to liberate Toledo (see map 6), and in 1212, in the epic battle of Las Navas de Tolosa (Jaén), a military force comprising the combined armies of Castile, Navarre, and Aragon routs the Almohads, a group of Berber Muslims who had invaded Al-Ándalus in the twelfth century in order to unify the *taifas* and restore a more fundamentalist Islam. With this victory the northern kingdoms break the Muslim resistance, so that in very little time, under Fernando III el Santo and Alfonso X el Sabio, they are able to establish their dominion over large parts of the south (see map 7), taking all the important cities in western Andalusia, including Córdoba (1236), Jaén (1246), Sevilla (1248), Cádiz (1265), and Jerez (1265). The kingdom of Granada does succeed in maintaining its independence, but at the cost of becoming a tributary of Castile, which had absorbed Leon under Fernando III in 1230.

The various phases of the Reconquest, which have been compared with the unfolding of a fan or the hammering in of a wedge, are represented graphically in maps 4–7. They show how the territorial expansion of Castile is achieved primarily at the expense of the Muslims but also to some degree at the expense of the kingdoms of Leon and Aragon, whose own achievements in the Reconquest languish. According to Paul Lloyd (1987:176–77) and Simon Barton (2004:64), Castile is able to outperform the neighboring kingdoms in reconquering territory because of the more open social character of its operations, which offer talented and ambitious people from the lower strata of society the opportunity to liberate themselves

9. Here I follow Barton 2004:31–88.

from feudal structures and to improve their economic and social standing.

In view of the events surveyed in this chapter, it is clear that the three key events in the linguistic history of Spain are the introduction of Latin by the Romans, the Muslim invasion—which ends the primacy of the Visigoths—and the Reconquest, as a result of which Castilian, an isolated and peripheral northern dialect, spreads southward and establishes itself as the dominant language in large parts of the Peninsula. It is conceivable that without the Muslim invasion and the war of reconquest that it provoked, Castile and the Castilian dialect might have remained very far from the cultural and political centers of the Peninsula.

Rise of Castilian

We saw in the previous chapter that starting in the twelfth century, faced with the increasing inability of the inhabitants of the Iberian Peninsula to use traditional Latin, the previously unthinkable practice of writing documents in Romance arises. It is not surprising that many of the early works written in Castilian have religious themes, like the early *Auto de los reyes magos* (1150), a nonliturgical drama; the *Vida de Santa María Egipcíaca* (1210), a saint's life translated from French; and several works by the monk Gonzalo de Berceo, such as his *Vida de San Millán* (1240), written for the purpose of promoting the monastery of San Millán. More mundane pretensions also lead to the creation of works written in Romance vernacular. Among the learned works of this type are the *Razón de amor con los denuestos del agua y el vino* (1210), a poem that fits into the tradition of troubadour lyric imported from Provence and France, and two epic poems based on themes of classical history, the *Poema de Alexandre* (1201) and the *Libro de Apolonio* (1235). On a more popular level we find the *Poema de Mio Cid* (ca. 1200), an epic poem that portrays somewhat imprecisely but with great power the story of this great figure of medieval Castile.

Inés Fernández-Ordóñez (2004:382–83) notes that already during the reign Fernando III (1230–52) the Castilian vernacular supplants Latin as the language most commonly used by the royal chancery. She calculates that whereas at the beginning of this period only 7.2 percent of all documents are written in Castilian, by 1241 they represent a majority, and by the end of the period they reach 60 percent, a level showing that Castilian has become the de facto official language of the chancery. Fernando's son and successor Alfonso X generalizes this practice, reserving the use of Latin for communicating with other kingdoms.

There are various explanations for the decision to favor Castilian over Latin in royal dealings. Ray Harris-Northall (1999:162) believes that it might be a consequence of the high level of military activity that characterizes this period of the Reconquest. He speculates that already at the beginning of this period, vernacular Romance is probably used in the first drafts of all documents, which are then translated into Latin before formal promulgation. With time, and in view of the difficulties of administering a kingdom from the battlefield, this last step is skipped, although for a while Latin continues to be used in the initial and final formulas of documents. Werner Bahner (1966:29) identifies social and political factors that may have contributed to the transition from Latin to Castilian: "It was necessary to find an official language that could unite Spaniards, Mozarabs, Jews, and Muslims. And keeping in mind the political and cultural circumstances of the period, this could only be the 'Castilian language.'"[10] Manuel González Jiménez (2004:373–74), finally, offers a more pragmatic explanation: "In these works, as before in the royal chancery, Alfonso X gave bold support to Romance, with no intention other than to convey his orders and culture to as wide a public as possible."[11]

Medieval Castilian reaches its zenith at the court of Alfonso X el Sabio (1252–84), which becomes a center of intense scientific and literary activity in which the king himself participates, bringing together teams of historians, scientists, translators, and even minstrels

10. "Había que buscar una lengua oficial que uniera a españoles, mozárabes, judíos y musulmanes. Y teniendo en cuenta las circunstancias políticas y culturales de aquella época, esta solo podía ser la 'lengua castellana.'"

11. "En estas obras, como antes en la cancillería regia, Alfonso X efectuó una decidida apuesta por el romance, sin otra intención que la de hacer llegar sus órdenes y la cultura a un público lo más amplio posible."

to produce a group of works that stand out for their quantity, quality, and variety. In the genre of historiography, special mention should be made of Alfonso's *Estoria de España*, the source of the majority of the medieval examples cited in this *Brief History*. There is also a legal work, the *Siete Partidas*, as well as scientific works such as the *Lapidario* (on gemology) and the *Libro de las cruces* (on astronomy).

The role of the king varies between poet—he is the author of the *Cantigas de Santa María*, a narrative written in Galician with occasional poems of praise—and, according to Lapesa (1981:240), editor, to judge by a passage from the 1276 *Libro de la Ochava Esfera*: "He removed the expressions that he felt were superfluous or duplicated and that were not written in correct Castilian, and he added others that were more appropriate; and as for the language, he himself corrected it."[12] Pedro Sánchez-Prieto Borja (2004:424), on the other hand, feels that scholars have exaggerated "the romantic vision of the personal participation of the king".

What is called *castellano drecho* in this passage, according to Echenique Elizondo (2003:343–47; 2005:314) is yet another Castilian koiné, initiated by Fernando III and embraced by Alfonso X, which with time becomes the standardized form of Medieval Castilian. Standardization, as defined by Fernández-Ordóñez (2004:381), is a process comprising three phases: election of the variety to be standardized, development of the variety so that it meets all linguistic needs, and codification. Thus, once Castilian is chosen, Alfonso authorizes his collaborators to elaborate and supplement the language through "an astonishing effort to make Castilian a language apt not only for legal, historical and literary discourse, but also to convey new scientific concepts"[13] (González Jiménez 2004:374). The codification phase is the most difficult, because, as Fernández-Ordóñez comments (2004:399), due to the number and diversity of the collaborators at the Alphonsine court, it was not possible to

12. "tollo las razones que entendio eran sobejanas et dobladas et que non eran en castellano drecho, et puso las otras que entendio que complian; et cuanto en el lenguaje, endreçolo el por sise."

13. "un asombroso esfuerzo para hacer del castellano una lengua apta tanto para discurso jurídico, histórico y literario, como para aprehender conceptos científicos nuevos".

establish overnight new orthographic, morphological, syntactic, and lexical standards. However, despite these limitations, Rafael Lapesa (1981:245–46) believes that by the time the Alphonsine school reaches its end, "Castilian prose had been definitively created. The enormous effort that had gone into the Alphonsine oeuvre had converted it into a cultural vehicle."[14]

....

Questions

1. Characterize the contribution of each of the pre-Roman languages to modern Castilian.
2. Distinguish between Romanization and Latinization.
3. What are the sources of words of Germanic origin in the Spanish vocabulary?
4. What are the three key events in the linguistic history of Spain? Explain the importance of each.
5. Why does Castilian become the de facto official language of the royal chancery—replacing Latin in this function—at such an early date?
6. How would modern-day Spain and Spanish be different without the contributions of Fernando III and Alfonso X?
7. Compare the Roman invasion and domination of the Iberian Peninsula with similar historical events that you know about. What similarities and differences do you see?
8. Compare the process of language shift that took place on the Iberian Peninsula after the Roman invasion with a similar situation that you know about. What similarities and differences do you see?

14. "la prosa castellana quedaba definitivamente creada. La enorme gimnasia que supone la obra alfonsí la había convertido en vehículo de cultura."

The Latin Language

4

As we have seen, the Spanish language is only the most recent in a series of stages in the evolution of a linguistic organism that has existed since before the beginning of recorded history. At the moment when the organism first appears, it is the language of a group of villages on both sides of the Tiber River in central Italy, which later forms the nucleus of the city of Rome. Because of the importance of this city and the empire that is born there, Latin becomes the European language of culture par excellence for more than a millennium. The many texts written in Latin throughout this period represent an incomparable resource for students of historical linguistics, especially those who specialize in the history of the Romance languages. These texts make it possible to compare the various stages in the life of this organism and to allow these stages to teach us what principles have determined the evolution of all its components, largely free of the need to reconstruct the forms of an original protolanguage.

Since the following chapters treat the linguistic evolution of Castilian, it is desirable to describe here, at the beginning, the linguistic features of the language that served as the starting point for this evolution. For this reason I present here, after a brief historical characterization, the principal phonological, morphological, and syntactic traits of Latin.

Stages in the History of Latin

Due to the existence of a group of words shared among the Italic, Germanic, and Celtic branches of the Indo-European family, linguists posit a time when the subpopulation that eventually splits into these groups was living in central Europe and speaking a language that might be termed "Proto-Italic/Germanic/Celtic". Later, around the tenth century BC, one group of this population migrates toward Latium, the central west region on the Italian Peninsula where Rome is subsequently founded.[1]

The PRELITERARY period ends and the PRECLASSIC begins in the third century BC, when a Greek slave named Livius Andronicus translates Homer's *Odyssey* into Latin. The influence of Greek is evident among the authors of this period, such as Plautus and Terence. In the political sphere, Rome establishes itself during this period as the dominant power on the Peninsula.

The high point of Roman literature, the CLASSICAL period, 100–14 BC, coincides with the consolidation of Roman political power throughout the Mediterranean basin. From this era date works by some of the most brilliant authors in Latin literature: Cicero, Sallust, Catullus, Virgil, Horace, and Ovid.

Shortly after the founding of the Roman Empire in 27 BC and the subsequent spread of the Latin language throughout Europe and North Africa, the decline of Latin literature begins during the so-called POSTCLASSICAL period (14 BC to AD 200). During the LATE PERIOD (AD 200–600) the uniformity of Latin is increasingly threatened. On the stylistic or diaphasic axis, incipient diglossia is becoming increasingly obvious. While the written form of the language maintains its uniformity, regional or diatopical differences multiply in the vernacular. Indeed it may be assumed that the vernacular is markedly different in each region, due to factors such as the presence of indigenous languages, the date and degree of Romanization, social class and geographic origin of the Roman colonists, and the varying degrees of isolation in which they live.

At the beginning of the MEDIEVAL or LOW period, known as the High Middle Ages (7th to 13th centuries), the existence of a single orthographic system for all registers of the language suggests that speakers are not clearly conscious of the diglossic tendencies, considering them to be a question of register more than of language. Later on, however, the practice of writing all documents in Latin

---

1. My source here is "Latin Language (Lingua Latina)," www.orbilat.com /Languages/Latin/index.html (January 14, 2004).

ceases to be sustainable, and texts written in the vernacular begin to appear.

As a result of the move toward writing in the vernacular, written Latin is relegated to the sphere of religion and used as a lingua franca among diplomats and scholars. During the RENAISSANCE period (14th through 16th centuries) some authors—notably Petrarch in Italy and Thomas More in England—try to recover in their literary works the glory of the Latin of the classical era through imitation of the best authors, but despite their efforts Latin ceases to be used in diplomacy during the MODERN period (17th and 18th centuries), and by the nineteenth century, the beginning of the CONTEMPORARY period, it is abandoned as the language of instruction in universities. Latin loses its last important function in the twentieth century when, for the first time, vernacular languages are permitted in the Catholic liturgy.

Phonology

VOWELS. In its common or classical form, Latin has ten vocalic **phonemes** (minimal distinctive phonological units), five long and five short, distributed as follows:

	FRONT	CENTRAL	BACK
high	i: i		u: u
mid		e: e	o: o
low		a: a	

The **phonemic** or functional nature of the feature of duration between short and long vowels is confirmed by a series of **minimal pairs**, i.e., pairs of words with different meanings whose form differs in only one phoneme (Lloyd 1987:71):

/i:/	*fidēs* 'you will trust'	/i/	*fidēs* 'faith'
/e:/	*lēvis* 'smooth'	/e/	*levis* 'light'
/a:/	*mālum* 'apple'	/a/	*malum* 'bad' (ac. sg.)
/o:/	*ōs* 'mouth'	/o/	*os* 'bone'
/u:/	*fūris* 'thief' (gen. sg.)	/u/	*furis* 'you rage'

To this set of vowels we add three relatively common **diphthongs**, groups of vocalic elements that are pronounced in a single syllable:

/oe/[2] (written œ or *oe*), /ae/ (æ or *ae*), and /aw/ (*au*). The segments that accompany the vowels in these diphthongs, /e/ and /w/, are commonly referred to as **glides**.

CONSONANTS. The inventory of Latin consonants is presented below. It is remarkably simple compared to that of Castilian. It lacks the affricate **mode of articulation** and the palatal **place of articulation**, as well as **voiced** fricatives. On the other hand, note the presence in many cases of **geminate** counterparts (indicated here in parentheses and exemplified below).

	BILABIAL	LABIO DENTAL	DENTAL	ALVEOLAR	VELAR	GLOTTAL	LABIO VELAR
unvoiced stop	p(p)		t(t)		k(k)		kʷ
voiced stop	b		d(d)		g(g)		gʷ
fricative		f(f)		s(s)		h	
nasal	m(m)			n(n)			
lateral				l(l)			
tap (trill)				r(r)			

For some consonants, as for vowels, the feature of quantity or duration is phonemic, as can be deduced from minimal pairs such as the following (Lloyd 1987:79):

aditus	'access'	*additus*	'added'
catus	'sharp'	*cattus*	'cat'
ager	'field'	*agger*	'rampart'
casa	'hut'	*cassa*	'empty' (f. nom. sg.)
caleō	'to be warm'[3]	*calleō*	'to be experienced'
ferum	'wild' (m. ac. sg.)	*ferrum*	'iron'
anus	'old woman'	*annus*	'year'

---

2. Several authorities, including Andrew Sihler (1995:55) and Sidney Allen (1978:60–62), insist that the second element of the diphthongs corresponding to *ae* and *oe* was /e/. This is not a case of **syneresis** because there is no possibility of hiatus (as in Sp. *maestro* 'teacher', which can be pronounced as two or three syllables).

3. In Latin studies, the first-person singular form of verbs—rather than the infinitive—is customarily used as the default citation form.

Orthography and Pronunciation

Latin **orthography** is largely phonemic; that is, letters correspond with phonemes and vice versa. However, it does present some difficulties for Spanish speakers.

- Long and short vowels are not distinguished in orthography. This information must be sought in a dictionary or school edition in which long vowels are marked with a macron: *ā ē ī ō ū*.
- Similarly, it is necessary to distinguish between single and geminate consonants, a difference that, in spite of being indicated orthographically, is usually ignored by speakers of Spanish and English.
- The letter *v* (and its equivalent *u* in consonantal functions) is pronounced /w/, ex. *vacca*, *uacca* /'wak ka/ 'cow'.
- The letter *c* always represents the unvoiced velar stop /k/, even before front vowels, ex. *cēra* /'keː ɾa/ 'wax') and *circa* /'kiɾ ka/ 'approximately'.
- The letter *g* always represents the voiced velar stop /g/, even before front vowels, cf. *genus* /'ge nus/ 'lineage', *gingīva* /gin 'gi wa/ 'gum'.
- The letter *i* in initial position before another vowel represents the consonant /j/, ex. *iustus* /'jus tus/ 'just'.

The orthography also fails to indicate stress or accentuation. Of the three factors that determine accentuation—high pitch, duration, and intensity—the first two were traditionally considered most important in Latin, for which reason it is customary to label Latin stress as "musical".

Nevertheless, accentuation is perfectly predictable in Latin. First of all, the question of stress is irrelevant to monosyllabic words: *hic* 'this', *tam* 'so (much)', *grex* 'flock', *sīc* 'just so'. Other than these, in Latin there are no **oxytonic** words, that is, words stressed on the final syllable. In bisyllabic words, stress always falls on the penultimate syllable, meaning that they are **paroxytonic**: *grandis* 'large', *liber* 'book', *contrā* 'against', *amor* 'love', *rubor* 'redness'.

The stress pattern of words of three or more syllables is determined by the "heavy" or "light" nature of the penultimate syllable.

- A word is paroxytonic if its penultimate syllable is heavy (or long, according to the more traditional terminology). A syllable is heavy if its vowel is long by nature (as in *currēbāmus* 'we were running', *recitāre* 'to recite', *octāvus* 'eighth') or is a diphthong (*concaedēs* 'piles of cut branches'), or if it ends in a consonant (*quadrāgintā* 'forty', *invictus* 'invincible', *ancilla* 'maid', *epigramma* 'inscription').

- If the penultimate syllable is light—that is, its nucleus is a short vowel—the word is **proparoxytonic** (stressed on the antepenultimate syllable): *curriculum* 'race', *gracilitās* 'thinness', 'simplicity', *grammaticus* 'grammarian', *decuriō* 'decurio, officer who has command over ten cavalrymen', *insipiens* 'silly'.

Note that in Latin, unlike in Spanish, the letters *e*, *i*, and *u* represent vowels rather than glides in words such as *decuriō* /de ˈku ri oː/, *insipiens* /in ˈsi pi ens/, both pronounced as four syllables. The only exceptions are the diphthongs *ae*, *oe*, and *au*, which are equivalent to long vowels: *incaenō* 'to dine in', *incautus* 'uncautious', both paroxytonic. In *longinquitās* /lon ˈgin kʷi tas/ 'distance', /kʷi/ is not considered to contain a diphthong, so that the word is pronounced proparoxytonically.

SAMPLE TEXT. Below I present a Latin text (the beginning of Caesar's *Commentāriī dē bellō Gallicō* or *Commentaries on the Gallic War*, his most important work), accompanied by an interlinear phonemic transcription that will serve to illustrate some of the guidelines explained above. (See the morphosyntactic analysis of this same text at the end of this chapter for a translation into English.)

> *Gallia est omnis dīuīsa in partēs trēs, quārum ūnam incolunt*
> *Belgae, aliam*
> /ˈgal li a est ˈom nis diː ˈwiː sa in ˈpar teːs treːs | ˈkwaː rum ˈuː nam*
> ˈin ko lunt ˈbel gae | ˈa li am/
> *Aquītānī, tertiam quī ipsōrum linguā Celtae, nostrā Gallī appellantur.*

/a kʷi: 'ta: ni: | 'teɾ ti am kʷi: ip 'so: ɾum 'lin gʷa: 'kel tae | 'nos tɾa:
'gal li: ap pel 'lan tuɾ/

Hī omnēs linguā, institūtīs, lēgibus inter sē differunt.

/hi: 'om ne:s 'lin gʷa: | ins ti 'tu: ti:s | 'le: gi bus in teɾ 'se: 'dif fe
ɾunt/

*Gallōs ab Aquītānīs Garumna flūmen, ā Belgīs Matrona et
Sēquana*

/'gal lo:s ab a kʷi: 'ta: ni:s ga 'ɾum na 'flu: men | a: 'bel gi:s 'ma tɾo
na et 'se: kwa na/

dīvīdit. Hōrum omnium fortissimī sunt Belgae.

/di: 'wi: dit | 'ho: ɾum 'om ni um foɾ 'tis si mi: sunt 'bel gae/

Nominal Morphology

NOUNS. Latin **nominal morphology**, the study of the component parts and functions of nouns, adjectives, and pronouns, operates on the basis of a **case system**, in which endings or **inflections** signal the grammatical function or **case** of the nominal element in question. Thus in the sentence *amīcus venit* 'the friend comes', the ending *-us* of *amīcus* 'friend' indicates that this word has the function of subject, while in the sentence *amīcum videō* 'I see the friend', the ending *-um* indicates that *amīcum* is serving as direct object of the verb.

The six cases of Latin, together with their principal (but not sole) syntactic functions, are as follows:

- **nominative** indicates the subject of the sentence: *amīcus venit* 'the friend comes'
- **genitive** denotes possession: *pater amīcī est* '[he] is the father of the friend'
- **dative** denotes the indirect object of the verb: *Caesar dōnum amīcō dat* 'Caesar gives the gift to the friend'
- **accusative** denotes the direct object of the verb (*amīcum videō* 'I see the friend') as well as direction (*Romam eō* 'voy a Roma')
- **ablative** denotes a series of semantic relations such as separation, instrument, place, and accompanimient, often accompanied by a preposition (*cum amīcō veniunt* 'they come with a friend'), but not always (*cornū occidit* 'she/he killed with a horn')

- **vocative** is used to address another person directly: *audī*, *amīce* 'listen, friend' (due to its infrequency, this case is omitted in the paradigms cited below)

A series of factors complicate the use of the Latin case system. First, note that the endings of *amicus* correspond to only one of five inflexional **paradigms** that existed in Latin. Nominal paradigms are typically called **declensions**, which are parallel to verbal **conjugations**. Thus in order to assign the correct case ending or inflexion to a noun in a given context, one must know, besides the case desired, the declension to which it belongs. In order to facilitate learning, a tradition has arisen whereby the declensions of Latin nouns are identified by their nominative and genitive singular forms—for example, as *amīcus, amīcī* (or abbreviated, *amīcus -ī*). Here the gentitive form is key, in two ways. First, it helps distinguish among declensions whose nominative forms are identical; consider the nominative ending *-us*, which signals the nominative singular in several declensions: *amīcus -ī* (second), *tempus -oris* (third), *frūctus -ūs* (fourth). Second, it marks imparisyllabic nouns, whose singular nominative form differs from all the others, as in *flūmen* 'river', nominative singular, beside *flūmin-is* (genitive singular), *flūmin-ī* (dative singular), *flūmin-ibus* (dative and ablative plural). As shown by these examples, the root of the genitive singular is used in cases other than the nominative.

Another complication in the use of the case system is **syncretism**, the concentration of two or more grammatical functions in a single case ending. Among the examples cited, we find syncretism in the forms *amico* (dative and ablative singular) and *flumin-ibus* (dative and ablative plural). When a syncretic form appears in a sentence, the grammatical context is key to determining which of the multiple functions is in operation. For example, in the sentence *Caesar dōnum amīcō dat*, we interpret *amīcō* as a dative rather than an ablative, since the verb *dat* requires a subject (*Caesar*), a direct object (*dōnum*), and an indirect object, the person to whom the gift is given (*amīcō*). In *Caesar dōnum ab amīcō recipit* 'Caesar receives a gift from a friend', the presence of the preposition *ab*, expressing origin, plus the meaning of the verb ('receives'), lead us to interpret *amīcō* as an ablative expressing the person from whom the gift originates.

The third complication is gender. The third conjugation has masculine (*rex, rēgis* 'king'), feminine (*lex, lēgis* 'law'), and neuter (*cor, cordis* 'heart') examples that are not formally distinguishable. The first declension is formed primarily by feminine nouns, such as *lūna -ae* 'moon', but there are occasional masculine nouns, such as *pīrāta -ae* 'pirate'. Conversely, in the second declension masculine nouns are dominant (*amīcus -ī* 'friend'), but there are feminine examples (*pīnus -ī* 'pine').

Finally, some of the declensions have subclasses other than those related to gender. In the second declension, for example, there are nouns such as *puer* (not **puerus), *puerī* 'boy', and in the third *pater*, *patris* (not **pateris). Another important example: the genitive form of third-declension nouns may include an *-i-* (the so-called *i*-stems), cf. *cīv-ium* 'of the citizens', *flumin-ium* 'of the rivers', beside the non-*i*-stems *lūc-um* 'of the lights', *sorōr-um* 'of the sisters'.

The forms of the five Latin declensions are shown below in abbreviated form, that is, without the vocative forms and omitting some minor subclasses, together with a list of nouns that are declined according to each paradigm.

First declension

lūna -ae
f. 'moon'

SG.

nom.	lūn-a
gen.	lūn-ae
dat.	lūn-ae
ac.	lūn-am
abl.	lūn-ā

PL.

nom.	lūn-ae
gen.	lūn-ārum
dat.	lūn-īs
ac.	lūn-ās
abl.	lūn-īs

ADDITIONAL EXAMPLES

feminine: *aqua -ae* 'water', *barba -ae* 'beard', *casa -ae* 'hut', *fēmina -ae* 'woman', *fenestra -ae* 'window', *filia -ae* 'daughter', *fortūna -ae* 'fortune, luck', *fossa -ae* 'ditch', *lingua -ae* 'tongue', 'language', *mēnsa -ae* 'table', *puella -ae* 'girl', *rosa -ae* 'rose', *terra -ae* 'land'

masculine: *agricola -ae* 'farmer', *incola -ae* 'inhabitant', *nauta -ae* 'sailor', *pīrāta -ae* 'pirate', *poēta -ae* 'poet'

Second declension

	amīcus -ī	puer -ī	dōnum -ī
	m. 'friend'	m. 'boy'	n. 'gift'
SG.			
nom.	amīc-us	puer	dōn-um
gen.	amīc-ī	puer-ī	dōn-ī
dat.	amīc-ō	puer-ō	dōn-ō
ac.	amīc-um	puer-um	dōn-um[4]
ab.	amīc-ō	puer-ō	dōn-ō
PL.			
nom.	amīc-ī	puer-ī	dōn-a
gen.	amīc-ōrum	puer-ōrum	dōn-ōrum
dat.	amīc-īs	puer-īs	dōn-īs
ac.	amīc-ōs	puer-ōs	dōn-a
ab.	amīc-īs	puer-īs	dōn-īs

ADDITIONAL EXAMPLES

feminine: *fāgus -ī* 'beech tree', *fraxinus -ī* 'ash tree', *pīnus -ī* 'pine tree'

masculine: *ager, agrī* 'field', *animus -ī* 'soul', *campus -ī* 'field', *cervus-ī* 'stag', *equus -ī* 'horse', *filius -iī* 'son', *lectus -ī* 'bed', *lupus -ī* 'wolf', *oculus -ī* 'eye', *populus -ī* 'people, nation', *vīcīnus -ī* 'neighbor'

neuter: *labrum -ī* 'lip', *oppidum -ī* 'town square', *pōmum -ī* 'apple', *templum -ī* 'temple'

4. The nominal and accusative forms of neuter nouns of all declensions are identical both in singular (here *dōnum*) and plural (*dōna*). Neuter plurals always end in *-a* (cf. also *flūmina* 'rivers', *tempora* 'times', *genua* 'knees').

Third declension

	cīvis -is m. 'citizen'	soror -ōris f. 'sister'	flūmen -inis n. 'river'
SG.			
nom.	cīv-is	soror	flumen
gen.	cīv-is	sorōr-is	flumin-is
dat.	cīv-ī	sorōr-ī	flumin-ī
ac.	cīv-em	sorōr-em	flumen
ab.	cīv-e	sorōr-e	flumin-e
PL.			
nom.	cīv-ēs	sorōr-ēs	flumin-a
gen.	cīv-ium	sorōr-um	flumin-ium
dat.	cīv-ibus	sorōr-ibus	flumin-ibus
ac.	cīv-ēs	sorōr-ēs	flumin-a
ab.	cīv-ibus	sorōr-ibus	flumin-ibus

ADDITIONAL EXAMPLES[5]

feminine: *lēx, lēgis* 'law', *lībertās -ātis* 'liberty', *lūx, lūcis* 'light', *māter -tris* 'mother', *nātiō -ōnis* 'nation', *nox, noctis* 'night', *pars, partis* 'part', *urbs, urbis* 'city'

masculine: *doctor -ōris* 'teacher', *dux, ducis* 'guide', 'leader', *frāter -tris* 'brother', *homō -inis* 'human', *hostis -is* 'enemy', *leō, leōnis* 'lion', *mīles, mīlitis* 'soldier', *mōns, montis* 'mountain', *pater -tris* 'father', *rēx, rēgis* 'king'

neuter: *caput, capitis* 'head', *corpus -oris* 'body', *iter, itineris* 'journey', *mare -is* 'sea', *nōmen -inis* 'name', *opus, operis* 'work', *tempus -oris* 'time'

Fourth declension

	frūctus -ūs m. 'fruit'	genū -ūs n. 'knee'
SG.		
nom.	frūct-us	gen-ū
gen.	frūct-ūs	gen-ūs
dat.	frūct-uī	gen-ū
ac.	frūct-um	gen-ū
ab.	frūct-ū	gen-ū

5. So-called *i*-stems are underlined.

PL.

nom.	frūct-ūs	gen-ua
gen.	frūct-uum	gen-uum
dat.	frūct-ibus	gen-ibus
ac.	frūct-ūs	gen-ua
ab.	frūct-ibus	gen-ibus

ADDITIONAL EXAMPLES

feminine: *acus -ūs* 'needle', *domus -ūs* 'house', *manus -ūs* 'hand', *nurus–ūs* 'daughter-in-law', *socrus–ūs* 'mother-in-law'

masculine: *arcus -ūs* 'bow (for arrows)', *gradus -ūs* 'step', *lacus -ūs* 'lake', *magistrātus–ūs* 'magistrate', *metus -ūs* 'fear', *senātus -ūs* 'senate'

neuter: *cornū -ūs* 'horn'

Fifth declension

rēs -ēī
f. 'thing'

SG.

nom.	rēs
gen.	rē-ī
dat.	rē-ī
ac.	re-m
ab.	rē

PL.

nom.	rēs
gen.	rē-rum
dat.	rē-bus
ac.	rē-s
ab.	rē-bus

ADDITIONAL EXAMPLES

feminine: *fidēs, fidēī* 'faith', *māteriēs -ēī* 'material', *spēs, spēī* 'hope', *speciēs -ēī* 'aspect'

masculine: *diēs, diēī* 'day'

Here are a few simple sentences made up of these nouns plus the verbs *videt* 'she/he sees' and *dat* 'she/he gives'. If a citizen sees a boy, we will say *cīvis puerum videt*, where *cīvis* is in nominative case and *puerum* accusative. In the opposite case we will say *puer cīvem videt* 'the boy sees the citizen' (*puer*, nominative; *cīvem*, accusative). To say that a man gives a thing to a sister, we will say *homō rem sorōrī dat* (*homō*, nominative; *rem*, accusative; *sorōrī*, dative), and if the moon gives light to the town square, *lūna lūcem oppidō dat* (*lūna*, nominative; *lūcem*, accusative; *oppidō*, dative).

ADJECTIVES. Latin adjectives are declined according to the same paradigms and principles applied to nouns, but in a simplified and more regular way. First, there are no adjectives that are declined according to the fourth or fifth declensions. Second, the forms of a very common type of adjective follow the first declension for feminine forms and the second for masculine and neuter forms: *magna* (f.), *magnus* (m.), *magnum* (n.) 'large'. Note that these types of adjectives are cited with the nominal forms of the three genders.

	1ST DECL. F.	2ND DECL. M.	2ND DECL. N.
SG.			
nom.	*magn-a*	*magn-us*	*magn-um*
gen.	*magn-ae*	*magn-ī*	*magn-ī*
dat.	*magn-ae*	*magn-ō*	*magn-ō*
ac.	*magn-am*	*magn-um*	*magn-um*
abl.	*magn-ā*	*magn-ō*	*magn-ō*
PL.			
nom.	*magn-ae*	*magn-ī*	*magn-a*
gen.	*magn-ārum*	*magn-ōrum*	*magn-ōrum*
dat.	*magn-īs*	*magn-īs*	*magn-īs*
ac.	*magn-ās*	*magn-ōs*	*magn-a*
abl.	*magn-īs*	*magn-īs*	*magn-īs*

ADDITIONAL EXAMPLES

altus -a -um 'tall', *antīquus -a -um* 'ancient', *bellus -a -um* 'pretty', 'handsome', *bonus -a -um* 'good', *clārus -a -um* 'clear', *dignus -a -um* 'worthy', *dūrus -a -um* 'hard', *falsus -a -um* 'false', *ferus -a -um* 'wild', *grātus -a -um* 'grateful', *infirmus -a -um* 'weak', *invictus -a -um* 'unconquered', 'invincible', *laetus -a -um* 'cheerful', *malus -a -um* 'bad', *multus -a -um* 'much', 'many', *novus -a -um* 'new', *Rōmānus -a -um* 'Roman', *sānus -a -um* 'healthy', *tantus -a -um* 'so large'

A large group of adjectives of the third declension follows the model of *fortis* 'strong', 'valiant', except that in the adjective declension the ablative singular is always identical to the dative (*-ī*) and the ending of the gentive plural is always *-ium*. The adjectives of this group are usually cited according to gender—for example, *fortis, -e*, where *fortis* is masculine and feminine, *forte* neuter. Adjectives ending in *-ēns* are cited as *-ēns, -entis*.

	F. & M.	N.
SG.		
nom.	*fort-is*	*fort-e*
gen.	*fort-is*	*fort-is*
dat.	*fort-ī*	*fort-ī*
ac.	*fort-em*	*fort-e*
abl.	*fort-ī*	*fort-ī*
PL.		
nom.	*fort-ēs*	*fort-ia*
gen.	*fort-ium*	*fort-ium*
dat.	*fort-ibus*	*fort-ibus*
ac.	*fort-ēs*	*fort-ia*
abl.	*fort-ibus*	*fort-ibus*

ADDITIONAL EXAMPLES
brevis -e 'brief', 'short', *facilis -e* 'easy', *gravis -e* 'heavy', *humilis -e* 'low', 'humble', *intelligēns, intelligentis* 'intelligent', *lēnis -e* 'smooth', *omnis -e* 'all', *potēns, potentis* 'powerful', *similis -e* 'similar'

Adjectives agree with their noun antecedents in gender and number (as in Spanish) but also in case, though they maintain their own declension. Examples:

a. Noun of the first or second declension, adjective of the third declension

Puer fortis est. 'The boy is strong.'
Puella fortis est. 'The girl is strong.'

Puer rosās amicō fortī dat. 'The boy gives the roses to the valiant friend.'

Puer dōnum grave puellīs fortibus dat. 'The boy gives the heavy gift to the valiant girls.'

b. Noun of the third declension, adjective of the first or second declension

Rēx altus est. 'The king is tall.'

Māter alta est. 'The mother is tall.'

Urbem magnam videō. 'I see the large city.'

Puer cīvibus altīs dōnum dat. 'The boy gives the gift to the tall citizens.'

PRONOUNS. Here only personal pronouns will be discussed (*I*, *you*, *he*, *him*, *her*, etc.). The matter is complicated by the fact that Latin lacks specific forms for third-person pronouns. To make up for their absence, demonstrative pronouns are used, like *hic* 'this one', *iste* 'that one (by you)', *ille* 'that one (over there)'. Only the declension of *ille* will be shown here, together with the declension of the first- and second-person pronouns. At the same time, it should be stressed that in Latin, as in Spanish, the use of personal pronouns is optional. In both languages their presence indicates an intention to express emphasis or opposition, or to avoid ambiguity.

	1ST P.	2ND P.	3RD P.		
			M.	F.	N.
SG.					
nom.	*ego*	*tū*	*ille*	*illa*	*illud*
gen.	*meī*	*tuī*	*illīus*	*illīus*	*illīus*
dat.	*mihi*	*tibi*	*illī*	*illī*	*illī*
ac.	*mē*	*tē*	*illum*	*illam*	*illud*
abl.	*mē*	*tē*	*illō*	*illā*	*illō*
PL.					
nom.	*nōs*	*vōs*	*illī*	*illae*	*illa*
gen.	*nostrum, nostrī*	*vestrum, vestrī*	*illōrum*	*illārum*	*illōrum*
dat.	*nōbīs*	*vōbīs*	*illīs*	*illīs*	*illīs*
ac.	*nōs*	*vōs*	*illōs*	*illās*	*illa*
abl.	*nōbīs*	*vōbīs*	*illīs*	*illīs*	*illīs*

EXAMPLES

ego tibi (vōbis) librōs dō 'I give books to you (sg., pl.)', *tū mē non vides* 'you do not see me', *amīcī nōs non amant* 'the friends do not love us'.

Verbal Morphology

In contrast to the nominal morphology, Latin **verbal morphology** is not so radically different from that of Spanish. Both verbal systems have the indicative, subjunctive, and imperative moods, the active and passive voices, irregular verbs, and the categories of person, number, tense, and aspect that determine the conjugations.

However, the Latin verbal system does differ from that of Spanish in some key points.

- Latin has four conjugations rather than three like Spanish (*-ar, -er, -ir*). Below are presented the paradigms of the present indicative of the four Latin conjugations, corresponding to the following present active infinitives: *amāre* 'to love', *dēbēre* 'to be under an obligation to', *cēdere* 'to yield', and *audīre* 'to hear'.

	1ST CONJ.	2ND CONJ.	3RD CONJ.	4TH CONJ.
1st p., sg.	*am-ō*	*dēb-eō*	*cēd-ō*	*aud-iō*
2nd p., sg.	*am-ās*	*dēb-ēs*	*cēd-is*	*aud-īs*
3rd p., sg.	*am-at*	*dēb-et*	*cēd-it*	*aud-it*
1st p., pl.	*am-āmus*	*dēb-ēmus*	*cēd-imus*	*aud-īmus*
2nd p., pl.	*am-ātis*	*dēb-ētis*	*cēd-itis*	*aud-ītis*
3rd p., pl.	*am-ant*	*dēb-ent*	*cēd-unt*	*aud-iunt*

- Latin has fewer tenses than Spanish does. In the indicative, it lacks the conditional (*amaría* 'she/he would love'), present perfect (*ha amado* 'she/he has loved'), preterite perfect (*hubo amado* 'she/he had loved'), and conditional perfect (*habría amado* 'she/he would have loved'). In the subjunctive, it lacks the present perfect (*haya amado* 'she/he may have loved').
- In most tenses, the **passive voice** is expressed by a synthetic verb form: *amātur* '(she/he) is loved', *amābitur* '(she/he) will be loved'. Only in certain tenses, the perfect and past perfect, is it expressed through a verbal phrase, *esse* 'to be' + past participle:

amāta est '(she/he) was loved' or *amāta erat* '(she/he) had been loved'.

Syntax

The following points highlight some syntactic differences between Latin and Spanish.

- Word order is less constrained in Latin. Subjects are not necessarily placed before objects, and adjectives are not always found next to their antecedents. This is possible in Latin because its nominal morphology makes up for the lack of syntactic rules. Consider this example: *dōna puellārum videō laetārum* 'I see the gifts of the cheerful girls' (lit. 'gifts of girls I see cheerful'). Since the verb *videō* appears in first-person singular form (the pronoun *ego* 'I' is optional), *dōna* has to be accusative, despite appearing in initial position. Of the two nouns *dōna* and *puellārum*, only the latter, in spite of its position, can be the antecedent of the genitive adjective *laetārum*, judging by its meaning and its agreement in terms of gender, number, and case.
- Most commonly, however, the Latin verb appears in final position. Exceptions to this tendency are due to stylistic strategies, such as the desire to stress a particular word more than usual. In the sentence cited above, for example, the fact that the words *dōna* and *laetārum* appear in initial and final position indicates that they are being emphasized.
- **Subordination** (where in sentences comprising two clauses, one—the subordinate clause—depends logically and grammatically on the other, the main clause) is achieved in Latin in various ways, for example with a conjunction: *ut* 'so that' (*hoc facit ut urbem capiat* 'he does this in order to capture the city'), *sī* 'if' (*sī id facit, prūdens est* 'if he does it, he is prudent'), *quod* 'that', 'because' (*doleō quod remansī* 'I'm sorry that I stayed'). There is also a subordinating construction that operates without a conjunction, the so-called **accusative and infinitive**. In these cases, after verbs of speaking and understanding such as *dīcō -ere* 'to say', *putō -āre* 'to consider', and *crēdō -ere* 'to believe', the

subject of the subordinate clause is typically expressed in the accusative, and the verb in the infinitive, as in *putō illōs hominēs sine amīcīs miserōs esse* 'I consider those men to be miserable without friends'. The English structure is clearly parallel.

Text Analysis

In order to illustrate the operation of some of the aspects of Latin grammar described in this chapter, an interlinear morphological analysis of the already cited extract from the *Comentāriī dē bellō Gallicō* is presented below. The analysis indicates meaning, declension (except where a word is irregular in this respect, as is *hic* 'this'), case, gender, number, conjugation, and voice.

Gallia	*est*	*omnis*	*dīvīsa*	*in*	*partēs*	*trēs*
Gaul	is	all	divided	into	parts	three
1st decl.		3rd decl.	1st decl.		3rd decl.	
nom. f. sg.		nom. f. sg.	nom. f. sg.		ac. f. pl.	

quārum	*ūnam*	*incolunt*	*Belgae,*	*aliam*	*Aquītānī,*
of which	one	inhabit	Belgae	other	Aquitani
1st decl.	1st decl.	3rd conj.	1st decl.	1st decl.	2nd decl.
gen. f. pl.	ac. f. sg.	act. voice	nom. m. pl.	ac. f. sg.	nom. m. pl.

tertiam	*quī*	*ipsōrum*	*linguā*	*Celtae,*
third	who	own	language	Celts
1st decl.		2nd decl.	1st decl.	1st decl.
ac. f. sg.	nom. m. pl.	gen. m. pl.	abl. f. sg.	nom. m. pl.

nostrā	*Gallī*	*appellantur.*
ours	Gauls	are called
1st decl.	2nd decl.	1st conj.
abl. f. sg.	nom. m. pl.	pas. voice

Hī	*omnēs*	*linguā,*	*institūtīs,*
These	all	language	institutions
	3rd decl.	1st decl.	2nd decl.
nom. m. pl.	nom. m. pl.	abl. f. sg.	abl. n. pl.

lēgibus	*inter*	*sē*	*differunt.*		
laws	among	themselves	differ		
3rd decl.			irreg.		
abl. f. pl.		ac. m. pl.	act. voice		
Gallōs	*ab*	*Aquītānīs*	*Garumna*	*flūmen,*	
Gauls	from	Aquitani	Garonne	River	
2nd decl.		2nd decl.	1st decl.	3rd decl.	
ac. m. pl.		abl. m. pl.	nom. f. sg.	nom. n. sg.	
ā	*Belgīs*	*Matrona*	*et*	*Sēquana*	*dīvīdit.*
from	Belgae	Marne	and	Seine	divides
	1st decl.	1st decl.		1st decl.	3rd conj.
	abl. m. pl.	nom. f. sg.		nom. f. sg.	act. voice
Hōrum	*omnium*	*fortissimī*	*sunt*	*Belgae.*	
these	all	most valiant	are	Belgae	
3rd decl.	3rd decl.	3rd decl.	irreg.	1st decl.	
gen. m. pl.	gen. m. pl.	nom. m. pl.	act. voice	nom. m. pl.	

(*Translation:* 'All Gaul is divided into three parts, one of which the Belgae inhabit, the Aquitani another, those who in their own language are called Celts, in ours Gauls, the third. All these differ from each other in language, customs, and laws. The River Garonne separates the Gauls from the Aquitani, the Marne and the Seine separate them from the Belgae. Of all these, the Belgae are the most valiant.')

The following features are notable in this extract:

- agreement in gender (f.), number (sg.), and case (nom.) among *Gallia*, *omnis*, and *dīvīsa*
- the adjectives *ūnam*, *aliam*, *tertiam*, whose antecedent is the accusative singular *partem* (from the feminine noun *pars*, *partis* 'part')
- the instrumental ablative in *linguā* 'by means of their language' and *nostrā* 'by means of ours'
- the passive verb form *appellantur*, present indicative of *appellō -āre* 'to call'

- the tendency to place the verb last, cf. *appellantur, differunt, dīvīdit*
- the absence of articles, cf. *belgae* 'the Belgae'

....

Questions

1. Compare the phonemic inventories of Latin and Spanish. What are the principal differences?
2. Transcribe the following words phonemically, indicating accentuation.

fēmina 'woman'	*dēflōrescō* 'to wilt'
nōnus 'ninth'	*jūmentum* 'draught animal'
secō 'to cut'	*pedāneus* 'foot-sized'
incidō 'to fall into'	*imperātrix* 'woman in charge'
locusta 'lobster'	*provocātiō* 'provocation'
amor 'love'	*sumptuōsus* 'expensive'
intercēdō 'to intervene'	*crūdēliter* 'cruelly'
pellūcidus 'transparent'	*dīversitās* 'diversity'
spēs 'hope'	

3. Define and contrast the following terms: *case, case ending, declension, paradigm.*
4. What are the factors that complicate the use of the Latin case system?
5. Using the table of declensions, plus the preposition *in* 'in' (which governs the ablative case) and the verbs *dō* 'I give', *dās* 'you give', *dat* 's/he gives', *dant* 'they give', *videt* 's/he sees', *vident* 'they see', *laborat* 'he works', *habet* 's/he has', *est* 'is', and *sunt* 'are', translate the following sentences into Latin.

   a. *El amigo ve al muchacho en el campo.* 'The friend sees the boy in the field.'
   b. *El rey da el regalo al ciudadano.* 'The king gives the gift to the citizen.'
   c. *La ciudad del rey tiene ciudadanos.* 'The king's city has citizens.'

d. *El amigo del muchacho ve las chozas de la ciudad.* 'The boy's friend sees the city's huts.'

e. *El cuerpo del ciudadano está en el campo.* 'The citizen's body is in the field.'

f. *Los amigos de los ciudadanos dan los cuernos a los hijos de los reyes.* 'The citizen's friends give the horns to the kings' sons.'

g *Los frutos de los campos están en la ciudad.* 'The fruits of the fields are in the city.'

h *Los ciudadanos de la ciudad ven el río.* 'The citizens of the city see the river.'

i *Los amigos ven los regalos del rey, los cuerpos de los ciudadanos y los frutos de los campos.* 'The friends see the king's gifts, the citizens' bodies, and the fruits of the fields.'

6. Using the same materials plus the tables of adjective declensions, translate the following sentences into English (and/or Spanish).

a. *Frāter sānus sorōribus laetīs dōna dat.*

b. *Fēminae intelligentēs urbem magnam vident.*

c. *Pater rēgis in domū magnō est.*

d. *Fīliī Rōmānōrum hostēs nātiōnis vident.*

e. *Tempus spēī et metūs venit.*

j. *Nautae intelligentēs terram hostium vident.*

k. *Nōbīs lēgēs et lībertātem senātus dat.*

l. *Domūs antīquae inter montēs altōs et urbem magnam sunt.*

m. *Agricola fortis multōs diēs in campō labōrat.*

7. For each of the nouns in the sentences in the previous exercise, identify gender, number, case and declension.

Example: *homō* (m., sg., nom., 3rd), *fēminam* (f., sg., accus., 3rd) *videt* 'the man sees the woman'

8. Using the forms of the demonstrative pronoun *ille* 'that one' for the third-person pronouns, translate the following sentences into Latin (keeping in mind that subject pronouns are optional):

a. *Aquélla ve la ciudad.* 'That one (f.) sees the city.'
b. *Aquél me ve.* 'That one (m.) sees me.'
c. *Aquéllas te ven.* 'Those (f.) see you.'
d. *Tú ves aquéllas.* 'You see those (f.).'
e. *Yo te doy aquéllas.* 'I give you those (f.).'
f. *Tú me das aquéllas.* 'You give me those (f.).'

5

From Latin to Medieval Castilian: Phonology

Nature of Phonological Change

All of the observations made in chapter 1 on language change in general—its inexorability, its dependence on the heterogeneity of the language and competition among variants, its essentially social and gradual character—also apply to phonological change in particular. However, because of its physical nature—as a product of the human vocal apparatus—phonological changes are idiosyncratic in many ways.

Given the fundamental differences between vowels and consonants, it is not surprising that they are subject to different kinds of innovations. In the vowel evolution between Latin and Spanish, the factor that sets in motion the majority of innovations is the adoption of a stress-based accentual system in the place of the former "musical" system (Lapesa 1981:76). This explains why some **tonic**, that is, stressed, vowels have undergone diphthongization, dividing into glide and vowel as in Lat. *porcu* 'pig' > Cast. *puerco* (change 12), and the weakening of the majority of the **atonic** (unstressed) vowels, which undergo changes in quality (changes 3 and 5) or are elided (changes 8, 18, and 20). Consonant changes, on the contrary, are usually conditioned by the phonological environment, that is, by their position in the word and by the sounds that surround them. For example, word-initial consonants tend to be more resistant to change, while medial consonants—especially those in **intervocalic** position—are the least resistant. Here the most important principle is **assimilation**, where a consonant absorbs one or more traits of a contiguous sound. Lat. *cantātu* 'sung'[1]

---

1. Astute readers will notice that the ending of *cantātu* (like that many other words cited in this chapter) does not correspond to any of the Latin case forms cited

becomes Cast. *cantado* when its intervocalic /t/ absorbs the sonority of the vowels that border it. Similarly, when the unstressed vowel /e/ of *semita* 'path' is lost (*/ˈse me da/ > */ˈsem da/ > /ˈsen da/), the bilabial nasal consonant /m/ assimilates to the following /d/, becoming dental.

It is also important to emphasize interactions among vowels and consonants. In the history of Spanish, for example, many consonantal innovations came about because the vowels /e/ and /i/ before another vowel were transformed into the glide /j/ (change 5). This is the first step in the complicated evolution whereby the Latin consonant /k/ is transformed into Cast. /θ/ (Lat. *lancea* > Cast. *lanza* 'lance'). Another example is the loss or **syncope** of the atonic vowel /e/ in Lat. *umeru* (change 8), which provokes the introduction of an epenthetic /b/ (change 21) in Med. Cast. *ombro* 'hombro'.

A distinction should be made between purely **phonetic** changes and changes that are **phonological** or phonemic. For example, the change in *cantado*—from [kan̪ ˈta do] to [kan̪ ˈta ðo]—lacks phonemic implications, because it does not create a significant distinction between the phoneme /d/ and others in the consonantal system: [d] and [ð] are allophones that do not contrast in any context. On the other hand, the change that is commonly called **yeísmo**, by which /ʎ/ changes to /j/, does affect the phonemic system, because it involves the loss of a whole series of oppositions in which /ʎ/ is a participant, in particular the one with /ʝ/, cf. *halla* 'she/he finds' and *haya* 'she/he may have', *callo* 'callus' and *cayo* 'cay'. This phenomenon is referred to as **merger**. The opposite case, whereby a single phoneme divides into two, is called **split**, as when Lat. /k/ splits into Castilian /k/ (Lat. *casa* /ˈka sa/ > Sp. *casa* /ˈka sa/ 'house') and /θ/ (Lat. *cēra* /ˈke: ra/ > Sp. *cera* /ˈθe ra/ 'wax').

One more important aspect of phonological change is the fact that changes of this kind occupy a limited span of time. They go into effect at a certain moment, are transmitted through the lexicon

---

in chapter 4. This is due to the fact that the ending of *cantātu* is an amalgamation of nonnominative forms. This aspect of the morphological development of spoken Latin nominal forms is explained in chapter 6.

and the speech community, and then cease to be in force. We know, for example, that the assimilatory change by which Lat. /t/ becomes Cast. /d/ in intervocalic position is no longer in force by the thirteenth century, because intervocalic /t/ in learned Greek and Latin words that enter the Castilian vocabulary during that century is not affected: *anatomía* 'anatomy', *catarro* 'head cold', *poeta* 'poet', *átomo* 'atom'.

The fact that changes have a limited temporal existence requires determining the order in which they are applied. We will see below (change 15) that the Latin geminate consonante /tt/ changes to /t/ in Castilian, cf. *gutta* 'drop' > *gota*. Necessarily, this change must take place after the change /t/ > /d/ exemplified by *cantātu* > *cantado*, since otherwise the final result of *gutta* would be **goda*. I will have occasion to refer to this aspect of phonological change repeatedly in this chapter and again in chapter 7.

Most Important Phonological Changes through Medieval Castilian

This section presents some of the phonological changes, in chronological order, that explain the transformation of Latin words such as *porcu*, *cantātu*, and *umeru* into their Medieval Castilian continuations *puerco*, *cantado*, and *ombro*. The list is limited to a selection of the changes that are considered most important, though a few more minor changes necessary for certain derivations are also included. The examples cited in each case include the intermediate steps that have already occurred up to that point in the evolution, plus—in parentheses—the final medieval form of the word.

1. Loss of final /m/
2. Loss of initial /h/
3. Vocalic mergers
4. Develarization of /w/ (> /β/)
5. Atonic /e/ in hiatus > /j/
6. /t/ and /k/ before /j/ > /ʦ/
7. /k/ before front vowels > /ʦ/
8. Syncope of intertonic vowels (first phase)

9. Palatalization of velar consonants in internal clusters
10. Assimilation of certain consonant clusters
11. Palatalization of consonants before /j/
12. Diphthongization
13. /f/ > /h/ in initial position
14. /ʎ/ > /ʒ/ (*rehilamiento*)
15. Lenition
16. Palatalization of geminate /l/ and /n/
17. Palatalization of initial /kl/, /pl/, /fl/
18. Syncope of intertonic vowels (second phase)
19. Loss of final /t/, /d/, /k/
20. Loss of final /e/
21. Simplification or reorganization of consonantal clusters
22. Prothesis before /s/ in initial clusters

1. Loss of final /m/. Textual evidence indicates that loss occurs already in the first century BC. In monosyllabic words, /m/ is sometimes lost (*iam* > *ya* 'already', *septem* > *siete* 'seven', and *sum* > Med. Cast. *so* 'I am') and sometimes retained as /n/ (*quem* > *quien* 'who', *tam* > *tan* 'so much', and *cum* > *con* 'with').

2. Loss of initial /h/. This change also dates from the first century BC. Examples: *homō* /'o mo:/ 'human being', *habēre* /a 'be: re/ 'to have'.

3. Vocalic mergers. Already in the spoken Latin of western Romania during the imperial era, a series of vocalic mergers occurs that is truly astounding in its scope. Through these mergers the thirteen vocalic phonemes of Latin (/a e i o u/, /a: e: i: o: u:/, and the three diphthongs /ae oe aw/) are reduced to seven in tonic or stressed position, to five in atonic or unstressed position (initial or final), and to three in **intertonic** position (unstressed, neither initial nor final). Perhaps the most notable aspect of this transformation is the loss of the distinctive character of vocalic duration or quantity. After these changes, vowels are distinguished exclusively by their quality or timbre, a change that entails the introduction of a new degree of vowel height—evident in the mid low vowels, front (/ɛ/) and back (/ɔ/), both of which eventually undergo diphthongization (see change 12).

a. Tonic vowels

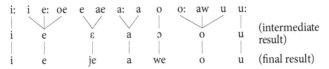

b. Initial atonic vowels

c. Final atonic vowels

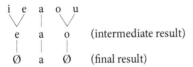

d. Intertonic vowels

i e   a o u
 \ /   \ /
  e   a   o   (intermediate result)
  | | |
  Ø   a   Ø   (final result)

Examples

TONIC VOWELS

a. tonic

LAT.		SP.
fīlia	>	*hija* 'daughter'
site	>	*sed* 'thirst'
cēra	>	*cera* 'wax'
poena	>	*pena* 'pain'
bene	>	/bɛn/ (> *bien* 'well')
caelu	>	/ˈkɛ lo/ (> *cielo* 'sky')
cāru	>	*caro* 'dear'
manu	>	*mano* 'hand'
bonu	>	/ˈbɔ no/ (> *bueno* 'good')
flōre	>	*flor* 'flower'
causa	>	*cosa* 'thing'
bucca	>	*boca* 'mouth'
dūru	>	*duro* 'hard'

b. atonic, initial

hībernu	>	*invierno* 'winter'
plicāre	>	*llegar* 'to arrive'
sēcūru	>	*seguro* 'sure', 'secure'
seniōre	>	*señor* 'lord'
amīcu	>	*amigo* 'friend'
mōmentu	>	*momento* 'moment'
dolōre	>	*dolor* 'pain'
suspecta	>	*sospecha* 'suspicion'
mūtāre	>	*mudar* 'to change'

c. atonic, final

vēnī	>	**vini* (> *vine* 'I came')
Iovis	>	*jueves* 'Thursday'
patrēs	>	*padres* 'fathers', 'parents'
mūtāre	>	*mudare* (> *mudar* 'to change')
cantās	>	*cantas* 'you sing'
fīlia	>	*hija* 'daughter'
cito	>	Med. Cast. *cedo* 'pronto'
cantō	>	*canto* 'I sing'
sēcūru	>	*seguro* 'sure', 'secure'
manūs	>	**manus* (> *manos* 'hands')

d. atonic, intertonic

asinu	>	**aseno* > *asno* 'ass'
umeru	>	**omero* > *ombro* 'shoulder'
orphanu	>	*huérfano* 'orphan'
temporānu	>	**temporanu* > *temprano* 'early'
populu	>	/ˈpɔ bo lo/ > *pueblo* 'town', 'people'

4. Develarization of /w/ (> /β/). Lat. /w/ loses its velar element to produce /β/ at a very early date, perhaps in order to integrate itself better with the other **bilabial** consonants. Example: *vacca* /ˈwak ka/ > /ˈβak ka/ (Med. Cast. *vaca* /ˈβa ka/ 'cow'), *clāve* /ˈkla: we/ > /ˈkla βe/ (> Med. Cast. *llave* /ˈλa βe/ 'key').

5. Atonic /e/ in hiatus > /j/. Already in the early history of spoken Latin, there is a strong tendency to reduce unstressed /e/ to a glide

/j/[2] when it occurs in **hiatus**, that is, in contact with a vowel from another syllable. As can be seen from the Castilian equivalents in the examples cited, the presence of /j/ in these contexts leads to palatalization—and in some cases, further changes—of the preceding consonants. Examples:

vīnea /'wi: ne a/ > /'wi nja/ (> esp. *viña* /'βi ɲa/ 'vine')
lancea /'lan ke a/ > /'lan kja/ (> Med. Cast. *lança* /'lan tsa/ 'lance')
puteu /'pu te u/ > /'po tjo/ (> Med. Cast. *pozo* /'po dzo/ 'well')
fāgea /'fa ge a/ > /'fa gja/ (> Med. Cast. *faya* /'ha ja/ 'beech tree')

6. /t/ and /k/ before /tj/ > /ts/. Both /t/ and /k/ palatalize when they absorb, by assimilation, a following /j/. There may have been a period of merger as /tʃ/,[3] before **depalatalization** as /ts/:

puteu /'pu te u/ > /'po te o/ > /'po tjo/ (> /'po tʃo/) > /'po tso/ (> cast. med. *pozo* /'po dzo/ 'well')
lancea /'lan ke a/ > /'lan kja/ (> /'lan tʃa/) > cast. med. *lança* /'lan tsa/ 'lance'

7. /k/ (> /tʃ/) > /ts/ before front vowels. /k/ (but not /t/) also palatalizes before the stressed front (palatal) vowels /ɛ/, /e/, /i/, as well as atonic /e/, probably producing an intermediate stage /tʃ/, which then depalatalizes into /ts/:

caecu /'kae ku/ > /'kɛ ku/ (> /'tʃɛ ku/) > Med. Cast. *ciego* /'tsje go/ 'blind')
cēra /'ke: ɾa/ > /'ke ɾa/ (> /'tʃe ɾa/) > Med. Cast. *cera* /'tse ɾa/ 'wax'
circa /'kiɾ ka/ > /'keɾ ka/ (> /'tʃeɾ ka/) > Med. Cast. *cerca* /'tseɾ ka/ 'near'
lūcēs /'lu:ke:s/ > /'lu kes/ (> /'lu tʃes/) > /'lu tses/ (> Med. Cast. *luzes* /'lu dzes/ 'lights')

---

2. The glide /j/ is distinguished from the consonant /j/. Traditionally, the glide /j/ is given the name **yod**.

3. /kj/ > /tʃ/ in Italian (*lancea* > *lancia*); for /tj/ > /tʃ/, cf. English *got you* > *gotcha*.

8. Syncope of intertonic vowels (first phase). As indicated above, Latin vocalic phonemes are reduced to only three—/e/, /a/, and /o/—when in intertonic position. It should be added that twice later on—once early and then again after lenition (change 15)—two of these vowels, /e/ and /o/, undergo syncope in this position.[4] Due to its greater sonority, /a/ is maintained even in this position, as can be seen in the example *orphanu > huérfano* 'orphan'.

> *temporānu* /tem po 'ɾa: nu/ > /tem po 'ɾa no/ > *temprano* /tem 'pɾa no/ 'early'
>
> *populu* /'po pul u/ > /'pɔ po lo/ > /'pɔ plo/ (> cast. *pueblo* /'pwe blo/ 'town', 'people')
>
> *asinu* /'a si nu/ > /'a se no/ > *asno* /'as no/ 'ass, donkey'
>
> *consūtūra* /kon su: 'tu: ɾa/ > /kon so 'tu ɾa/ > /kons 'tu ɾa/ (> *costura* /kos 'tu ɾa/ 'sewing')

9. Palatalization of velar consonants in internal clusters. The phoneme /k/ palatalizes not only before /j/ (change 5) and front vowels (change 7) but also before alveolar consonants in interior clusters, producing /ʎ/, /ʃ/, /ʧ/, and /ɲ/. For example, the cluster /kl/ that results from the vowel syncope in /a 'pi ku la/ > /a 'pe kla/ 'bee' evolves into /ʎ/ at this stage:

> /kl/ > /ʎ/: *apicula* /a 'pi ku la/ > /a 'pe ko la/ > /a 'pe kla/ > /a 'pe ʎa/ (> Med. Cast. *abeja* /a 'be ʒa/ 'bee')
>
> /ks/ > /ʃ/: *dīxī* /'di: ksi:/ > Med. Cast. *dixe* /'di ʃe/ 'I said'
>
> /kt/ > /ʧ/: *strictu* /'stɾik tu/ > /'stɾe ʧo/ > (Med. Cast. *estrecho* /es 'tɾe ʧo/ 'narrow')
>
> /gn/ > /ɲ/: *ligna* /'lig na/ > Med. Cast. *leña* /'le ɲa/ 'firewood'
>
> /gl/ > /ʎ/: *tēgula* /'te: gu la/ > /'te go la/ > /'te gla/ > /'te ʎa/ (> Med. Cast. *teja* /'te ʒa/ 'tile')

---

4. Harris-Northall (1990) describes the syncope of intertonics as a unitary tendency that was applied to an ever-increasing number of phonetic environments over a period of several centuries. Practical reasons dictate that they be presented here in two phases.

10. *Assimilation of certain consonantal clusters.* There is a series of early assimilations that in some cases have geminates as their products:

/ps/ > /ss/: *ipse* /ˈip se/ > /ˈep se/ > Med. Cast. *esse* /ˈes se/ 'that one'

/pt/ > /tt/: *septem* /ˈsep tem/ > /ˈsep te/ > /ˈsɛp te/ > /ˈsét te/ (> *siete* /ˈsje te/ 'seven')

/mb/ > /mm/: lat. tard. *palumba* /pa ˈlum ba/ > /pa ˈlom ba/ > /pa ˈlom ma/ > (*paloma* /pa ˈlo ma/ 'dove')

/mn/ > /nn/: *damnu* /ˈdam nu/ > /ˈdam no/ > /ˈdan no/ (> *daño* /ˈda ɲo/ 'harm')

In other cases, the resulting consonants are simple:

/ns/ > /s/: *mēnsa* /ˈmeːn sa/ > /ˈmen sa/ > /ˈme sa/ (> Med. Cast. *mesa* /ˈme za/ 'table')

11. *Palatalization of /l/ and /n/ before /j/.* Among the first palatalizations due to change 5 are the following:

aliu /ˈa li u/ > /ˈa le o/ > /ˈa ljo/ > /ˈa λo/ (> Med. Cast. *ajo* /ˈa ʒo/ 'garlic')

vīnea /ˈwiː ne a/ > /ˈβi ne a/ > /ˈβi nja/ > Med. Cast. *viña* /ˈβi ɲa/ 'vine'

12. *Diphthongization of tonic /ɛ/ and /ɔ/.* After the beginning of the strong palatalizing tendency in consonants, but before lenition (for which see below), the vocalic inventory of Ibero-Romance, which long before has been reduced to the five vowels /aeiou/ in atonic position, is also reduced to five in tonic position, when the low mid vowels /ɛ/ and /ɔ/ diphthongize, becoming respectively, in Castilian, /je/ and /we/. Castilian has **diphthongization** in both **open syllables** (i.e., those ending in a vowel) and **closed syllables** (ending in a consonant), whereas in both French and Italian it is limited to open syllables.

Examples of /ɛ/ > /je/

bene /ˈbe ne/ > /ˈbɛ ne/ > /ˈbje ne/ (> *bien* /bjen/ 'well')

metu /ˈme tu/ > /ˈmɛ to/ > /ˈmje to/ (> *miedo* /ˈmje do/ 'fear')

ferru /'fe ru/ > /'fɛ ro/ > /'fje ro/ (> *hierro* /'hje ro/ 'iron')
septem /'sep tem/ > /'sep te/ > /'sɛp te/ > /'sɛt te/ > /'sjet te/
 (> Med. Cast. *siete* /'sje te/ 'seven')

Examples of /ɔ/ > /we/
bonu /'bo nu/ > /'bɔ no/ > *bueno* /'bwe no/ 'good'
rota /'ro ta/ > /'rɔ ta/ > /'rwe ta/ (> *rueda* /'rwe da/ 'wheel')
ossu /'os su/ > /'ɔs so/ > /'wes so/ (> *hueso* /'we so/ 'bone')
solidu /'so li du/ > /'sɔ le do/ > /'sɔl do/ > *sueldo* /'swel do/
 'salary'

13. Initial /f/ > /h/. Still in the prehistory of Castilian (tenth century), initial /f/ tends to become /h/: /fa 'ri: na/ > /fa 'ri na/ > Med. Cast. *farina* /ha 'ri na/ 'flour', /'fi: ku/ > /'fi ko/ > /'hi ko/ > Med. Cast. *figo* /'hi go/ 'fig'). This pronunciation is maintained until the sixteenth century, when /h/ is lost (by **apheresis**) in initial position. The words in question continue to be written with the letter *f* until the fifteenth century, when it is replaced by *h*, which is still current. Note that initial /f/ is retained before /r/ (*frīgidu* > *frío* 'cold'), /w/ (*fonte* > *fuente* 'spring'), and sometimes /l/ (*flōre* > *flor* 'flower').

14. Rehilamiento of /ʎ/ to /ʒ/. In primitive Castilian, the /ʎ/ produced by changes 9 and 11 undergoes a change called *rehilamiento*, the production of a vibration at the place of articulation that is additional to that of the vocal cords,[5] producing /ʒ/; see the previously cited *apicula* (> /a 'be ʎa/) > Med. Cast. *abeja* /a 'be ʒa/ 'bee', *tēgula* (> /'te ʎa/) > Med. Cast. *teja* /'te ʒa/ 'tile' and *aliu* (> /'a ʎo/) > Med. Cast. *ajo* /'a ʒo/ 'garlic'. We will see later on that this sound changes to /ʃ/ and finally to /x/ in the Spanish of the seventeenth century.

15. Lenition. This change, which affects all stop consonants in intervocalic position,[6] entails a reduction in articulatory energy. The results of this reduction are complex.

---

5. Steven Lee Hartman (1992:434) remarks that, acoustically, *rehilamiento* is equivalent to increased stridency.

6. This change also affects intervocalic clusters of stop plus /r/: cf. *patre* /'pa tre/ > *padre* /'pa dre/ (['pa ðre]) 'father'.

First, voiced stops become fricatives and in some cases even disappear:

/b/ > [β]: *cibu* /'ki bu/ > /'ke bo/ > /'ʦe bo/ > Med. Cast. *cevo* ['ʦe βo] 'bait'

/d/ > [δ] (> /Ø/): *crūdu* /'kru du/ > /'kru do/ > *crudo* ['kru δo] 'raw', *sedēre* /se 'de: ɾe/ > /se 'de ɾe/ > [se 'δe ɾe] > Med. Cast. *seer* /se 'eɾ/ 'to sit', *quadrāgintā* /kwa dɾa: 'gin ta:/ > /kwa dɾa 'gen ta/ > [kwa δɾa 'ɣen ta] > Med. Cast. *quaraenta* /kwa ɾa 'en ta/ 'forty')

/g/> [ɣ] (>/Ø/): *plāga* /'pla: ga/ > /'pla ga/ > (*llaga* ['λa ɣa] 'wound'), *lēgāle* /le: 'ga: le/ > /le 'ga le/ > [le 'ɣa le] > *leal* /le 'al/ 'faithful', *pigritia* /pi 'gɾi ti a/ > /pe 'gɾe te a/ > /pe 'gɾe tja/ > /pe 'gɾe ʦa/ > [pe 'ɣɾe ʦa] (> Med. Cast. *pereza* /pe 're dza/ 'laziness')

Later on, unvoiced stops become voiced. It appears that the weakening tendency lasts long enough for them to become fricatives as in the previous case, but not to the point of suffering syncope.

/p/ > /b/ > [β]: *cūpa* /'ku: pa/ > /'ku pa/ > /'ku ba/ > *cuba* ['ku βa] 'cask'), *capra* /'ka pɾa/ > /'ka pɾa/ > /'ka bɾa/ > *cabra* ['ka βɾa] 'goat'

/t/ > /d/ > [δ]: *catēna* /ka 'te: na/ > /ka 'te na/ > /ka 'de na/ > *cadena* [ka 'δe na] 'chain', *patre* /'pa tɾe/ > /'pa tɾe/ > /'pa dɾe/ > *padre* ['pa δɾe] 'father'

/k/ > /g/ > [ɣ]: *sēcūru* /se: 'ku: ɾu/ > /se 'ku ɾo/ > /se 'gu ɾo/ > *seguro* [se 'ɣu ɾo] 'sure', *socru* /'su kɾu/ > /'sɔ kɾo/ > /'swe kɾo/ > /'swe gɾo/ > *suegro* ['swe ɣɾo] 'father-in-law'

Finally, geminate stops become simple:

/pp/ > /p/: *cuppa* /'kup pa/ > /'kop pa/ > *copa* /'ko pa/ 'cup'
/tt/ > /t/: *gutta* /'gut ta/ > /'got ta/ > *gota* /'go ta/ 'drop'
/kk/ > /k/: *siccu* /'sik ku/ > /'sek ko/ > *seco* /'se ko/ 'dry'

Some scholars think that other, similar changes to nonocclusive sounds are due to the same process of lenition. For example, the sonorization of intervocalic /s/ and /ʦ/ implies a reduction of energy parallel to that shown in the **occlusive** (stop) examples:

/s/ > /z/: *casa* /'ka sa/ > Med. Cast. /'ka za/ 'house'

/ts/ > /dz/: *lūcēs* /'lu: ke:s/ > /'lu kes/ > /'lu tses/ > Med. Cast. *luzes* /'lu dzes/ 'lights'

Another example: the reduction of the geminates /ss/ and /mm/:

/ss/ > /s/: *ossu* /'os su/ > /'ɔs so/ > Med. Cast. *huesso* /'we so/ 'bone'[7]

/mm/ > /m/: *flamma* /'flam ma/ > /'flam ma/ (> *llama* /'ʎa ma/) 'flame'

16. Palatalization of geminate /l/ and /n/. Once change 14 (/ʎ/ to /ʒ/) is no longer viable, /ʎ/ is again produced when geminate /ll/ palatalizes: *caballu* /ka 'bal lu/ > /ka 'bal lo/ > *caballo* /ka 'ba ʎo/ 'horse'. Geminate /nn/ palatalizes as well: *annu* /'an nu/ > /'an no/ > *año* /'a ɲo/.

17. Palatalization of /kl/, /pl/, /fl/ in initial position. The process whereby the cluster /kl/ produces /ʎ/ by assimilation in interior groups has already been explained (change 9). The cluster /kl/ also palatalizes in initial position, in cases such as *clāve* /'kla: we/ > /'kla βe/ > *llave* /'ʎa βe/ 'key', as do initial /pl/ (*plānu* /'pla: nu/ > /'pla no/ > *llano* /'ʎa no/ 'level') and /fl/ (*flamma* /'flam ma/ > /'fla ma/ > *llama* /'ʎa ma/ 'flame'). While in the case of /kl/ the palatal outcome is explicable as an assimilation between the two segments /k/ (velar) and /l/ (alveolar), there is no analogous explanation for the clusters /pl/ and /fl/. For this reason, Lloyd (1987:225) hypothesizes that their palatalization reflects an analogical generalization indicative of a perceived parallelism among these similar clusters.

18. Syncope of intertonic vowels (second phase). In some cases, it is obvious that lenition has to occur before the intertonic vowel is lost, since otherwise we would expect, for example, a derivation *bonitāte* /bo ni 'ta te/ > **/bon 'ta te/ (change 8) > **/bon 'ta de/ (change

---

7. Clearly, the change /s/ > /z/ ends before /ss/ > /s/, as otherwise this word would have been pronounced **/wé zo/ in Medieval Castilian.

15) > **/bon 'tad/ (change 20). For this reason linguists posit a late application of this phase of syncope, after the beginning of lenition.

> *bonitāte* /bo ni 'ta: te/ > /bo ne 'ta te/ > /bon e 'da de/ > *bondad* /bon 'dad/ 'kindness'
> *comite* /'ko mi te/ > /'kɔ me te/ > /'kwe me te/ > /'kwe me de/ > (esp. med. *cuende* /'kwen de/, var. *conde* 'count')
> *līmitāre* /li: mi 'ta: ɾe/ > /li me 'ta ɾe/ > /li me 'da ɾe/ > /lim 'da ɾe/ (> *lindar* /lin 'daɾ/ 'to border on')

19. Loss of final /t/, /d/, /k/. Examples: /t/ (*fābulat* /'fa: bu lat/ > /'fa bo lat/ > /'fa blat/ > /'ha blat/ Med. Cast. > *habla* /'ha bla/ 's/he speaks'), /d/ (*ad* /ad/ > *a* /a/ 'to'), /k/ (*dīc* /di:k/ > /dik/ > *di* /di/ 'say').

20. Loss of final /e/. During the tenth and eleventh centuries (Penny 2002:58), final /e/ suffers **apocope** when occurring after the majority of single consonants in Castilian:

> *pāne* /'pa ne/ > *pan* /pan/ 'bread'
> *mare* /'ma ɾe/ > /mar/ /maɾ/ 'sea'
> *mercēde* /mer 'ke: de/ > /meɾ 'ke de/ > /meɾ 'tse de/ > / esp. med. *merced* /meɾ 'tsed/ 'mercy'

In contrast, it is preserved after final consonantal clusters:[8]

> *parte* /'paɾ te/ > *parte* /'paɾ te/ 'part'
> *viride* /'wi ɾi de/ > /'we ɾe de/ > /'βe ɾe de/ > *verde* /'βeɾ de/ 'green'
> *comite* > *conde* /'ko mi te/ > /'kɔ me te/ > /'kwe me te/ > /'kwe me de/ > /'kwem de/ (> esp. med. *cuende* /'kwen de/, var. *conde* 'count')

---

8. In Medieval Castilian, the loss of final /e/ is common even in this context, cf. *grand* for *grande* 'large', *delant* for *delante* 'in front of', *art* for *arte* 'art'. Lloyd (1987:320–21) attributes this tendency to the prestige of bilingual speakers of Gallo-Romance, who during this era hold important ecclesiastical offices in Spain. When this prestige diminishes in the fourteenth century, apocope also becomes rare in this environment.

21. Simplification or reorganization of consonantal clusters. As a result of the second phase of loss of intertonics (change 18), a new group of hard-to-pronounce consonant clusters arises. These are simplified, reorganized, or supplemented in order to alleviate this problem. In groups of nasal + liquid consonants, a transitional consonant is inserted through **epenthesis**, as in *hombro* (/'u me ɾu/ > /'o me ɾo/ > /'om ɾo/ > /'om bɾo/ 'shoulder'). In *hambre*, epenthesis is preceded by **dissimilation** (whereby one of two similar sounds undergoes a change that makes it less similar to the other): (*/'fa me ne/ > /'fam ne/ > /'ham ne/ > /'ham ɾe/ > *hambre* /'ham bɾe/ 'hunger'). **Metathesis** is also common: (*cumulu* /'ku mu lu/ > /'ko mo lo/ > /'kom lo/ > *colmo* /'kol mo/ 'height'), as is assimilation (*comite* /'kwem de/ > Med. Cast. *cuende* /'kwen de/ 'count').

22. Prothesis before /s/ in initial clusters. The initial clusters /sp/, /st/, and /sk/, permitted in Latin, are now judged to be ill-formed, motivating a change that disarticulates the clusters through the addition of an additional syllable with vowel /e/:

> *sperāre* /spe 'ra: ɾe/ > /spe 'raɾ/ > *esperar* /es pe 'raɾ/ 'to wait', 'to hope'
> *stāre* /'sta: ɾe/ > /staɾ/ > *estar* /es 'taɾ/ 'to be'
> *schola* /'sko la/ > /'skɔ la/ > /'skwe la/ > *escuela* /es 'kwe la/ 'school'

Phonological Derivations

This very simplified list of phonological changes is sufficient to depict the evolution of a large number of words in a step-by-step procedure called **derivation**. This involves applying relevant changes, in order, to a Latin form such that they produce the corresponding medieval form. This exercise is admittedly somewhat artificial: since a step-by-step derivation cannot show the overlap of changes, no claim can be made as to the reality of the intervening stages between Latin and Medieval Castilian. In spite of this caveat, chronological derivations are clearly an indispensable as a pedagogical tool, as they represent the best possible method of illustrating the most fundamental concepts of phonological change. A set of examples is presented below.

FORMS	NUMBER OF CHANGE	EXPLANATION
Lat. *vēritāte*		
/we: ɾi 'ta: te/		Latin form
/we ɾe 'ta te/	3	vowel mergers
/βe ɾe 'ta te/	4	/w/ > /β/
/βe ɾe 'da de/	15	lenition
/βeɾ 'da de/	18	second loss of intertonics
/βeɾ 'dad/	20	apocope of final /e/
Med. Cast. *verdad*		
Hisp. Lat. *capitia*		
/ka 'pi ti a/		Latin form
/ka 'pe te a/	3	vowel mergers
/ka 'pe tja/	5	atonic /e/ in hiatus > /j/
/ka 'pe tsa/	6	/tj/ > /ts/
/ka 'be dza/	15	lenition
Med. Cast. *cabeza*		
Lat. *populu*		
/'po pu lu/		Latin form
/'pɔ po lo/	3	vowel mergers
/'pɔ plo/	8	first loss of intertonics[9]
/'pwe plo/	12	diphthongization
/'pwe blo/	15	lenition
Med. Cast. *pueblo*		
Lat. *umbilīcu*		
/um bi 'li: ku/		Latin form
/om be 'li ko/	3	vowel mergers
/om 'bli ko/	8	first loss of intertonics
/om 'bli go/	15	lenition
Med. Cast. *ombligo*		

9. In this and some other cases the timing of the syncope is irrelevant.

Exceptions to Regular Phonological Change

The above list of twenty-two phonological changes that take place between the spoken Latin of the classical period and thirteenth-century Castilian serves to follow sequentially the evolution of many common words. However, the list is not suited to derive equally common words such as *noche* 'night' (< *nocte*), *lecho* 'bed' (< *lectu*), *hoja* 'leaf' (< *folia*), and *ojo* 'eye' (< *oculu*). For example, following the evolution of *nocte* through the cited changes, we derive **nueche instead of *noche*, because it is expected that tonic short /o/ (> /ɔ/) will diphthongize to /we/. This gap is due to a simplification that I have made, omitting from the list a change called **metaphony**, in which the quality of a vowel is modified by that of a nearby vowel. The list of changes also fails to provide the tools to derive *sepa* 'she/he may know' from *sapiam* or *obrero* 'worker' from *operāriu*, due to the omission of yet another change that stipulates metathesis between certain vowels and consonants (*sapiam* > /ˈsaj pam/, *operāriu* > /o pe ˈraj ɾu/) with subsequent **fusion** of /aj/ to /e/ (/ˈsaj pam/ > /ˈse pa/, /o pe ˈraj ɾu/ > /o pe ˈɾe ɾo/).

There are five more categories of words whose derivation cannot be achieved with our list of twenty-two changes.

LEARNED AND FOREIGN TRANSMISSION. The introduction to this chapter stressed the fact that phonological changes are of limited duration. In order to illustrate this, some words were cited that were incorporated into the Spanish language after the end of the viability of lenition, among them *catarro* and *átomo*. Clearly, if these words had formed part of the language since the beginning, by the medieval era they would have been pronounced **/ka ˈda ro/ and, perhaps, **/ˈan do/ (with metathesis). For this reason, it is necessary to distinguish between loanwords, that is, words transmitted to Spanish through **learned** or foreign channels, and words that were transmitted through **popular** channels directly from spoken Latin. There is a third category, so-called **semilearned** words, which, in spite of being transmitted through popular channels, preserve some features of their Latin counterparts due to being closely identified with them in some learned context, usually religious. Among the examples that could be cited are *ángel* 'angel', from *angelus* /ˈan ge lus/, where the expected popular outcome is **/ˈan xo/ (cf. Port. *anjo* 'angel'), and as a learned word **/ˈan xe lo/. Another example: *siglo* 'century', from *saeculum* (/ˈsae ku lum/), instead of expected popular **/ˈse xo/ or **/ˈsje xo/, or as a learned word, **/ˈse ku lo/.

INCOMPLETE PHONOLOGICAL CHANGES. Some scholars cite, for the category of semilearned words, the example *cruz* 'cross' (< Lat. *cruce*), whose expected popular outcome would be ***croz* /kroθ/ in Modern Spanish. However, Lloyd (1987:27, 182) shows that *cruz* is one of a long list of words in which Latin short tonic /u/ develops into Sp. /u/ instead of the expected /o/—cf. *summa > suma* 'sum', *jugu > yugo* 'yoke', *mundu > mundo* 'world', *furtu > hurto* 'theft', and *sulcu > surco* 'furrow'. Since some of these words can hardly be associated with an ecclesiastical context, we conjecture that the change /u/ > /o/ is incomplete—that it loses viability before being propagated through the entire vocabulary. Other incomplete changes in Spanish: initial /fl/, which produces /ʎ/ in some cases (*flamma > llama* 'flame') but also /fl/ (*flōre > flor* 'flower') and /l/ (*flaccidu > lacio* 'limp, weak'), and /ɔ/ followed by a nasal vowel, which sometimes diphthongizes (*fonte > fuente* 'spring'), sometimes does not (*monte > monte* 'mountain', *homine > omne* 'human being'), and sometimes does both (*comite > Med. Cast. cuende, conde* 'count'; *quōmodo > cuemo, como* 'how').

ANALOGICAL INTERFERENCE. As we shall see repeatedly in the next chapter, when we consider morphological change, many exceptions to regular phonological change are due to the operation of **analogical change**. Frequently, the effects of analogy—through which the form of a word is affected by that of a word or group of words associated with it—are detected in nominal or verbal paradigms. For example, applying our twenty-two changes to the forms of the Latin imperfect of verbs ending in *-āre* (*-ābam, -ābās, -ābat, -ābāmus, -ābātis, -ābant*), we would expect to see, in Spanish, *-aba, -abas, -aba,* ***-abámos,* ***-abádes, -aban*. The fact that these forms are in fact pronounced *-ábamos* and *-ábais* is due to the regularization of the stress pattern of the paradigm: the accent stays invariably on the same syllable. On other occasions, the influence of a single strongly associated word may be sufficient to cause an analogical innovation, as when *siniestro*, the Spanish counterpart of Lat. *sinistru* 'left', appears with a phonologically inexplicable diphthong due to the analogical influence of its semantic opposite, *diestro* 'right' (< *dextru*).

PHONOLOGICAL EFFECTS OF GRAMMATICALIZATION. Grammaticalized words commonly lose part of their phonological substance, as in Eng. *I'm going to* [ˈgowjŋ tu] *Boston* vs. *I'm gonna* [ˈgʌ nə] *eat*. This phenomenon explains why, in the formation of the clitic pronouns, Lat. *illum, illam* become *lo, la* (rather than ***ello*, ***ella*), and why *habeō, habēmus* result in *he, hemos* (rather than ***heo*, ***habemos*).

TRANSPARENCY OF MORPHOLOGICAL STRUCTURES. The fact that speakers are able to recognize the prefix *re-* and the root *pon-* explains why lenition fails to apply to the intervocalic /p/ in words such as **reponere* (> *reponer*).

Text Analysis

An interlinear phonological transcription of folio 164r of Alfonso's *Estoria de España* is presented here as a way of illustrating Alphonsine orthography. The sounds that most clearly distinguish Medieval Castilian from Modern Spanish are underlined. See the morphological analysis of this same text at the end of chapter 6 for a translation.

Sobre aquellas nueuas el Çid enuio luego por sus parientes
/ˈso bɾe a ˈke ʎas ˈnwe βas el ˈt͜si dem ˈbjo ˈlwe go poɾ sus pa ˈɾjen tes/

& sus amjgos. Et mostroles lo quel el Rey enuiara dezir,
/e su sa ˈmi gos | e mos ˈtɾo les lo ke lel ˈrej em ˈβja ɾa de ˈd͜ziɾ/

& dixo les de como non le diera el Rey mas de nueue dias
/e ˈdi ʃo les de ˈko mo non le ˈdje ɾa el ˈrej ˈmas de ˈnwe βe ˈdi as/

de plazo en quel saliesse de la tierra.
/de ˈpla d͜zo en kel sa ˈlje se de la ˈtje ɾa/

ALPHONSINE ORTHOGRAPHY

The first writers who dare to write in Romance vernacular have to face the fundamental problem of finding orthographic representations for Romance sounds that did not exist in Latin. The early solutions are eccentric and chaotic, but thanks to the thirteenth-century chancery of Alfonso X el Sabio, the process of creating a regularized orthography was initiated. Below are some of the most important medieval sound/letter correspondences.

PHONEME	LETTER(S)	EXAMPLE(S)
/i/	i, y, j	*dia, ymagen, antjguas*
/ʦ/	c, ç, z	*cibdat, cabeças, marzo*
/ʣ/	z	*ligereza, fizo*
/z/	-s-	*casa, vicioso*
/s/	s-, -s, -ss-	*siempre, los, fuessen*
/ʃ/	x	*dexassen, dixiemos*
/ʒ/	g, j, i	*ymagen, fijo, meior*
/β/	u, v	*uezinos, vida*
/h/	f-	*fizo, fijo*
/ɲ/	nn	*montannas, anno*
/ʎ/	ll	*llamado, fallamos*

Et que querie saber dellos quales querien yr con el, o quales fincar.
/e ke ke 'rje sa 'beɾ 'de ʎos 'kwa les ke 'rje 'niɾ ko 'nel | o 'kwa les hin 'kaɾ/

Et dixo Aluar Hannez Minnaya: Sennor, todos yremos con uusco, & dexaremos Castiella,
/e 'di ʃo al 'βaɾ 'ha ɲeʣ mi 'na ja | se 'ɲoɾ | 'to do si 're mos kon 'βus ko | e de ʃa 're mos kas 'tje ʎa/

& ser uos emos uassallos leales. Et esto mismo le dixieron todos los otros,
/e 'seɾ βo 'se mos βa 'sa ʎos le 'a les | e 'es to 'mis mo le di 'ʃje ɾon 'to dos lo 'so tros/

& quel non desampararien por ninguna guisa.
/e kel 'non de sam pa ɾa 'rjen poɾ nin 'gu na 'gi za/

El Çid quando les esto oyo gradescio gelo mucho.
/el 'ʦid 'kwan do le 'ses to o 'jo gɾa de 'ʦjo ʒe lo 'mu ʧo/

Et dixoles que si el tiempo uiesse que gelo gualardonarie el muy bien.

/e ˈdi ʃo les ke si el ˈtjem po ˈβje se ʒe lo gwa laɾ do na ˈrje ˈel muj ˈbjen/

Otro dia salio el Çid de Viuar con toda su companna.

/ˈo tɾo ˈdi a sa ˈljo el ˈt͡sid de βi ˈβaɾ kon ˈto da su kom ˈpa ɲa/

Et dizen algunos que cato por agüero, et saliente de Viuar que ouo corneia diestra,

/e ˈdi d͡zen al ˈgu nos ke ka ˈto po ɾa ˈgwe ɾo | e sa ˈljen te de βi ˈβaɾ ke ˈo βo koɾ ˈne ʒa ˈdjes tɾa/

et a entrante de Burgos que la ouo siniestra. Et que dixo estonces a sus amigos /fol. 164v/

/e a en ˈtran te de ˈbuɾ gos ke la ˈo βo si ˈnjes tɾa | e ke ˈdi ʃo es ˈton t͡se sa su sa ˈmi gos/

& a sus caualleros: Bien sepades por cierto que tornaremos a Castiella

/e a sus ka βa ˈʎe ros | ˈbjen se ˈpa des poɾ ˈt͡sjeɾ to ke toɾ na ˈre mo sa kas ˈtje ʎa/

con grand onrra & grand ganancia, si Dios quisiere.

/kon gran ˈdon ra e grand ga ˈnan t͡sja | si ˈdjos ki ˈzje ɾe/

Et pues que entro en Burgos fuesse pora la posada do solie posar,

/e pwes ke en ˈtɾo en ˈbuɾ gos ˈfwe se po ɾa la po ˈza da do so ˈlje po ˈzaɾ/

mas non le quisieron y acoger. Ca el Rey lo enuiara defender

/mas non le ki ˈzje ɾo ni a ko ˈʒeɾ | ka el ˈrej lo em ˈβja ra de fen ˈdeɾ/

quel non acogiessen en ninguna posada en toda la uilla, nin le diessen uianda ninguna.

/kel non a ko ˈʒje se nen nin ˈgu na po ˈza da en ˈto da la ˈβi ʎa | nin le ˈdje sen ˈβjan da nin ˈgu na/

. . . .

Questions

1. Apply, in chronological order, the twenty-two phonological changes presented in the chapter to the following words, to illustrate their phonological evolution between Latin and Me-

dieval Castilian. Begin, in each case, with a transcription of the Latin base.

fīliu > hijo	*strictu > estrecho*	*auricula > oreja*	*dēlicātu > delgado*
capanna > cabaña	*corticia > corteza*	*anniculu > añejo*	*cuniculu > conejo*
caput > cabo	*catēnātu > candado*	*cova > cueva*	*sagitta > saeta*
decimu > diezmo	*clausa > llosa*	*dentēs > dientes*	*laborāre > labrar*
condūxī > conduje	*ferru > hierro*	*meliōre > mejor*	*īnsula > isla*
scōpa > escoba	*fōrma > horma*	*mēnses > meses*	*scrīptu > escrito*
solidu > sueldo	*līmitāre > lindar*	*petra > piedra*	*spōnsu > esposo*
lūce > luz	*probant > prueban*	*stagnu > estaño*	*lumbrīce > lombriz*
rēgāle > real	*lūmine > lumbre*	*romānice > romance*	*modulāre > moldar*
uncia > onza	*ruptu > roto*	*vermiculu > bermejo*	*gutta > gota*
vigilāre > velar	*cista > cesta*	*lumbu > lomo*	*tauru > toro*
manica > manga	*satiōne > sazón*	*capillu > cabello*	*monēta > moneda*
cēpulla > cebolla	*sēcūru > seguro*	*littera > letra*	*audīre > oír*
negat > niega	*spīna > espina*	*fibra > hebra*	*aperīre >*
perdit >	*tenet >*	*causa >*	
peccāre >	*volat >*	*venit >*	

2. Following the description of Alphonsine orthography in this chapter, provide a transcription of the medieval pronunciation of the following words.

plazo	*fincar*	*nueue*
aquellas	*decir*	*dixo*
dexaremos	*Castiella*	*bozes*
gelo	*corneia*	*fuesse*
ganancia	*quisiere*	*fazer*
uilla	*acogiesen*	*Cid*
desenganno	*uso*	*fuerça*
peso	*doze*	*caballeros*
fijos	*uençudos*	*mojones*

3. Explain why the twenty-two changes listed fail to provide correct derivations of the following words:

mobile > móvil	*mittere > meter*	*mītigāre > mitigar*
flaccidu > lacio	*summa > suma*	*comite > conde*

illu > lo

sinistru > siniestro

flōre > flor

mundo > mundo

mundu > mundo

plicem > llegue

clavu > clavo

homine > hombre

lectu > lecho

repausāre > reposar

platea > plaza

From Latin to Medieval Castilian: Morphology and Syntax

6

Interdependence of Morphological and Syntactic Changes

This chapter could be entitled "From Latin to Medieval Castilian: Grammar", since grammar has traditionally been understood as the study of both **morphology**, which has to do with the component parts of words and their grammatical functions, and **syntax**, which is concerned with the placement of words in sentences. I combine the two linguistic components here because in practice they tend to be interdependent. This interdependency can be seen in many of the topics mentioned below in the historical study. For example, the loss of the nominal case endings leads to a reduced flexibility in the order of words, while eliminating the need to make adjectives agree with their antecedents in terms of case. Grammaticalization creates new categories of words such as articles and clitic pronouns, which in turn require the development of new syntactic rules.

We shall see below that there is a general tendency in the morphosyntactic evolution of Spanish. While Latin is a predominantly **synthetic** language—in the sense that it prefers to use **inflection** to signal grammatical categories such as gender, number, case, tense, and mood—Medieval Castilian is more of a mixed language in this respect, due to the effects of grammaticalization, through which a strong **analytic** component is introduced, in which grammatical functions are performed by independent words. The replacement of synthetic with analytic structures is most common in the nominal system. For the Latin word *amīcī*, for example, Castilian substitutes the prepositional phrase *del amigo* 'of the friend'; for Lat. *fortior*, the phrase *más fuerte* 'stronger'. If indeed the synthetic element remains strong in the Castilian verbal system (the ending *-aba* of *hablaba* 'I used to speak', for example, still indicates person, number, tense, aspect, and mood), even here there are analytic substitutes: for Lat.

amābō, Medieval Castilian substitutes the phrase *amar e* 'I shall love', and for *amātur*, the phrase *es amado, -a* 's/he is loved'.

Nominal Morphology

NOUNS. Important transformations occur in all parts of the nominal system, especially in the categories of case, declension, and gender.

Case. We saw in chapter 4 that Latin nominal **morphosyntax** functions primarily on the basis of a case system, in which nominal endings are used to signal syntactic functions within the sentence. In spoken Latin, this system experiences a progressive degradation, disappearing completely before the appearance of the first documents written in Hispano-Romance.

The decay of the case system has two principal causes, closely interrelated.

First of all, there are indications that already in the common era of Latin, efforts are made in the spoken language to complement the case system with prepositional constructions: *dē* + ablative replaces the genitive (*dē illīs* for *illōrum* 'of them'), *cum* + ablative replaces the instrumental ablative (*cum cornū* for *cornū* 'by means of a horn'), *ad* + accusative is used for the dative to express a recipient (*ad illōs* for *illīs* 'to them'). According to Lapesa (1981:71), these substitutions are found even in the most archaic Latin and in the most literary registers.

Second, some of the early phonological changes have the effect of increasing syncretism, that is, of neutralizing the differentiating potential of the endings. For example, the apocope of /m/ in the singular form of the accusative case of all declensions (*lūnam, lupum, lūcem, frūctum, rem*) makes them indistinguishable from other cases: the form *luna* 'moon', from the first declension, now functions as the nominative, accusative, and ablative singular, while *luce* 'light', from the third declension, serves as both ablative and accusative singular. Vowel mergers are another important factor in this connection. Due to this series of changes, the first intermediate stage (for which see the table below) is created, in which, for example, /'lo po/ serves as accusative singular (originally *lupu(m)* [/'lu pum/ 'wolf']) and as dative and ablative singular (originally *lupō* [/'lu po:/]).

These two causes—the phonological and the syntactic—are interrelated, because each one gives impetus to the other. The degradation of the case endings through phonological change inevitably makes the problem of syncretism more serious, intensifying the need to supplement the endings with prepositional constructions. At the same time, the possibility of using complementary prepositional constructions diminishes the importance of the endings in the communication of the syntactic information that originally only they contained.

The example of ancient Gallo-Romance—in which a two-case system was maintained well into the thirteenth century—leads us to assume that that such a system could have existed in primitive stages of Ibero-Romance, with nominative and **oblique** cases, where the latter, based on the accusative, is used for all functions other than subject and vocative. This is the second intermediate stage in the table. However, by the time the first documents appear in Ibero-Romance—the final stage—this system has become even further simplified, eliminating the nominative forms and leaving only the oblique: *lobo* (sg.) and *lobos* (pl.).

	ORIGINAL FORM	1ST INTERM. STAGE	2ND INTERM. STAGE	FINAL STAGE
nom.	lup-us	lop-os	lob-os	
gen.	lup-ī	lop-e		
dat.	lup-ō	lop-o		
ac.	lup-um	lop-o	lob-o	lob-o
ab.	lup-ō	lop-o		
PL.				
nom.	lup-ī	lop-e	lob-e	
gen.	lup-ōrum	lop-oro		
dat.	lup-īs	lop-es		
ac.	lup-ōs	lop-os	lob-os	lob-os
ab.	lup-īs	lop-es		

Declensions. The phonological and morphological changes just portrayed have important repercussions for the declensions. There are now no longer multiple forms for each noun (singular and plural of the nominative, genitive, dative, accusative, ablative, and vocative) but only two (singular and plural of the oblique form). The reduction is actually even more radical. Given their similarity with the nouns of the second declension, those of the fourth declension— not very numerous in any case— lose their independence and merge with the second declension: the accusative of fourth-declension *lacum* 'lake' becomes /'la ko/, and the plural *lacūs* becomes /'la kos/, forms perfectly parallel to /'lo po/ (< *lupum*), /'lo pos/ (< *lupōs*) of the second declension. At the same time, the few nouns of the fifth declension merge with the nouns of two other declensions, either the third (*facie[m] > faz* 'bundle') or the first (*die[m] > día* 'day').

The result of the foregoing is that by the beginning of the Hispano-Romance period, only three varieties of nouns are left: those that end in *-a*, *-as*, mostly feminine and reflecting the first and fifth declensions; those that end in *-o*, *-os*, mostly masculine and reflecting the second and fourth; and those that end in *-e* (or, due to the frequent loss of final /e/, a consonant), *-es*, without a clear gender affiliation, which derive from the third and fifth declensions. Thus the three noun classes of Castilian persist as relics of the Latin declensions: *luna, lunas*; *lobo, lobos*; *parte, partes* (*luz, luces*).

Gender. The gender system also suffers a radical change: it is reduced from three to two when all neuter nouns are reinterpreted as either masculine or feminine. This simplification has two causes. First, neuter nouns do not always denote inanimate objects, as might be expected, which implies that no semantic criterion is applied in the assignment of gender. Latin neuter nouns can refer to groups of human beings (*vulgus -ī* 'the common people', *praesidium -iī* 'guard, escort'), to the human body (*corpus -oris* 'body') and its parts (*ōs, ōris* 'mouth'), and to other living things (*pōmum -ī* 'apple'), even human beings (*scortum -ī* 'leather', prostitute'). Although they frequently refer to things and abstractions (*remedium -iī* 'remedy'), so do nouns that are feminine (*ratiō-ōnis* 'reason') or masculine (*rūmor -ōris* 'rumor', 'gossip'). Second, the neuter gender in the singular is not associated with any specific form, as shown by the diversity of the neuter nouns cited above, plus the following: *tempus -oris* 'time', *cornū -ūs* 'horn', *caput -itis* 'head', *mare -is* 'sea', *nōmen -inis* 'name'.

Some neuter nouns ending in *-e* or a consonant become masculine (*nombre*), while the majority of neuter nouns in *-um* become masculine since after the vocalic convergences, they end in *-o* exactly as the masculine nouns do (*templum > templo*, like *lupum > lobo*). In all these cases the plural form in *-s* is due to analogy with masculine nouns, since it cannot derive from the neuter plurals in *-a* (*nomina* replaced by *nombres*; *templa* by *templos*).

In a few cases, neuter nouns are transmitted to Romance as feminine. Notable among these are monosyllabic words that end in a consonant, such as *mel -lis > miel* 'honey', *sal -is > sal* 'salt', and *lac -tis > leche* 'milk' (also *mar -e > mar* 'sea', which has always vacillated between feminine and masculine; cf. the expression *en alta mar* 'on the high seas'). The majority of the polysyllabic neuters that become feminine, however, do so when their plural in *-a* is reanalyzed (i.e., falsely analyzed) as a first-declension singular. Among the examples of this confusion are the following:

> *braza* 'length of measure equivalent to 1.6718 meters' (< *bracchia*, pl. of *bracchium -iī* 'arm')
> *leña* 'firewood' (< *ligna*, pl. of *lignum -ī* 'wood')
> *obra* 'work' (< *opera*, pl. of *opus -eris* 'work')
> *boda* 'wedding' (<*vōta*, pl. of *vōtum -ī* 'vow')
> *hoja* 'leaf' (< *folia*, pl. of *folium -iī* 'leaf')

In some cases a collective sense remains as a relic of the original plurality. This is clear in the cases of *leña*, *obra*, and *hoja* (which can mean 'foliage'). *Braza* is collective in the sense that it denotes a measure of two arms' length, while a *boda* may be named for the vows made reciprocally by bride and groom.

ADJECTIVES. Due to their similarity to the first three noun declensions, the adjective declensions evolve in a completely parallel way. Taking *altus -a -um* 'tall' as an example of the first and second declensions, we eliminate first the entire neuter component (*-um*) and then the nominative forms (*altus -a*), leaving only the oblique feminine *alta/altas* and masculine *alto/altos*. The transformation of the third-declension adjectives is analogous: *fortis*, which does not reflect the difference between masculine and feminine, is reduced to the oblique forms *forte/fortes* (> Sp. *fuerte/fuertes* 'strong').

A good example of the transfer of complexity from the morphological to the syntactic component through grammaticalization is the evolution of Latin comparative and superlative adjectival forms. In Classical Latin these grades are indicated through the synthetic endings *-ior* (neuter *-ium*) for the comparative and *-issimus -a -um* for the superlative. Examples: *fortis* 'strong', *fortior* 'stronger', *fortissimus* 'very strong', 'strongest'. As reflected by the Spanish equivalents of these forms, in spoken Latin the comparative and superlative endings are replaced by analytical syntactic constructions comprising, in the comparative, the elements *más* 'more' (< *magis*) + the positive form of the adjective (*más fuerte* 'stronger'), and in the superlative, the elements *muy* + positive form of the adjective (*muy fuerte* 'very strong') or the definite article (duly agreeing with its antecedent) + *más* + positive form of the adjective (*el más fuerte* 'the strongest [one]', *las más fuertes* 'the strongest [ones]').

A few of the most frequently employed Latin comparatives do manage to survive, at times together with the analytic forms (*menor* 'smaller' = *más pequeño* 'smaller'):

meliōre (comparative of *bonus* 'good') > *mejor* 'better'
maiōre (comparative of *magnus* 'large') > *mayor* 'greater'
pēiore (comparative of *malus* 'bad') > *peor* 'worse'
minōre (comparative of *parvus* 'small') > *menor* 'smaller'

PRONOUNS. We have seen that the twelve forms of the noun paradigm are reduced to only two, singular and plural of the oblique case. In the pronominal system, the case system is retained to a greater degree, though of course the paradigms do undergo some significant changes. Here we will consider the evolution of the Latin personal pronouns of first, second, and third person.

First person. The chart below shows, in four columns, Latin pronouns, the products of their phonological evolution, the words used in Medieval Castilian to perform the respective functions, and the same words in Modern Spanish.

	LATIN PRONOUN	ETYMOLOGICAL RESULT	EQUIVALENT IN MEDIEVAL CASTILIAN	EQUIVALENT IN MODERN CASTILIAN
SG.				
nom.	ego	yo	yo	yo
gen.	Meī	—	de mi	de mí
dat.	mihi	mi[1]	me	me
ac.	mē	me	me	me
abl.	mē	—	(por) mi, conmigo	(por) mí, conmigo
PL.				
nom.	nōs	nos	nos	nosotros
gen.	nostrum, nostrī	—	de nos	de nosotros
dat.	nōbīs	—	nos	nos
ac.	nōs	nos	nos	nos
abl.	nōbīs	—	(por) nos	(por) nosotros
			con nosotros	con nosotros

In the singular, *ego* becomes *yo* regularly. The accusative/ablative *mē* also persists, but now functioning as accusative (*Juan me ve* 'Juan sees me') and dative (*Juan me da la carta* 'Juan gives me the letter'). The Latin dative pronoun *mihi* lives on in the medieval form *mi*, but with a new function: it no longer functions as a dative but instead as a prepositional **complement**[2]—Med. Cast. *para mi* 'for me', *por mi* 'for my sake', *de mi* 'of me'. This last form replaces the Latin genitive singular *meī*.

Judging by examples such as *para mi, por mi*, one would logically expect ****con mi** instead of *conmigo*. Whence the anomaly? As we shall see, this is just one of many examples of speakers' attempts to "repair the damage" occasioned by phonological change. According to Rini's

1. This result is anomalous, as the expected result of *mihi* would be **me.
2. For the prepositions to be followed by an originally dative form is also a novelty, since in Latin prepositions govern only ablative (*dē mē* 'from me', *sine mē* 'without me', *prō mē* 'for me') or accusative (*ante mē* 'in front of me', *contrā mē* 'against me', *post mē* 'after me').

explanation (1992:34–83), Latin *cum* combines with the ablative *mē*, but normally in inverse order, that is, as a postposition: *mēcum* 'with me'. Following the phonetic changes indicated above, /'me: kum/ becomes, successively, /'me: ku/ (loss of final /m/), /'me ko/ (vowel mergers), and /'me go/ (lenition). Soon after this evolution begins, the preposition (*cum* >) *con* becomes unrecognizable, for which reason speakers feel compelled to reinstate it at the beginning, probably as **conmego* (cf. Med. Port. *comego*). In Medieval Castilian, even before the first written documents, this form changes to *conmigo* by analogy with the variant *mi* that is used with all the other prepositions. This same sequence of events also explains the second- and third-person forms *contigo* 'with you' and *consigo* 'with himself/herself'. Also in parallel, on the basis of Lat. *nobiscum* 'with us', is the evolution of the Castilian plural *conuusco*, whose tonic /u/ has not been completely explained. In any case, this form is lost before the end of the medieval period.

In the plural, *nos* 'we' (< Lat. *nōs*) persists as a nominative until the fourteenth century, when, by analogy with the new form *uoso-tros* (for which see below), the innovation *nosotros* appears. In the oblique functions, first *nos* (and later *nosotros*) acts as a preposi-tional complement, while accusative *nos* performs, as does singular *me*, the functions of accusative (*Juan nos ve*) and dative (*Juan nos da la carta*). The Latin gentive *nostrum/nostrī* and the dative/ablative *nōbīs* are lost.[3]

Second person. Again the Latin paradigm of second-person pro-nouns is cited below, followed by the three additional categories.

	LATIN PRONOUN	ETYMOLOGICAL RESULT	EQUIVALENT IN MEDIEVAL CASTILIAN	EQUIVALENT IN MODERN CASTILIAN
SG.				
nom.	tu	tu	tu	tú
gen.	tuī	—	de ti	de ti
dat.	tibi	ti	te	te
ac.	tē	te	te	te
abl.	tē	—	(por) ti, contigo	(por) ti, contigo

3. The word *nuestro* 'our, ours' comes from *nostrum*, oblique form of the posses-sive adjective *noster -trī*.

PL.

nom.	võs	uos	uos	vosotros
gen.	nostrum, nostrī	—	de uos	de vosotros
dat.	võbīs	—	uos	os
ac.	võs	uos	uos	os
abl.	nõbīs	—	(por) uos	(por) vosotros

Clearly, the changes here are more extensive. Let us consider first the evolution of the nominative pronouns, reproduced here in schematic form.

Latin

SINGULAR	PLURAL
tū	*võs*

Late Latin and Early Medieval Castilian

	SINGULAR	PLURAL
familiar	*tu*	*uos*
formal	*uos*	*uos*

Late Medieval Castilian

	SINGULAR	PLURAL
familiar	*tu/uos*	*uosotros*
formal	*uuestra merced*	*uuestras mercedes*

The difference between the first two stages is due to the introduction of a distinction between formal and informal singular pronouns. It is theorized that this change might have arisen when certain persons began to refer to themselves as *nõs* 'we' instead of *ego* 'I', perhaps because they represented a group of people. Logically, a person who refers to himself or herself with the plural first-person pronoun, *nõs*, has to be addressed with the second-person plural pronoun *võs*. The result of this change is the creation of a more complex system—similar to that of Modern French—in which the applicability of *tū* (Fr. *tu*) is reduced to the familiar singular only, while *võs* (Fr. *vous*) continues to perform the functions of second-person plural while also assuming the new function of second-person singular in formal situations.

By the late Middle Ages a new problem arises, due to the gradual erosion of the deference communicated by *uos*. As a result, *uos* becomes practically synonymous with *tu* in the singular, thereby extending its uses to all four slots on the grid. This problem, which threatens to erase the familiar-formal distinction, is resolved in two ways. First, to differentiate between singular and plural familiar *uos*, the word *otros* is added to the plural form to produce the unequivocally plural *uosotros*.[4] Second, to combat the lack of a clear distinction between familiar and formal, formal *uos* is abandoned in favor of a series of honorific titles such as *señoría* 'your lordship' and *merced* '(your) mercy', most commonly *uuestra merced* 'your mercy', with its plural *uuestras mercedes* 'your mercies'. It is ironic that by the end of the fifteenth century a system has arisen in which *uos*—formerly ubiquitous—has been reduced to a single function, the one traditionally performed by *tú*.

Now let us consider the oblique forms, where the changes are analogous but not identical to those that took place in first person. In singular, as in the case of *mi*, *ti* (< Lat. *tibi*) is no longer used as dative but as a prepositional complement (*a ti* 'to you', *para ti* 'for you', *por ti* 'for your sake', etc.; exception: *contigo* 'with you'), while the accusative/ablative *tē*, just like *mē*, assumes the functions of accusative (*Juan te ve* 'Juan sees you') and dative (*Juan te da la carta* 'Juan gives the letter to you'). Genitive *tuī* is lost. In the plural, Lat. *vōs* serves only as accusative and not as accusative/ablative, as in the cases of *mē* and *tē*. The genitive variants *vestrum*, *vestrī* and the dative/ablative *vōbīs* are lost. Regarding *vōs*, it has a bipartite evolution. In its new function as prepositional complement, it remains unchanged for a time (*a uos* 'to you', *de uos* 'of you', *para uos* 'for you') until it becomes *uosotros* (*a uosotros* 'to you', *de uosotros* 'of you', *para uosotros* 'for you'). In the accusative and dative functions, beginning in the fifteenth century, the innovative variant *os* (*Juan os ve* 'Juan sees you', *Juan os da la carta* 'Juan gives you the letter') becomes generalized.

4. This solution is also found in popular French (*vous autres*). As Miguel Calderón Campos and Francisca Medina Morales (2010:211) show, before *uos otros* becomes established, Medieval Castilian experimented with *uos mismos* 'you same ones', *uos solos* 'you alone', and *uos todos* 'you all', this last example clearly parallel to American English *you all*. Once *uosotros* was established, *nosotros* was formed by analogy.

Third person. We saw in chapter 4 that Latin lacks third-person pronouns. For this reason, in order to refer to third persons, speakers of Latin use demonstrative pronouns. The list of possible Latin pronouns includes *hic* 'this one', *iste* 'that one (near you)', *ille* 'that one (over there)'.[5] In almost all varieties of Western spoken Latin, a new category of personal pronoun, corresponding to third person, is formed on the basis of one of these: *ille*.

As in the case of *ego* and *tū*, *ille* has its own paradigm, which is severely reduced in its evolution to Medieval Castilian. Let us consider, first, subject pronouns.

	M.	F.	N.
SG.			
nom.	*ille* > Cast. *él*	*illa* > Cast. *ella*	*illud* > Cast. *ello*
PL.			
ac.	*illōs* > Cast. *ellos*	*illās* > Cast. *ellas*	

Notice, above all, that the singular forms of Medieval Castilian derive from nominative (if it had been the accusative, we would say **ello* [< *illum*] instead of *él*), while the plural forms derive from the accusative (the nominatives *illī*, *illae* would have evolved to **elle* > **él* instead of *ellos* and *ellas*). The final /e/ of *ille* is lost and the final /o/ of *illud* is preserved, in accordance with the vowel changes examined in chapter 5 and the effects of grammaticalization. The genitive and ablative forms do not persist.

The same paradigm is also the source of the so-called **clitic** pronouns—atonic pronouns that are obligatorily linked with verbs to denote direct and indirect objects—according to the following table:

	M.	F.	N.
SG.			
dat.	*illī* > Cast. *le*	*illī* > Cast. *le*	
ac.	*illum* > Cast. *lo*	*illam* > Cast. *la*	*illud* > Cast. *lo*

5. When *hic* loses this function in Medieval Castilian, there is a readjustment of demonstrative functions: second-person *iste* 'that one' becomes first-person *este*; intensive *ipse* 'he himself' becomes second-person *ese*; *ille* combines with **accu-* (< *eccum* 'here') to produce third-person *aquel*.

PL.

dat.   *illīs* > Cast. *les*   *illīs* > Cast. *les*

ac.   *illōs* > Cast. *los*   *illās* > Cast. *las*

No clitic pronouns derive from the nominative, since they function only as verbal complements: *verlas* 'to see them', *hablarle* 'to speak to him/her', et cetera. Regarding the clitics' phonetic evolution, one notices above all the apheresis of the first syllable, again a consequence of the process of grammaticalization.

In terms of morphology, one is struck by the survival of the forms of the dative, whose development in the atonic environment produces, according to the table, *le* (< *illī*) in singular and *les* (< *illīs*) in plural. The table does not explain, however, why both *le* and *les* are replaced by *se* when preceeding direct object clitic pronouns: *Juan se lo da a María* 'Juan gives it to María', *Juan se las presenta a María y Elena* 'Juan introduces them to María and Elena'. This anomaly is explained by the phonological evolution of the Latin combinations *illī + illum* (*illam, illōs, illās*): (1) /'il li: 'il lum/ > /'il li: 'il lu/ (apocope of final /m/), (2) /'el li 'el lo/ (vowel mergers), (3) /el 'ljel lo/ (glide formation), (4) /'lje lo/ (phonological erosion due to grammaticalization), (5) /'ʎe lo/ (palatalization of /l/ before /j/), and (6) /'ʒe lo/ (*rehilamiento*). This last stage is that of Medieval Castilian, where it is orthographically represented as *ge lo* or *gelo*.[6] Consider Alphonsine examples such as the following: *a quantos le demandauan algo, todo gelo otorgaua* 'whoever asked for something, he granted it all to him/her/them'; *puso ge los delante que los comiessen* 'he placed it before him/her/them to eat'; *e tolliege las luego* 'and then he took it away from him/her/them'.

Several hypotheses have been proposed to explain the subsequent replacement of *ge lo* by *se lo* by the first half of the sixteenth century (Keniston 1937:73). The factor that impels this adjustment is probably the grammatical and semantic isolation of the pronoun *ge*. Unlike all the other clitic pronouns (*se, te, nos*, etc.), *ge* could not be used alone but had to be followed by another pronoun. It was also ambiguous, since it refers to an indirect object that might be singular or plural. It would thus have been more logical to replace *ge* with

---

6. There is no separate medieval equivalent of the plural *illīs +illum*.

le and *les* (****le lo*, ****les lo*) in order to reestablish the etymological order, but it was eventually replaced by *se* instead. Penny (1993:137) attributes the change to two factors: a tendency to confuse the sibilants (/ʒ/ >) /ʃ/ and /s/ in the sixteenth century and the erroneous identification with reflexive constructions like *se lo comió* 'she ate it up', *se lo imagina* 'he imagines it'. Arias (2006:307), on the contrary, rejects the identification with reflexive *se lo* on the grounds that it was less frequent that *ge lo*. For him (309), this innovation reflects a preference for less **marked** or common sounds in words with purely grammatical content.

The linguistic myth (see sidebar) that purports to explain the use of *se lo* for *le lo* does not take into account the existence of medieval *ge lo*. The traditional explanation that is offered for the solution *se lo*, according to which the sequence *le + lo* is cacophonous or ugly sounding, is disproved on the one hand by the existence of the word *lelo* 'foolish' and on the other by the many phrases that contain a pronoun plus a neuter article, as in *decirle lo que quiero* 'to tell him what I want', *describirle lo buenas que son* 'to describe to her how good they are'.

Another notable feature of Medieval Castilian is the use of dative *le* for the accusative when the referent is a masculine human being. This phenomenon, called *leísmo*, is still very much alive in the Castilian spoken in northern Spain. The hypotheses that have been proffered to explain this anomaly are conveniently summarized in Flores Cervantes 2006:676–77. Traditionally, scholars have considered that *leísmo* reflects the substitution of the etymological criterion (accusative *lo*; dative *le*) for a gender criterion (masculine *le*; feminine *la*; neuter *lo*), as a way of making personal pronouns parallel with other pronominal and demonstrative series such as *él, ella, ello*; *este, esta, esto*; *ese, esa, eso*, et cetera. Other analysts have suggested that *leísmo* reflects aspects of the pronominal system of the Astur-Leonese variety (absorbed by Medieval Castilian as part of the process of koineization), in which the difference between things (represented by the neuter pronoun *lo*) and persons (represented by *le*) is fundamental. Finally, a communicative hypothesis has been proposed, according to which the different pronouns reflect different levels of participation in an event—less in the case of *lo* and more in the case of *le*.

Below are presented a series of medieval examples of the phenomenon, where in many cases *le* appears in apocopated form and agglutinated—that is, bound to another word.

> *y este segundo Hercules llamaron le por sobrenombre Sanao* 'and this second Hercules was given the nickname Sanao'
> *ellos tomaron le estonce e leuaron le antel rey Leomedon* 'they captured him then and took him before King Leomedon'
> *e uenciol Annibal e fuxo Senpronio a Roma* 'and Hannibal defeated him and Sempronius fled to Rome'
> *e a Magon enuiol preso a Roma con otros omnes onrados* 'and he sent Mago as a prisoner to Rome with other honest men'

Finally, note the survival of the neuter pronouns *ello* and *lo*. These two pronouns differ from the others in not having noun antecedents (as there are no longer any neuter nouns in Spanish). As a consequence, *ello* and *lo* have been adapted to refer not to nouns but to matters that are not entirely conceptualized, specified, or determined, in sentences such as *lo de tu suegra* 'the matter of your mother-in-law' (Garcés Gómez 2002).

ARTICLES. Like some other languages, Latin works perfectly well without articles. The determination of a referent is deduced from the context:

> *Amīcōs videō.* 'I see the/some friends'
> *Homō potēns est.* 'The man is powerful.'

When more precise reference becomes necessary, demonstrative adjectives can be employed:

> *Illōs amīcōs videō.* 'I see <u>those</u> friends (over there).'
> *Ille homō potēns est.* '<u>That</u> man (over there) is powerful.'

Over time, as in the case of the third-person personal pronouns, the demonstrative *ille* becomes dominant in this usage in Western spoken Latin.[7] The usage becomes so frequent that *ille* ends up reduc-

---

7. The only exception is Medieval Mallorcan, whose feminine article *sa* derives from *ipsa* 'she herself'.

A LINGUISTIC MYTH: THE SUPPOSED CACOPHONY OF THE PRONOUN COMBINATION ***LE LO

The historical explanation for the anomalous use of *se* for *le* and *les* is somewhat complex. First, the Latin sequence *illī illu* undergoes a series of phonetic changes that produce *ge lo* (/'ʒe lo/) in Medieval Castilian; second, *ge lo* is replaced by *se lo* in the Spanish of the sixteenth century. Given this complexity, it is not surprising that another, simpler explanation has arisen, which, in spite of being completely false, is widely accepted in the Spanish-speaking world. According to this explanation, which completely ignores the existence of medieval *ge lo*, *se lo* replaces ***le lo* for reasons of euphony. In other words, it is alleged that the phonetic sequence /'le lo/ is not natural in Spanish or that it even sounds bad.

According to Montrose Ramsey (1902:196), for example, *se* replaces *le* "to avoid the concurrence of two short syllables beginning with *l*". Even the much more recent grammar by John Butt and Carmen Benjamin (1988:126) mentions this explanation: "This phenomenon is traditionally blamed on the cacophony of too many *l*'s."

The great Venezuelan poet and philologist Andrés Bello ([1847] 1951:946) contradicts this stylistic explanation when, commenting on the loss of ancient *ge lo*, he adds that "lo mejor hubiera sido sin duda adoptar, para el dativo oblicuo, las combinaciones *le lo, le la* . . . , nada ingratas al oído" ('undoubtedly it would have been best to adopt, for the dative case, the combinations *le lo, le la* . . . , not at all unpleasant to the ear').

The counterexample *dile lo lelo que es* 'tell him how silly he is', in which four short syllables with initial /l/ are easily pronounced in sequence (cf. additional examples such as *dile lo que piensas* 'tell her what you think', *dile lo mucho que lo quieres* 'tell him how much you love him', *diles lo antes possible* 'tell them as soon as possible', in which *lo* is a neuter article), shows that the traditional explanation is a myth. In sum, if it is true that ***le lo doy* "sounds bad", it is not because of the sequence of sounds it entails but simply because it is grammatically incorrect.

ing its demonstrative force to the point of becoming a mere marker of definiteness, to refer to things identifiable by the hearer by the context: *Ayer llegó una carta. La carta está en el escritorio.* 'A letter arrived yesterday. The letter is on the desk.'

The derivation of the forms of the Castilian definite article from the Latin paradigm of *ille* is portrayed in the following chart:

	M.	F.	N.
SG.			
nom.	*ille* > Cast. *el*	*illa* > Cast. *ela* > *el, la*	*illud* > Cast. *lo*
PL.			
ac.	*illōs* > Cast. *elos* > *los*	*illās* > Cast. *elas* > *las*	

As in the case of the subject pronouns, the singular forms of the article derive from the nominative and the plural forms from the accusative. Their anomalous form is due to the phonological erosion characteristic of grammatical (and grammaticalized) words. The neuter form *lo* is used before adjectives to make them into nouns, as in *lo bueno de la situación* 'the good thing about the situation', *lo fascinante de él* 'the fascinating thing about him'.

Another interesting phenomenon regarding the articles is the use of the apparently masculine form *el* before feminine nouns that begin with a vowel. Note that in the table on definite articles the results of the feminine nominative demonstrative *illa* are *el* and *la*. In other words, in Castilian, one of the feminine **allomorphs** (variants of **morphemes** or minimal units of meaning) of the definite article is *el*. This allomorph is typically[8] used, well into the sixteenth century, before feminine nouns beginning with a vowel, as exemplified by the following, taken from the *Poema de Mio Cid:*

> *saco el pie del estribera* (38) 'he took his foot out of the stirrup'
> *en mano trae desnuda el espada* (471) 'he carries the naked
>   sword in his hand'
> *ca fecha es el arrancada* (609) 'because the battle has been won'

8. This is only a tendency, however. Even in Alphonsine prose we find exceptions: *la estoria [historia], la era, la encarnación, la eglesia* [iglesia], *la onrra* [honra].

assi fera lo de Siloca, que es del otra part (635) 'the same thing
    will happen at Jiloca on the other side'
e grande es el almofalla (660) 'and the army is large'
e tanxo el esquila (1673) 'and he gave the alarm'
salios le de sol espada (1726) 'he escaped from under his sword'
aun uea el ora que uos meresca dos tanto (2338) 'I hope I may
    have the chance of repaying you twice over'

After the sixteenth century, the modern system is imposed, according to which the use of feminine *el* is limited to feminine nouns that
begin with tonic /a/, such as *el águila* 'the eagle', *el agua* '(the) water',
and *el hambre* '(the) hunger'.

The indefinite article, for its part, derives from the accusative
forms of *ūnus* 'one': m. sg. *ūnu[m]* > *uno*, f. *ūna[m]* > *una*, m. pl.
ūnōs > *unos*, f. pl. *ūnās* > *unas*. The plural forms are used in Latin as
in Spanish—compare *similitūdinēs ūnārum rērum* and *semejanzas
de unas cosas* 'similarities of some things'.

Verbal Morphology

We have seen that in its evolution toward Medieval Castilian, Latin
nominal morphology undergoes a fundamental transformation:
the five noun declensions are reduced to three, the three genders
are reduced to two, and the case system is almost completely lost
(except in a few pronouns). In contrast, Latin verbal morphology
is transmitted to Medieval Castilian largely intact. Like their Latin
counterparts, Castilian verbs are conjugated according to the categories of person (first, second, third), number (singular, plural),
mood (indicative, subjunctive, imperative), aspect (imperfective,
perfective), and tense (present and past, among others). Still, there
are some changes, caused by factors such as the tendency of the language to become more analytic through grammaticalization, plus
phonological change and the measures taken to "repair" the irregu-
larities it produces. In this section, after a commentary on this last
topic, we will look at three of the most important changes: those
affecting conjugations, the passive voice, and tenses.

ANALOGICAL CHANGE. The Castilian verbal system offers a panoply of examples of analogical change. In this sense, consider the forms of the Latin second and third conjugations, here represented by *dēbeō, dēbēre* 'to have the obligation to' and *cēdō, cēdere* 'to yield', 'to withdraw' (together with first declension *amō, amāre* 'to love' and fourth declension *audiō, audīre* 'to hear').

Latin Conjugations

	1ST CONJ.	2ND CONJ.	3RD CONJ.	4TH CONJ.
1st p., sg.	*amō*	*dēbeō*	*cēdō*	*audiō*
2nd p., sg.	*amās*	*dēbēs*	*cēdis*	*audīs*
3rd p., sg.	*amat*	*dēbet*	*cēdit*	*audit*
1st p., pl.	*amāmus*	*dēbēmus*	*cēdimus*	*audīmus*
2nd p., pl.	*amātis*	*dēbētis*	*cēditis*	*audītis*
3rd p., pl.	*amant*	*dēbent*	*cēdunt*	*audiunt*

As we shall see below, these two conjugations are merged into a combined conjugation in Castilian. This combination, however, re-quires various adjustments that reflect the operation of a type of an-alogical change called **leveling**, by which the forms of a paradigm are regularized through mutual influence. In the second conjugation, the adjustment is limited to the first-person singular form, *dēbeō > debo*, in order to match the corresponding forms of the verbs of the third conjugation (and of the first, cf. *amō* 'I love'). In the third conjugation, all the plural forms change, following the forms of the second, *dēbēmus* (> *debemos*), *dēbētis* (> *debéis*), and *dēbent* (> *de-ben*), such that the final forms are *cedemos, cedéis* and *ceden* rather than the expected **cendos, **cedes, and **cedon.

Another example is *plicāre* 'to fold', which produces, through regular phonetic change, *llegar* 'to arrive' in Castilian. While the forms of the present indicative are phonologically regular (*plicō > llego* 'I arrive', *plicās > llegas* 'you arrive', etc.), the corresponding subjunctive forms show the effects of leveling: *llegue* and *llegue-mos* cannot result from *plicem, plicēmus* through regular phono-logical development, as they would otherwise be **llez and **lle-cemos.

CONJUGATIONS. With the fusion of the second and third conjugations, the four Latin conjugations are reduced to three. The Castilian paradigms are shown here:

Castilian Conjugations

	1ST CONJ.	2ND CONJ.	3RD CONJ.
1st p., sg.	*amo*	*debo, cedo*	*oigo*
2nd p., sg.	*amas*	*debes, cedes*	*oyes*
3rd p., sg.	*ama*	*debe, cede*	*oye*
1st p., pl.	*amamos*	*debemos, cedemos*	*oímos*
2nd p., pl.	*amades > amáis*	*debedes > debéis* *cededes > cedéis*	*oides > oís*
3rd p., pl.	*aman*	*deben, ceden*	*oyen*

The majority of the Latin forms cited above are transparently related to their Castilian counterparts through the phonological changes examined in chapter 5. As we have just seen, the forms that cannot be explained in this manner (e.g., *dēbeō* and *cēdunt* vis-à-vis *debo* and *ceden*) are due to the effects of analogy. The same can be said of the infinitive *cedere*, which, were it not for leveling, might have produced **cedre.[9]

PASSIVE VOICE. It was mentioned in chapter 4 that Latin generally employed synthetic forms to express the passive voice—that is, through a verbal base and inflections. Consider, for example, the present indicative passive forms corresponding to the regular verbs cited above.

	1ST CONJ.	2ND CONJ.	3RD CONJ.	4TH CONJ.
1st p., sg.	*amor*	*dēbeor*	*cēdor*	*audior*
2nd p., sg.	*amāris*	*dēbēris*	*cēderis*	*audīris*
3rd p., sg.	*amātur*	*dēbētur*	*cēditur*	*audītur*
1st p., pl.	*amāmur*	*dēbēmur*	*cēdimur*	*audīmur*
2nd p., pl.	*amāminī*	*dēbēminī*	*cēdiminī*	*audīminī*
3rd p., pl.	*amantur*	*dēbentur*	*cēduntur*	*audiuntur*

9. For *oigo* see Penny 1993:172–73.

Thus, *amor* (/'a mor/) means 'I am loved', *amāris* 'you are loved', *amātur* 'she/he is loved', and so on.

However, the passive forms are not synthetic in all tenses. In the perfective or preterite tenses, an analytic construction is used, based on the past participle plus a form of the verb *sum* (*esse*) 'to be'. The perfective construction *amātus sum*, therefore, means 'I was loved' or 'I have been loved'. In the paradigm corresponding to the perfect tense of the verb *amō* (*amāre*) 'to love' presented below, note that in this tense there is agreement in gender and number between subject and participle. Thus a woman would say *amāta sum* 'I was loved', and several women would say *amātae sumus* 'we were loved'.

The synthetic forms of the passive voice paradigms do not persist in Castilian. Rather, the perfect tenses are taken as a model for the construction of a series of analytic paradigms. One of the essential elements of this adaptation is a change in the semantic interpretation of the perfective paradigm: *amātus sum* (> *soy amado*) is now interpreted as present tense, in the sense 'I am loved' rather than 'I was loved'.

1st p., sg.	*amātus sum* 'I was loved' → 'I am loved'
2nd p., sg.	*amātus es* 'you were loved' → 'you are loved'
3rd p., sg.	*amātus est* 'he was loved' → 'he is loved'
1st p., pl.	*amātī sumus* 'we were loved' → 'we are loved'
2nd p., pl.	*amātī estis* 'you were loved' → 'you are loved'
3rd p., pl.	*amātī sunt* 'they were loved' → 'they are loved'

TENSES. It goes without saying that in a brief history there is no space for a detailed analysis of the evolution of all Latin and Castilian verbal tenses and moods. Instead I will present a miscellany of topics, chosen on the one hand for their global importance and on the other for their relevance to the morphosyntactic analysis of Medieval Castilian, especially as represented in the Alphonsine text analyzed below. Topics are (1) tenses transmitted relatively intact between Latin and Medieval Castilian, (2) tenses that underwent semantic changes in their evolution, and (3) compound tenses.

Many tenses remained relatively unchanged between the two phases of the language. To illustrate this point, the correspondences between the first-person singular forms of Lat. *amō* (*amāre*) and its reflex, Cast. *amar* 'to love', are presented below. Since the passive voice has already been described, here only the tenses of the active voice will be discussed.

	LATIN	MEDIEVAL CASTILIAN
INDICATIVE		
present	*amō*	*amo*
imperfect	*amābam*	*amaua*
preterite	*amāvī*	*amé*
past perfect	*amāveram*	*amara*
SUBJUNCTIVE		
present	*amem*	*ame*

Two comments are necessary here. First, speakers of Modern Spanish will be surprised to see the form *amara* identified as an indicative past perfect, that is, as an equivalent of *había amado* 'I had loved', since today, as we know, *amara* is used almost exclusively as a form of the imperfect subjunctive equivalent to *amase*. We shall see in chapter 7—where details and examples are provided—that the indicative use of this form continues to the beginning of the fifteenth century, when the modern meaning becomes dominant. Second, it should be added that while the endings of the Medieval Castilian imperfect indicative are very similar to those of Modern Spanish for first-conjugation verbs (*amaua, amauamos*, etc.), there is a period during which the second and third conjugations have two competing sets of endings: beside traditional *comia* /ko 'mi a/, *comiamos*, etc., one also finds *comie* /ko 'mje/, *comiemos*. For more information on the origin and use of this medieval variant, very common in Alphonsine prose, see Malkiel 1959, Lloyd 1987:361–62, and Henriksen 2008.

We just saw that *amara* undergoes a change of meaning toward the end of the medieval period. Other tenses undergo similar changes earlier on, during the transition from spoken Latin to Romance. The Latin past perfect subjunctive *amāssem* (also *amāvissem*), for example, is preserved in Romance, but from the beginnings of written Castilian it is used as an imperfect subjunctive, as in Med. Cast. *amasse* (Modern *amase*). Another tense that is transmitted to the Romance period with a different value is the Latin future perfect indicative, which becomes a future subjunctive in Castilian: *amāverit > amare, comēderit > comiere*, et cetera (cf. Veiga 2006:140–42). This new tense, whose further evolution is described in chapter 7, appears with great frequency in Alphonsine texts, as we shall see.

COMPOUND TENSES. In chapter 4 it was noted that Latin has fewer tenses than Castilian, lacking, among others, the conditional (*amaría* 'I would love') and the perfect forms of the indicative present (*he amado* 'I have loved'), preterite (*hube amado* 'I had loved'), and conditional (*habría amado* 'I would have loved'). This imbalance between Latin and Romance is due primarily to the coining of a series of new Romance tenses, called **compound tenses** because they are bipartite, constructed from the auxiliary verb *auer* 'to have' plus either a past participle (as in the case of *auie amado* 'I/he/she had loved') or an infinitive (*amar e* 'I shall love') of another verb.

The compound tenses are a major manifestation of the replacement of synthetic by analytic structures and, at the same time, of the grammaticalization of the verb *auer*, which in both Latin (*habēre*) and Medieval Castilian had the meaning 'to have, to possess', as shown in the following examples:

> *no an dignidat ninguna* 'they have no dignity whatever'
> *la onra que an los caualleros* 'the honor that gentlemen have'
> *non auedes uos otros por que temer* 'you have no reason to be afraid'
> *ouieron un Rey los moros que ouo nombre Zama* 'the Moors had a king who had the name Zama'

It is also possible to "have" an action finalized, as shown by the following sentences, where there is agreement between the name of the action (in the form of a participle) and the direct object thus affected:

> *des que ouo fechas aquellas dos ymagenes* 'after he had all these images done'

> *otros muchos logares de que no auemos escriptos los nombres* 'many other places whose names we don't have written down'
>
> *pues que Tarif ouo la batalla uençuda* 'after Tarif had the battle won'

Already in primitive Castilian, *auer* experiences a semantic innovation by which the auxiliary function is added at the same time that the denotation of possession begins to be lost. In this new function, the verb communicates exclusively grammatical information such as tense, person, and number. Since the idea of possession is absent in these cases, there is no longer any reason to make the action agree with the thing affected. In the following sentences, therefore, we see the final stage of the process of grammaticalization.

> *e assi cuemo ouieron cauado grand pieça en fondon* 'and as they had dug a lot in the bottom'
>
> *quando estas palauras ouieron dicho aquellos mandaderos* 'when the commanders had said these words'
>
> *assi auien uençudo a los Romanos* 'in this way they had defeated the Romans'
>
> *et gradescio mucho a los moros las buenas razones quel auien dicho* 'and he thanked the Moors heartily for the useful things they had said to him'

This explanation of the grammaticalization of *auer* presupposes a transitive context, but clearly the process ends up affecting intransitive contexts as well, in which there is no possibility of possession (*he ido* 'I have gone', *he subido* 'I have risen', etc.). We also note that the grammaticalization of *auer* makes possible the creation of a series of new compound tenses, since it can be conjugated in all possible tenses. In one case, the new compound tense replaces a synthetic Latin tense, when the past perfect *amāveram* (> *amara*) yields to *auie* (*auia*) *amado* after a period during which the two tenses are synonymous. Other tenses are completely new, such as the preterite perfect (*ouieron atado* 'they had tied') and the present perfect (*an perdudo* 'they have lost').

The grammaticalized verb *auer* also figures in constructions with the present active infinitive. The combination *habeō amāre* was probably used initially to express obligation ('I have to love'), but since obligatory actions usually translate into future actions, soon this combination is used to express future tense in large parts of the western Romance area.[10] In this auxiliary meaning, the forms of Medieval Castilian *auer* undergo a phonological reduction typical of grammaticalized forms, with the following results: *habeō > e, habes > as, habet > a, habēmus > auemos > emos, habētis > auedes > eis, habent > an.* At first these forms continue to be interpreted as independent of the infinitives that they accompany, as is shown by the following examples–taken from Alphonsine prose and the *Poema de Mio Cid*, both from the thirteenth century—in which a clitic pronoun appears between the two parts of the compound future:

> *Seer uos an perdonados uuestros pecados.* 'Your sins will be forgiven.'
> *Poder lo as fazer.* 'You will be able to do it.'
> *Ser uos emos uassallos leales.* 'We will be loyal vassals to you.'
> *Vengar nos emos dellos del mal que nos an fecho.* 'We will avenge ourselves for the wrong they have done to us.'

Later on, the forms of *auer* turn into inflectional endings, losing their status as independent words. Thus the synthetic Latin future (*illum amābō* 'I shall love him'), after becoming analytic in Medieval Castilian (*amar lo e*), is once again synthetic in Modern Spanish (*lo amaré*),[11] such that intercalated words are no longer allowed.

The imperfect tense forms of *habēre* (*habēbam, habēbās, habēbat*) are transformed, analogously, into the endings of the conditional (*-ia* /i a/, *-ias, -ia* or their medieval variants *-ie* /'je/, *-ies, -ie* parallel to the alternative endings of the imperfect indicative). The conditional is a completely new tense in Romance whose original

---

10. Another factor that may have figured in this evolution was the fact that some forms of the Latin future were not sufficiently differentiated: thus in the third conjugation the future *cēdet* could be confused with the present *cēdit*, and in the first conjugation the future *amābit* was very similar to the perfect *amāvit*.

11. History is repeating itself in Modern Spanish: the future *amaré* is being seriously threatened by the verbal periphrasis *voy a amar*.

function was to refer to the future from a moment in the past, as in *dijo que vendría* 'she/he said that she/he would come' (transposition to the past of 'she/he says that she/he will come').

Principal Syntactic Innovations

In this section I will comment on some of the principal syntactic innovations that took place in the transition from Latin to Medieval Castilian. We begin with word order and the use of reflexive constructions in a passive sense, then turn to a series of syntactic products of grammaticalization: the evolution of conjunctions, the development of the adverbializing suffix *-mente* and the prepositional "personal *a*", and the evolution of the syntax of clitic pronouns. Examples are taken from the *Estoria de Espanna* of Alfonso X el Sabio (Kasten, Nitti, and Jonxis-Henkemans 1997).

To illustrate trends in WORD ORDER, I refer to the text whose phonological analysis appeared at the end of chapter 5 and which is morphologically analyzed at the end of the present chapter. Apart from the placement of clitic pronouns, to be explained below, we find a situation very similar to that of Modern Spanish, a language that, in comparison with English, offers quite a bit of freedom in word order. In the main clauses of our sample text we find several examples of the order "subject-verb":

> *el Çid enuio* 'the Cid sent'
> *todos yremos* 'we shall all go'
> *El Çid . . . gradescio* 'the Cid . . . thanked'

We also find examples of the order "verb-subject", especially where verbs are preceded by a conjunction or adverb (English glosses reflect the Spanish word order):

> *et esto mismo le dixieron todos los otros* (lit., 'and this same thing to him told all the others')
> *otro dia salio el Çid de Uiuar* (lit., 'the next day went out the Cid from Vivar')
> *et dizen algunos* (lit., 'and say some')
> *quando aquello uio el Çid* (lit., 'when that saw the Cid')

Here we find no examples of the main verb in final position, where it usually appears in Latin, except where there is no complement, as in *si Dios quisiere* 'if God wishes', and neither do we find examples of the radically free order permitted by Latin. Adjectives, for example, always appear next to their noun antecedents in Medieval Castilian: *ninguna guisa* 'no way', *uassallos leales* 'loyal vassals', *otro dia* 'the next day', *corneia diestra* 'crow on the right', *grand onrra* 'great honor'.

Already at this stage the so-called **passive reflexive**, in which the passive element is expressed impersonally (without an agent) through a reflexive construction, is well established in Castilian (Real Academia Española 1973:3.5.6b; Elvira 2002):

> *compusiemos este libro de todos los fechos que fallar se pudieron della* 'we wrote this book from all the relevant information that could be found'
>
> *conuiene que uos digamos primero quamanna es europa, e quantas otras tierras se encierran en ella* 'we need to tell you first how large Europe is, and how many other lands are included in it'
>
> *e fizieron se muy grandes pueblos* 'and they became very large towns'
>
> *hya oystes desuso contar de cuemo se partieron los lenguages en Babilonna la grand* 'you already heard above how the languages diverged in great Babylon'
>
> *dixol que por desacuerdo se perdien las cosas e por acuerdo se deffendien* 'he told him that things were lost because of disagreements and that they were defended through agreements'

According to Félix Sepúlveda Barrios (1988:84), it is likely that this structure arose in western spoken Latin as another reaction (besides the development of the passive with *ser*) to the loss of the synthetic forms of the passive voice.

We have seen repeatedly that grammaticalization has served as a generator of morphological innovation in the evolution of Medieval Castilian. Given the close ties between morphology and syntax, it is not surprising that this phenomenon also played a fundamental role in syntactic change. The cases mentioned below may be added, therefore, to the many examples that have already been cited.

The Latin CONJUNCTION *ut* 'how', 'when', 'so that', is not transmitted into Castilian, but two others are preserved: *sī* 'if' continues to function as a conditional conjunction, while *quod* 'that' extends its range of meaning beyond that of 'cause'.[12] This is reflected in *que*, the Castilian derivative of *quod* (or more probably of *quid*, an originally interrogative pronoun that becomes confused with *quod*), whose greatly expanded sphere of usage includes the following types of clauses:

noun (i.e., functioning as noun, as here, where it is the direct object): *cuedando que assi passarien como ellos* 'thinking that they would pass as they [the others] had'

consecutive (expressing a consequence): *se leuanto entrellos una niebla tan espesa que a penas se deuisauan uno a otro* 'a fog arose among them so thick that they could barely see each other'

concessive (voicing an objection): *aquella cibdad pero que sea agora yerma & despoblada* 'that city though it may now be barren and depopulated'

causal (expressing cause): *non cates a su vista ni alteza de so estado, que lo aborreci* 'do not look upon his appearance or his high status, because I hated him'

final (expressing the objective of an action): *despues a la tercera noche guiso donna Sancha que se echasse el conde so padre & la condessa su madrastra* 'later, on the third night, Lady Sancha arranged for the count to attack her father and the countess her mother'

The conjunction *que* continues to be versatile in Castilian, although in the meantime the inventory of conjunctions has increased through the agency of grammaticalization, as in *aunque* 'although'

---

12. The so-called accusative and infinitive construction, as in *putō illōs hominēs sine amīcīs miserōs esse* 'I think those men are miserable without friends' persists in Castilian but is normally not employed with verbs of speaking and understanding, but instead with verbs of asking and commanding, e.g., *pedir, mandar, ordenar*, as in *mando los luego descabesçar* 'he gave the order to behead them later'.

and its now archaic synonym *maguer que*, also *porque* 'because', *con-que* 'so', *mientras (que)* 'while', *ya (que)* 'since' and *luego (que)* 'after'. See Hilty 2006 for more information on this topic.

Another case of grammaticalization is that of the SUFFIX *-mente*, used in Castilian to form adverbs from adjectival bases. Originally, *mente* was the ablative form of the feminine noun *mens, mentis* 'mind' and, as such, combined as an independent word with the feminine form of adjectives that described the mental state of a person, as in *tranquillā mente* 'with a tranquil mind', *studiōsā mente* 'with a studious mind'. The grammaticalization of this construction begins when the word is used with adjectives that cannot refer to mental states, as in *et nōndum tōtā mē mente recēpī* 'and still I have not completely recovered', and is completed[13] when, in the earliest Castilian texts, this morpheme is used as a suffix rather than an independent word. The early Castilian form of this suffix, *-mientre* (probably the product of the combination of *-mente* with the Latin adverbial suffix *-iter*), loses ground in the thirteenth century to the variant *-ment* and in the fourteenth to the modern variant *-mente*, both probably of dialectal origin.

Also grammaticalized is the preposition *a* in its functioun as the so-called PERSONAL *a* to mark direct objects that are either specific and personal (*veo a mi tío* 'I see my uncle') or personified (*tú temes al éxito tanto como al fracaso* 'you fear success as much as failure'), as opposed to *busco una secretaria* 'I'm looking for a secretary' (not specific) and *veo mi casa* 'I see my house' (not personal or personified). As shown by the following examples, this use of the preposition is not obligatory in the Alphonsine prose of the thirteenth century, although it is present in some cases.

> *e puso en cada logar omnes de so linage* 'and he put in each place men of his lineage'

---

13. Actually, the grammaticalization of *-mente* is not yet fully complete, given the three anomalies in its derivation: (1) the two elements maintain their own accent as though they were two independent words: *técnicamente, torpemente, febrilmente*, pronounced as *técnica mente, torpe mente, febril mente*; (2) the adjective bases must have feminine form; (3) in a sequence of adverbs, the suffix *-mente* is added only to the final one (*rápida y completamente* 'rapidly and completely').

mato en la carrera un ladron un omne onrado 'a thief killed an
   honest man on the highway'
echaron ende a todas las otras yentes 'they threw all the other
   people out of there'
no connocien ni temien a dios 'they neither knew nor feared
   God'

Among the possible explanations that Brenda Laca (2006:425–29)
enumerates for this phenomenon, which she calls "prepositional
accusative", is that of helping to distinguish between subject and object, as in the second of the examples cited above, in which it is not
completely clear who killed whom.

The creation through grammaticalization of the CLITIC PRO-
NOUNS brought with it the need for syntactic rules. An examination
of the position of clitic pronouns in our Alphonsine text show that
the rules in force during the medieval period differ from current
practice. For example, the medieval clitic follows the verb in the following examples:

et mostroles 'and he showed them'
& dixo les de como 'and he told them how'
gradescio gelo mucho 'he thanked them very much'

In contrast, the clitic appears before the verb, and sometimes sepa-
rated from it, in the following:

& ser uos emos uassallos leales 'and we shall be loyal vassals to
   you'
que gelo gualardonarie 'that he would reward them'
lo quel el Rey enuiara dezir 'what the king had ordered to be
   told to him'
les esto oyo 'he heard them (say) this'

In his detailed study of this topic, Dorien Nieuwenhuijsen
(2006:1364–68) cites a series of factors that determine the placement
of clitic pronouns during this period: (1) the importance of the antecedent of the clitic pronoun in the hierarchy of all the antecedents
in the sentence, (2) the hierarchy of grammatical persons, in which
pronouns of first and second person have priority over those of third

person, and (3) the distance between the clitic pronoun (especially third-person pronouns) and its antecedent. Nieuwenhuijsen concludes that "important" clitic pronouns and those that are placed furthest from their antecedents tend to be placed before their verbs.

Text Analysis

Below is a translation and morphosyntactic analysis of the same Alphonsine text that was phonologically analyzed in chapter 5. Particular emphasis is placed on the differences between the Medieval Castilian of the thirteenth century and Modern Spanish.

Sobre aquellas nueuas el Çid enuio luego por sus parientes
Al recibir aquellas noticias, el Cid envió luego por sus parientes
Upon receiving this news, the Cid then called for his relatives
& sus amjgos. Et mostroles lo quel el Rey enuiara dezir,
y sus amigos. Y les mostró lo que el rey había mandado que se le
    dijera
and his friends. And he told them what the king had ordered to be
        told to him,
    mostroles: postposed clitic pronoun
    quel: apocope and **agglutination** of *le*; separation of clitic pro-
        noun from verb
    enuiara: indicative past perfect
& dixo les de como non le diera el Rey mas de nueue dias
y les dijo cómo el rey no le había dado más de nueve días
and he told them how the king had not given him more than nine
        days'
    dixo les: postposed clitic pronoun
    diera: indicative past perfect
de plazo en quel saliesse de la tierra.
de plazo en que le saliese de la tierra.
time to leave the country.
    quel: apocope and agglutination of *le*
Et que querie saber dellos quales querien yr con el, o quales fincar.
Y que quería saber de ellos cuáles querían ir con él, o cuáles que-
        darse.

And he wanted to know from them who wanted to go with him, or
who would stay.

    querie /ke 'rje/: alternative imperfect ending

Et dixo Aluar Hannez Minnaya: Sennor, todos yremos con uusco, &
dexaremos Castiella,

Y dijo Alvar Háñez Miñaya: Señor, todos iremos con usted, y deja-
remos Castilla,

And Alvar Háñez Miñaya said: Sir, we shall all go with you, and we
shall leave Castile,

    yremos: synthetic future

    con uusco /kom 'bus ko/: plural form parallel to *conmigo*

& ser uos emos uassallos leales. Et esto mismo le dixieron todos los
otros,

y le seremos vasallos leales. Y esto mismo le dijeron todos los
otros,

and we will be loyal vassals to you. And all the others told him the
same thing,

    ser uos emos: analytic future with intercalated clitic pronoun

    uos: reflex of the Latin accusative functioning here as a dative

& quel non desampararien por ninguna guisa.

y que no le desampararían de ninguna manera.

and that they would not abandon him in any way.

    quel: apocope and agglutination of *le*; leísmo

    desampararien /de sam pa ra 'rjen/: synthetic conditional with
    alternative inflexion

El Çid quando les esto oyo gradescio gelo mucho.

El Cid cuando les oyó [decir] esto se lo agradeció mucho.

The Cid, when he heard them [say] this, thanked them very much.

    les esto oyo: clitic pronoun separated from verb

    gelo /'ʒe lo/: old form of *se lo*, derived from *illī illu*

Et dixoles que si el tiempo uiesse que gelo gualardonarie el muy bien.

Y les dijo que si tuviese la oportunidad se lo remuneraría él muy
bien.

And he told them that if he had the opportunity, he would reward
them very well.

    dixoles: postposed clitic

    gelo /'ʒe lo/: old form of *se lo*, derived from *illī illu*

gualardonarie /gwa larˉ do na ˈrje/: synthetic conditional with
 alternative inflexion

Otro dia salio el Çid de Uiuar con toda su companna.

Al otro día salió el Cid de Vivar con toda su compañía.

The next day the Cid left Vivar with his whole troop.

*Et dizen algunos que cato por agüero, et saliente de Uiuar que ouo
 corneia diestra,*

Y dicen algunos que buscó agüero, y que saliendo de Vivar tuvo
 una corneja a la derecha,

And some say that he looked for an omen, and that upon leaving
 Vivar he had a crow on the right,

saliente: present participle with the meaning of a gerund

*et a entrante de Burgos que la ouo siniestra. Et que dixo estonces a
 sus amigos* [fol. 164v]

y entrando en Burgos la tuvo a la izquierda. Y que dijo entonces a
 sus amigos

and upon entering Burgos he had one on the left. And that he said
 then to his friends

entrante: present participle with the meaning of a gerund

*& a sus caualleros: Bien sepades por cierto que tornaremos a
 Castiella*

y a sus caballeros: Que sepáis bien por cierto que volveremos a
 Castilla

and to his soldiers: You know well that we shall return to Castile

tornaremos: synthetic future

con grand onrra & grand ganancia, si dios quisiere.

con gran honra y gran ganancia, si Dios quiere.

with great honor and great profit, if God wishes.

quisiere: future subjunctive

Et pues que entro en Burgos fuesse pora la posada do solie posar,

Y después que entró en Burgos se fue para la posada donde solía
 alojarse,

And after he entered Burgos he went to the boarding house where
 he usually stayed,

fuesse: postposed clitic pronoun

solie /so ˈlje/: alternative ending of the imperfect

mas non le quisieron y acoger. Ca el Rey lo enuiara defender

pero no le quisieron acoger allí. Porque el rey había enviado [un
  mensaje] prohibiendo

but they refused to admit him there. Because the king had sent an
  order forbidding

  le: leísmo

  enuiara: indicative past perfect

*quel non acogiessen en ninguna posada en toda la uilla, nin le dies-
  sen uianda ninguna.*

que le acogiesen en ninguna posada en toda la villa, o que le diesen
  comida ninguna.

that he be admitted to any boarding house in the whole village, or
  that he be given food.

  quel: apocope and agglutination of *le*: leísmo

  non, *ninguna*, *nin*: negations induced by the negative meaning
  of *defender* 'to forbid'

Appendix: Lexical Archaisms in Alphonsine Prose

Below appears a brief list of some of the most important lexical **archaisms** (words that have become obsolete) that appear frequently
in thirteenth-century Alphonsine prose. Our experience is that for
native speakers of Modern Spanish, the Castilian of this period is
not hard to understand. In contrast to the true archaisms listed below, most medieval words are identical to their modern counterparts or differ very little in form or sense. For example, it is easy to
associate, on the basis of formal similarities, pairs of words such as
medieval *gradescer* and modern *agradecer* 'to thank', *rebatarse* and
arrebatarse 'to snatch', *fremoso* and *hermoso* 'beautiful', *uerguenna*
and *vergüenza* 'shame', *ascondudo* and *escondido* 'hidden', *periglo*
and *peligro* 'danger'. Semantically, it is not difficult to reinterpret
nueuas as *noticias* 'news' and *ferir* as *golpear* 'to strike'. A few archaic verb forms do cause difficulties, such as the preterite forms
yogo (from *yazer* 'to lie'), *sopo* (*saber* 'to know'), *ouo* (*auer* 'to have'),
plogo (*plazer* 'to please'), *troxo* (*traer* 'to bring'), and the future forms
morrá (*morir* 'to die'), *verná* (*venir* 'to come'), *terná* (*tener* 'to have'),
and *combrá* (*comer* 'to eat'). In other cases, the vacillating orthography of the medieval texts can be confusing, as in the cases of *ymaien*

(*imagen* 'image'), *uieios* (*viejos* 'old'), *beuir* (*vivir* 'to live'), *uuscar* (*buscar* 'to look for'), *boz* (*voz* 'voice'), and *regno* (*reino* 'kingdom'). Still, the modern reader tends to get used to these differences very quickly.

acorrer 'to succor'

abondado 'rich'

affincado 'firm, secure'

aina, ayna 'soon'

al 'something else'

am(b)idos 'unwillingly'

amortido 'fainted'

amos 'both'

apuesto 'elegant'

asmar 'to consider'

auer 'to have'

auol 'vile'

ca 'because'

carrera 'path', 'manner'

catar 'to look at'

comoquier que 'although'

conortar 'to console'

consennar 'to indicate'

cras 'tomorrow'

crebanto 'affliction'

cuedar 'to think'

cuemo 'how'

cuende 'count'

cueyta 'danger', 'pain'

cutiano 'daily'

defender 'to forbid'

dende 'from this'

departir 'to divide', 'to distinguish'

desque 'after'

desuso 'above', 'from above'

do 'where'

eguar 'to make equal'

ende 'from that'

enderesçar 'to favor'

enderescer 'to head'

enfinta 'feint'

engenno 'war machine'

escanno 'bench'

estorcer 'to escape a danger'

euar 'to look at'

fascas 'that is'

fazienda 'matter', 'action'

fi(n)car 'to stay'

fi(n)car los ynoios 'to kneel'

finiestra 'window'

fiuza 'loyalty'

guisa 'manner'

guisar 'to prepare'

hueste 'army'

lazrar 'to suffer'

librar 'to carry out'

lumazo 'cushion'

luua 'glove'

maguer 'although'

mancebo 'boy'

(auer) menester 'to need'

(meter) mientes 'to pay attention'

natura 'nature'

o 'where'

onde 'whence'

pagarse 'to enjoy'

pechar 'to pay a fine'

pesar 'to pain, upset'

plazer 'to please'

pleyto 'matter'

poridat 'discretion', 'secret'

premia 'coercion'

punnar 'to fight', 'to urge'

quedo 'quiet, unmoving'

quito 'free, exempt'

recabdo 'caution', 'value'

recelar 'to fear'

segudar 'to pursue'

semeiar 'to seem'

sieglo 'world'

siniestro 'left'

so 'below', 'I am'

soldada 'pay'

suso 'above'

tamanno 'so large'

toller 'to take away'

tornar 'to return'

trauar 'to grab', 'to enter a conflict'

trebeio 'diversion'

tuerto 'wrong, misdeed'

uegada 'time, instance'

uiçioso 'comfortable'

uuiar 'to manage'

y 'there'

yuso 'below'

Questions

1. What factors explain the loss of the Latin case system?
2. How do the five Latin declensions evolve in the transition to Hispano-Romance? What relics of the declensions are still present in Castilian?
3. What factors explain the loss of the Latin neuter gender?
4. What factors explain the distribution of originally neuter Latin nouns into the masculine and feminine genders in Castilian?
5. Explain the development and historical significance of the underlined words in the following sentences and phrases:

   a. *Et gradecieron gelo mucho los senados.* 'And the senates thanked him very much.'
   b. *E puso por ende con el su amizdad engannosa mientre.* 'And for this reason [he/she] made friends with him deceptively.'
   c. *Non auedes uos otros por que temer.* 'You have no reason to fear.'
   d. *& tomo las & dio con ellas en la mar de Affrica.* 'And he took them and set out with them into the African sea.'
   e. *Ascondudas so ell agua.* 'Hidden beneath the water.'
   f. *Amauan le todos.* 'Everyone loved him.'
   g. *Si tu por mi lo fiziesses.* 'If you would do it for me.'
   h. *Que fue muy loado por ello.* 'That he was very much praised for that.'
   i. *& auras contigo los prophetas con quien fabla el nuestro sennor dios.* 'And you will have with you the prophets with whom our Lord God speaks.'
   j. *Crecen cada dia e son mas fermosas. Es una de las meiores cosas del mundo.* 'They grow each day and they are more beautiful. It's one of the best things in the world.'
   k. *En ell armario de los libros fallaras lo que demandas.* 'In the book cabinet you will find what you are asking for.'
   l. *A manera de los que an uençuda alguna batalla.* 'In the manner of those who have won some battle.'

m. *Todas las yentes que son llamadas Capros.* 'All the peoples who are called Capros.'

n. *Ser uos emos vasallos leales.* 'We shall be loyal vassals to you.'

o. *E ellos mostraron le los libros de la eglesia.* 'And they showed him the church's books.'

p. *& el tenielos cercados dell otra part.* 'And he had them surrounded from the other side.'

q. *Creo que aquellos hombres son infelices sin amigos.* 'I think that those men without friends are unhappy.'

r. *Con grand onrra & grand ganancia, si dios quisiere.* 'With great honor and great profit, if God wishes.'

From Medieval Castilian to Modern Spanish

7

Political and Cultural History of Spain after the Middle Ages

After the rapid series of conquests that follows the victory at Las Navas de Tolosa, the Reconquest stagnates.[1] There are multiple causes: the need to consolidate militarily the victories achieved during the thirteenth century, the slow pace of repopulation, epidemics of the plague beginning in 1348, an economic downturn, the fact that the remaining Muslim potentates are vassals of Castilian monarchs, and finally, the political instability that devastates Castile during the fourteenth and fifteenth centuries under the dynasty of the Trastámara, an era characterized by weakness in the monarchy and resulting conflicts with the nobility. The reign of Juan II of Castile (1419–54), for example, is marked first by the regency of his mother, followed by that of his uncle, and finally by the influence of his *valido*, the constable Álvaro de Luna. Juan's son, Enrique IV the Impotent (1454–74), also allows himself to be manipulated by favorite members of the nobility, notably by Beltrán de la Cueva, to the point that the king's own daughter, Juana, is given the nickname Beltraneja because of her physical resemblance to the favorite and an almost universal belief in the king's impotence. For this reason, Enrique's sister, Isabel I la Católica (1451–1504), challenges Juana for the throne and eventually prevails after an armed conflict between their respective supporters, the Aragonese and the Portuguese.

The reign of Isabel (queen of Castile, 1474–1504; queen con-

1. Here I follow the narratives of Simon Barton (2004:85–88), Diego Marín (1969), and "Casa de Trastámara," *Biografías y Vidas*, n.d., www.biografiasyvidas .com/biografia/t/trastamara.htm. According to Diez, Morales, and Sabín (1980:179), the Reconquest should be considered completed by the end of the thirteenth century. See "Iberian Peninsula, 1270–1492," http://www.learnnc.org/lp/media/uploads/2007 /09/1492spain.jpg, for a map of Spain during this period.

sort of Aragon, 1479–1504) is of major importance in the history of Castile. Her marriage in 1469 to Fernando II (king of Aragon, 1479–1516) allows for the unification of a large part of the Peninsula (Castile, Aragon, Catalonia, Valencia) under one crown and one religion. Together, Isabel and Fernando, tradicionally called the Reyes Católicos or Catholic monarchs, take a series of measures that transform the weak, chaotic feudal system they inherit into a modern absolutist state, with its own army, a healthy treasury, and growing agricultural production.

Many of the most important events of the reign of the Reyes Católicos take place in the decisive year 1492. First, after an eleven-year war, they succeed in conquering Granada, thus ending the presence of this Muslim tributary and completing the task of the Reconquest, begun almost eight hundred years before. At the same time that they are driving out all political elements not in harmony with their idea of Spain, they resolve to rid Spain of all religions other than Catholicism as well, ordering the expulsion of the Jews (1492) and Muslims (1502) who refuse to convert. In order to judge the sincerity of the *conversos* who decide to convert rather than be expelled, they activate the Holy Inquisition, an organization approved by the pope in 1478 and placed under their control. Through this institution policies are enacted that, seen from a modern perspective, are clearly cruel and intolerant, but that at the time were an attempt—albeit a misguided one—to achieve a more unified and homogeneous nation. Also in 1492, Christopher Columbus disembarks on the shores of America, inaugurating a conquest of the New World that can be conceived as a continuation of the Reconquest of Spain. The fruits of this new campaign are sufficiently rich to make Spain the most powerful nation in the Western world.

These same events are important for the history of the language. With the expulsion of the Sephardic Jews, for example, a chapter in Spanish dialectology is initiated, since the exiles preserve their fifteenth-century Castilian in their new homelands in northern Africa, the Balkans, and the Middle East. Although their language, called Sephardi (Sp. *sefardí*, also *judeo-español* and *ladino*—see sidebar), is deeply affected by the languages with which it comes into contact, it also preserves many of its original features, making it the most archaic Spanish dialect. The discovery of America is even more significant, since it makes possible an immense expansion of the language and the eventual development of numerous and diverse American varieties.

The year 1492 is also interesting in a philological sense, since it marks the publication of two important works by the Sevillian humanist Antonio de Nebrija: the first part of his bilingual dictionary (Latin-Spanish, followed in 1495 by the Spanish-Latin part) and his *Arte de la lengua castellana*, the first grammar of a modern European language. Even at this late date the publication of a grammar of a vernacular language seemed pointless to many people, for whom Latin continued to be the written language par excellence. In the preface to his *Arte*, Nebrija recounts how the queen herself asked him about the usefulness of the work, to which he replied that "siempre la lengua fue compañera del imperio" (language has always been the handmaiden of Empire), adding that "despues que vuestra alteza metiesse debaxo de su iugo muchos pueblos barbaros & naciones de peregrinas lenguas: & co nel vencimiento aquellos ternian necessidad de recebir las leies: quel vencedor pone al vencido & con ellas nuestra lengua: entonces por esta mi arte podrian venir enel conocimiento della".[2] Here Nebrija is undoubtedly thinking of Africa rather than America.

It is also during the reign of the Reyes Católicos that it becomes common to refer to the language of Castile with a name—Spanish (*español*)—that symbolizes the central place this variety has assumed in the political life of the country. According to Amado Alonso (1942:15), toward the end of the fifteenth and beginning of the sixteenth centuries, many books are published in which Castilian is referred to as Spanish—for example, *Manual de nuestra Santa Fe Católica, en español* (1495), *Séneca Proverbia, en español, cum glosa* (1500), *Flor de virtudes, en español* (1502). However, he admits that "limitándonos ahora a la alternancia castellano-español en el

2. 'after your highness has placed many barbarous peoples and nations of outlandish languages under your yoke, and having been conquered they will need to receive laws that the victorious imposes on the vanquished and with them our language: thus through this my *Arte* they could come to know it'.

siglo XVI, 'castellano' es tan dominante, sobre todo en los primeros cincuenta años, que no hay por qué traer ejemplos".[3] On this topic, see Mondéjar Cumpián 2002.

In terms of culture, we see during the reign of the Reyes Católicos the first signs of the Renaissance, an originally Italian cultural revolution characterized by a strong interest in classical Greco-Latin culture. In literature, the moralizing and theological tone of the Middle Ages is abandoned in favor of the values of Greco-Roman antiquity, with a sense of human beings as creative personalities and essential components of nature, as well as an appreciation of life on earth over life in the hereafter.

Linguistically, two important tendencies become evident. First, there is an exaltation of the classical languages, leading to a rejection of medieval forms of Latin and Greek and a concomitant effort to imitate classical models more faithfully. Second, contemporary authors accept the challenge of renovating and enriching the syntax and lexicon of the vernacular languages through imitation of the stylistics of classical models and the adoption and adaptation of many learned **Latinisms** and **Hellenisms**—respectively, borrowings from ancient Latin and Greek.

The first great representative of the Renaissance style in Spain is Juan de Mena (1411–56), a prolific author whose *Laberinto de Fortuna* is considered by Cano Aguilar (1992:204) to be "la máxima muestra de la poesía humanista y latinizante, tanto en la forma como en el contenido".[4] Juan Luis Alborg (1972:364) mentions some of the most notable aspects of Mena's Renaissance stylistics, including the frequent use of the Latin **hyperbaton**, a rhetorical figure that artificially transplants into Castilian the freedom of word order characteristic of Latin. In Mena's writings we find *las maritales tragando cenizas* for *tragando las cenizas maritales* 'swallowing the marital ashes' and *divina me puedes llamar Providencia* for *me puedes llamar divina Providencia* 'you may call me divine Providence'. Additional

3. 'limiting ourselves to the alternation between *Castilian* and *Spanish* in the 16th century, *Castilian* is so dominant, especially during the first fifty years, that there is no need to cite examples.'

4. 'the highest example of humanist and Latinizing poetry, both in form and in content'.

Expelled from Spain in 1492, Spaniards of Jewish descent spread out over Europe, Asia, and Africa. Those who flee to Portugal suffer the misfortune of being expelled again in 1497. In some of the countries of the diaspora, as in the Netherlands and Italy, the Sephardic refugees assimilate to the local population. In other places, however, like Morocco and various parts of the Ottoman Empire (especially Salonika in Greece and Constantinople in Turkey), they manage to maintain their culture and language for several centuries. However, beginning with World War II these communities begin to break up, and their inhabitants are obliged to emigrate anew, often to America, and later on to Israel. As a consequence, Sephardi is suffering significant losses in number of speakers and spheres of usage.

In many of its features, Sephardi reflects the Hispano-Romance that was spoken on the Iberian Peninsula at the moment of expulsion at the end of the fifteenth century. The sibilants, especially, reflect fairly accurately those of the Castilian of that period (*coxo* 'cojo' /'ko ʃu/ 'lame', *fijo* 'hijo' /'fi ʒu/ 'son', and *casa* /'ka za/ 'house'), though the affricates are missing (*cinco* /'sin ko/ 'five', *dezir* /de 'zir/ 'to say'). Additionally, Sephardi is *yeísta* and has a tendency to drop /ʝ/ in the environment of a front vowel (*gallina* /ga 'i na/ 'hen'). The influence of Galician-Portuguese and Leonese is evident in other characteristics, such as the propensity to preserve initial /f/ and to close final unstressed /o/ (*fijo* /'fi ʒu/), and to preserve the consonant cluster /mb/ (*palombika* 'little dove') and the archaic use of an article before possessive adjectives (*la mi madre* 'my mother'). Notable, in pronominal use, is the use of *vos* as an equivalent of modern *vosotros* and the absence of *usted* in favor of *él* or *ella*.

To give an idea of the form that Sephardi takes in modern Israel, below I provide a passage taken from the electronic version of the magazine *Aki Yerushalayim* (July 13, 2005), where one notices that except for a few words (*mozotros* for *nosotros* 'we', *ainda* for *todavía* 'still'), the passage is perfectly comprehensible to a native speaker of Modern Spanish:

> La kultura djudeo-espanyola esta sufriendo aktualmente de los rezultados de un proseso de eskayimiento [*decaimiento*] ke empeso largos anyos atras i se esta kontinuando en muestros dias

---

AN ARCHAIC DIALECT *(continued)*

tambien. Ay ken [*quien*] pensa ke esta kultura esta agonizando i ke este es un proseso sosio-kultural kontra el kual no podemos azer nada. Mozotros akseptamos esta idea i esperamos ke ainda no es demazia tadre [*demasiado tarde*] para poder empidir ke despareska en las profundinas del ulvido esta ermoza kultura ke muestros padres transmetieron fidelmente de una jenerasion a la otra durante serka de 500 anyos.[†]

[†] The Judeo-Spanish culture is presently suffering the results of a process of decay that began years ago and is continuing in our day as well. Some people think that this culture is dying and that we are dealing with a sociocultural process against which nothing can be done. We do not accept this idea and we hope that it is still not too late to be able to stop the disappearance into the depths of oblivion of this beautiful culture that our ancestors faithfully transmitted from one generation to another for almost 500 years.

---

examples, taken from various authors of this period, include *pocos hallo que de las mías se paguen obras* for *hallo pocos que se paguen de las obras mías* 'I find few people who like my works', *las potencias del ánima tres* for *las tres potencias del ánima* 'the three powers of the soul', *generosa en lo ajeno dar* for *generosa en dar lo ajeno* 'generous in giving away what does not belong to her', *luminosas de pólvora saetas* for *saetas luminosas de pólvora* 'luminous arrows of powder'. A second notable feature of Mena's prose is the use of learned words, Latinisms and Hellenisms, that frequently fail to take root in the language: *novelo* for *nuevo* 'new', *vulto* for *rostro* 'face', *flutuoso* for *oscilante* 'oscillating', *esculto* for *esculpido* 'sculpted', *exilio* for *destierro* 'exile', and *poluto* for *sucio* 'dirty'.

One of the most important works of the Spanish Renaissance is published during the reign of the Reyes Católicos, namely, *La Celestina*, written by Fernando de Rojas and published in 1499. Linguistically, this work illustrates many of the Latinizing tendencies of the era. In the sentence *No creo ir conmigo el que contigo queda* (for *no creo que vaya conmigo el que contigo se queda* 'I don't think that anyone staying with you is going with me'), we see an imitation of the Latin structure of infinitive and accusative; in *que mi secreto dolor manifestarte pudiese* for *que pudiese manifestarte mi secreto dolor* 'that I could confess to you my secret pain', one observes the tendency to place the verb in sentence-final position; and in *algunas consolatorias palabras* for *algunas palabras de consuelo* 'some words of consolation' and *tu senectud* for *tu vejez* 'your ancient old age', we see the use of crude Latinisms.

When the Reyes Católicos die, the throne passes to the Habsburgs, in the person of Carlos I of Spain (1516–56, son of Juana la Loca—daughter of Isabel and Fernando—and her husband Felipe el Hermoso, Duke of Burgundy), and subsequently to Carlos's son Felipe II (1556–98). Their reigns coincide with the high point of the Spanish Empire, which stretches from America to northern Africa, Italy, Flanders, and even the Philippines. The Spanish people profit very little from the arrival of the tremendous wealth taken from the American possessions, however, because both father (Carlos I) and son (Felipe II) squander the new resources in a series of military campaigns mostly directed against the expansion of Protestantism. Speaking of Felipe II, Diego Marín writes (1969:131): "The preoccupation of defending Catholicism against the heresy that was threatening to reach his territory was the main theme of his politics. To this end he subordinates all the material interests of the country, because, as he declares stubbornly, 'I would rather lose all my lands and a hundred lives than be king over heretics'. His personal idiosyncrasy contributed more than anything to bankrupting Spain in long and futile European wars."[5]

Consequently, the seventeenth century is a period of grave political, military, economic, and social crisis, by the end of which Spain has become a second-rate power in Europe.[6] The heirs of the house of Habsburg show little interest in political matters, leaving the nation in the hands of trusted ministers or *validos*. The most

5. "La preocupación de defender el catolicismo contra la herejía que amenazaba extenderse a sus dominios fue la nota característica de su política. A ella subordina los intereses materiales del país, porque según declara con firmeza, 'antes perderé todos mis estados y cien vidas que tuviere que ser señor de herejes'. Su idiosincrasia personal . . . contribuyó más que nada a arruinar a España en largas y fútiles guerras europeas."

6. Here I follow Barton (2004:119–23).

corrupt of these is Francisco Gómez de Sandoval y Rojas, Duke of Lerma (1550–1625), during whose regime Spain suffers a grave demographic and economic crisis as a result of the expulsion between 1609 and 1614 of almost three hundred thousand *moriscos* (Moorish converts to Christianity) and the mortality provoked by continual wars, hunger, and plague. Another *valido*, Baltasar de Zúñiga (1561–1622), involves Spain in the Thirty Years' War, with the result that during the second half of the century, France takes advantage of Spain's weakness to seize all of the Spanish Crown's possessions in Europe.

The era of the Spanish Empire coincides with a period of intense and brilliant literary production, the so-called Siglo de Oro or Golden Age, which lasts from the coronation of Carlos I in 1516 to the death of Felipe IV in 1665. The most remarkable product of this era is the realist novel, especially the picaresque—a genre inaugurated by *Lazarillo de Tormes*, an anonymous novel of 1554—which focuses, not without humor, on the more sordid aspects of life. Miguel de Cervantes (1547–1616) combines the realism of this genre with a satire of the idealism of the chivalric novels in his monumental *El ingenioso hidalgo don Quijote de la Mancha* (1605–15). In the genre of poetry, one notes the contrast between the delicate, sober, and simple style of Garcilaso de la Vega (1501–36) and the condensed and complex style of Baroque poets such as Luis de Góngora y Argote (1561–1627). For a typical sample of this era, see the analysis of a poem by Góngora at the end of this chapter.

The seventeenth century also witnesses the publication of the first monolingual dictionary of Spanish, the *Tesoro de la lengua castellana o española* (1611) by Sebastián de Covarrubias. Since Nebrija, all dictionaries had been bilingual or multilingual (generally with the inclusion of Latin), since no one thought it was necessary to compile a dictionary of the vernacular, which everyone spoke anyway. Even Covarrubias feels the need to justify his work as a collection of etymologies. The work is very rich, however, not only in terms of vocabulary but also in meanings and literary citations adduced to illustrate them, for which reason it serves, a century later, as the major source in the compilation of the first dictionary of the Royal Spanish Academy.

The last Habsburg king, Carlos II, chooses as his successor his nephew Felipe de Anjou (1687–1746), of the house of the Bourbons, and this dynasty has remained in power in Spain, with some interruptions, up to the present day. The Bourbons try to modernize Spain, installing a centralist regime like that of France and importing the new spirit of the European Enlightenment, which is characterized by faith in reason and cultivation of knowledge. These measures create conflicts with regional and local authorities, on the one hand, and with the Church, on the other. In the eighteenth century, Spain's foreign policy continues to be disastrous, and by the beginnings of the nineteenth century it has lost the majority of its American colonies and is suffering the humiliation of being invaded by Napoleon's troops. This is also the beginning of a turbulent period of civil wars, coups d'état, and revolutions that culminates in the Second Republic (1931–36) and the Spanish Civil War (1936–39) and is prolonged in the dictatorship of general Francisco Franco, who remains in power until his death in 1975. This leads, then, to the definitive establishment of democracy in Spain.

For Fernando Lázaro Carreter (1949:208), one of the most urgent linguistic problems of the eighteenth century was to overcome the excesses of the Baroque, which had left the language "martirizada, exhausta, consumida en su propio delirio" ('tormented, exhausted, consumed in its own delirium'). One of the measures taken to combat this tendency is the establishment of the Royal Spanish Academy (Real Academia Española de la Lengua) in 1713 (approved by King Felipe V in 1714), whose motto, "limpia, fija y da esplendor" 'to lend purity, propriety and elegance', refers explicitly to the need to counter the excesses of the Baroque. This objective is made concrete in the production of the first dictionary of the Academy, *Diccionario de la lengua castellana* (now called *Autoridades*), published in six volumes between 1726 and 1737. With the second edition of the *Diccionario* (1780), the practice of publishing in a single volume, without citations, is initiated. Other notable editions include the fourth (1803), in which for the first time the letters *ch* and *ll* are listed independently of the letters *c* and *l*; the twenty-second (2001), in which this practice is abandoned; the eleventh (1869), from which for the first time Latin equivalents are omitted; the fifteenth (1925), in which the title changes from "Castilian" to "Spanish" language; the nineteenth (1970), from which proverbs are omitted; and the twentieth (1984), in which for the first time obscene words are included. Notably, since its beginnings the Academy has been steadily increasing the number of **Americanisms** included in the pages of the work.

Already in the first edition of the *Diccionario* the Academy begins to reform and modernize Castilian orthography, which had changed little since the Middle Ages. Geminate letters, as well as the letter ç, are discarded, and the letters *u* and *v* are reserved respectively for vocalic and consonantal use. Through its *Orthographia española*, published in several editions beginning in 1741, the Academy continues to reform the orthography. In the sixth edition (1779) of this work, the etymological criterion is abandoned in the spelling of words such as *theatro* (for *teatro* 'theater'), *rhetórica* (for *retórica* 'rhetoric'), and *mechánica* (for *mecánica* 'mechanics'), and by the eighth edition (1815), the majority of the pending questions have been resolved, including the distribution of *c* and *qu*, and the use of the letter *j* for the unvoiced velar fricative /x/.

Another eighteenth-century linguistic controversy, according to Lázaro Carreter (1949:162), is the continued use of Latin as the language of instruction in higher education,[7] in spite of the fact that students and professors alike are increasingly unable to express themselves in this language and fall more and more often into the "vice" of speaking Castilian. Many contemporary authors argue that Castilian is ready to assume the role of a language of learning, among them Gregorio Mayans (1699–1781), author of a Castilian rhetoric; Father Benito Jerónimo Feijoo (1676–1764); Fray Martín Sarmiento (1695–1772), author of the posthumous work *La educación de la juventud* (1798); and Gaspar Melchor de Jovellanos (1744–1811), who declares faithfulness to Latin to be an "idolatría ciega" ('blind idolatry') and under whose influence Castilian is finally recognized in 1813 as the language of instruction for university education.[8]

7. According to Coloma Lleal (1990:206), already in the thirteenth century municipal schools are providing primary education in the vernacular.

8. According to Jenny Brumme (2003:270): "No obstante la emancipación de la lengua vulgar, el latín mantuvo su prestigio. La enseñanza que, hasta finales del s. XVIII, estuvo totalmente en manos de las congregaciones y órdenes religiosas, sobre

Linguistic Changes

The following sections examine the principal linguistic changes through which Medieval Castilian is transformed into Modern Spanish. They are classified according to whether they are phonological, morphological, or syntactic in nature.

PHONOLOGICAL CHANGES. In this section, seven phonological changes are added to the twenty-two presented in chapter 5. All of them pertain to the consonantal system, since the vowel system of Spanish (in its standard form, at least)[9] is so stable that since the loss of final /e/ (change 20), it has not undergone any systematic changes. Contrary to the early tendency to multiply the number of consonantal phonemes through phonemic split, the cumulative effect of the postmedieval changes is the opposite: Through a series of mergers, the phonemic inventory is appreciably reduced, with the eventual loss of /β/ (as a phoneme, if not as an **allophone**), /ʤ/, /ʒ/, /z/, and, in some varieties, /ʎ/ and /θ/. Other consonantal phonemes undergo fundamental articulatory changes.

Principal phonological changes after Medieval Castilian

23. Loss of initial /h/
24. Merger of the phonemes /b/ and /β/

---

todo de los jesuitas, daba máxima importancia al aprendizaje del latín. Sólo con Carlos III (1759–88) se emprendió un largo proceso hacia la sustitución del latín por el castellano en las diversas instituciones de enseñanza." ('In spite of the emancipation of the vernacular language, Latin maintained its prestige. The instruction that until the end of the eighteenth century was completely in the hands of the congregations and religious orders, especially the Jesuits, gave maximum importance to the learning of Latin. Only with Carlos III (1759–88) was a long process begun toward the replacement of Latin by Castilian in the various educational institutions.')

9. Penny (2004:594–98) mentions some minor vocalic changes that take place during the fourteenth and fifteenth centuries, such as monophthongization (*Castiella* > *Castilla*), reversal of apocope (*-ment* > *-mente*), and the relatinization of some words (*sofrir* > *sufrir*, *cevil* > *civil*). In several modern-day varieties of Spanish we find certain phenomena of vowel reduction, such as **centralization** (['me sə] for *mesa* (['me sa] 'table'), **devoicing** (['tras tọs] for *trastos* (['tras tọs] 'junk'), and loss (['kɾok 'si] for *creo que sí* (['kɾe o ke 'si] 'I think so').

25. Deaffrication of /ʦ/ and /ʣ/
26. Devoicing of the voiced sibilants
27. /ṣ/ > /θ/
28. /ʃ/ > /x/
29. Yeísmo (/ʎ/ > /j/)

23. Loss of initial /h/. This is a repetition of change 2, except that this time the initial /h/ in question is a reflex of Latin initial /f/, transformed into /h/ through change 13. Thus, Lat. *farīna* /fa 'ri: na/, which in Medieval Castilian is pronounced /ha 'ri na/, now becomes /a 'ri na/ (Mod. Sp. *harina* 'flour'). By studying the distribution of the feminine allomorphs *el* and *la* of the definite article, Rini (2010) concludes that the loss of /h/ (*la hambre* /la 'ham bre/ → *el hambre* /e 'lam bre/ 'hunger') takes place during the period 1437–1560. Note that the glide /j/ of the diphthong /je/ becomes consonantal /j/ when it is left in initial position by the loss of /h/, as in *ferro* /'hje ro/ > /'je ro/ 'iron'.

24. Merger of the phonemes /b/ and /β/. This change captures the phonological repercussions of the fact that at this stage in the history of Castilian, the voiced bilabial fricative /β/ has two origins: (1) as product of the develarization of Lat. /w/ (change 4, through which *clāve* /'kla: we/ > /'kla βe/ 'key'), and (2) as result of the lenition of Latin /p/ and /b/ (change 15), through which *cūpa* /'ku: pa/ > /'ku ba/ > *cuba* ['ku βa] 'cask' and *cibu* /'ki bu/ > Med. Cast. *cevo* ['ʦe βo] 'bait'). After change 24, [β] is interpreted, irrespective of its origin, as an allophone of the phoneme /b/. In other words, if before this change the words *cabe* and *cave* were phonemically analyzed respectively as /'ka be/ and /'ka βe/, after the change both are analyzed as /'ka be/. According to Penny (2002:97), this process is completed by the middle of the 16th century.

25. Deaffrication of /ʦ/ and /ʣ/. Practically at the same time, a series of changes begins that fundamentally transforms the Castilian sibilants. The first of these is the **deaffrication** (loss of affricate character) of /ʦ/ and /ʣ/, whereby they become dental or **dorsodental** fricatives, as in *braço* /'bra ʦo/ > /'bra ṣo/ 'arm', *dize* /'di ʣe/ > /'di ẓe/ 'she/he says'. According to Paul Lloyd (1987:332), these new fricative sibilants differ from the already existent /s/ of *fablasse* [ha 'βla ṣe] 'spoke') and /z/ (*casa* ['ka z̺a] 'house') both in the place of articulation, more dental in the new forms and more alveolar in the older forms, and in the part of the tongue involved: while /s/ and /z/ are clearly **apical**, that is, articulated by the tip of the tongue, /s̺/ and /z̺/ are **dorsal**, articulated by the blade of the tongue, with the tip resting against the lower incisors. In other words, this new /s̺/ is similar to the sound that is used today in almost all of Spanish America. Note that this change has no phonological implications, since the segments affected continue to be contrastive.

26. Devoicing of the voiced sibilants. Also during the sixteenth century, unvoiced variants of the voiced sibilants are introduced and generalized. Thus *casa* 'house', previously pronounced /'ka za/ (apico-alveolar), is now pronounced /'ka sa/, while *dize* /'di z̺e/ (dental) yields to /'di s̺e/ 'she/he says' and *hijo* /'i ʒo/ to /'i ʃo/ 'son'. This change does have phonological implications, since the three voiced phonemes are lost (/z/, /z̺/, and /ʒ/) together with all the contrasts in which they participate. In other words, this change can be conceptualized as a triple merger of phonemes: of /s̺/ and /z̺/ (apical), /s̺/ and /z̺/ (dental) and /ʃ/ and /ʒ/ (palatal), in each case in favor of the former. Penny (2002:99) believes that the devoicing of sibilants begins in the northern part of the Castilian region as a spontaneous change, then spreads toward the south in the middle of the sixteenth century as northerners migrate en masse to the new capital, Madrid, where they evidently overwhelm the more conservative southern speakers with their new unvoiced variants of these phonemes.

27. /s̺/ > /θ/. In Castile, in the course of the sixteenth and the first half of the seventeenth centuries, the alvodental /s̺/ produced by changes 25 and 26 is displaced toward a maximally anterior place of articulation, becoming the unvoiced **interdental** fricative /θ/. Thus, the sibilant of Med. Cast. *braço* 'arm', originally pronounced as an affricate (/'bra ʦo/), then as an dorsodental fricative (/'bra s̺o/), is now interdental (/'bra θo/). The evolution of the sibilant of *dize* has one extra step, as it is also devoiced: /'di ʣe/ > /'di z̺e/ > /'di s̺e/ > /'di θe/.[10]

---

10. We shall see in chapter 9 that the sibilants have a separate evolution in Andalusian.

28. /ʃ/ > /x/. At approximately the same time, the place of articulation of Cast. /ʃ/ is displaced toward the back of the mouth, until it becomes velar /x/ or even uvular /χ/. Thus, *fijo* 'son', pronounced /'i ʒo/ after change 23, then /'i ʃo/ (after change 26), is now articulated /'i xo/ or /'i χo/.

29. Yeísmo (/ʎ/>/ʝ/). This last change, which arises at several points on the Peninsula, has still not spread to the entire Castilian-speaking territory, though it is characteristic of Madrid and most urban areas. This is the phenomenon through which the phoneme /ʎ/ merges with /ʝ/ (or one of its variants), thereby neutralizing the phonological opposition between the two sounds. Thus in *yeísta* areas, words like *halla* and *haya* are both pronounced /'a ʝa/.

Now let us trace the further evolution of *cabeza* 'head' and *fijo* 'son', derived through Medieval Castilian in chapter 5, plus that of *caballo* 'horse'.

Med. Cast. *cabeza* /ka 'be ʣa/

/ka 'be ʣa/	24	merger of /b/ and /β/
/ka 'be z̞a/	25	deaffrication if /ʣ/
/ka 'be s̞a/	26	devoicing of voiced sibilants
/ka 'be θa/	27	/s̞/ > /θ/

Mod. Sp. *cabeza*

Med. Cast. *fijo* /'hi ʒo/

/'i ʒo/	23	loss of initial /h/
/'i ʃo/	26	devoicing of voiced sibilants
/'i xo/	28	/ʃ/ > /x/

Mod. Sp. *hijo*

Med. Cast. *caballo* /ka 'ba ʎo/

| /ka 'ba ʎo/ | 24 | merger of /b/ and /β/ |
| /ka 'ba ʝo/ | 29 | yeísmo |

Mod. Sp. *caballo*

MORPHOLOGICAL CHANGES. This discussion has already anticipated some of the more important morphological changes. In

A LINGUISTIC MYTH: THE LISPING KING

In some places it is traditional to attribute the origin of the Castilian unvoiced interdental fricative /θ/ to the alleged eagerness of Spaniards to imitate the lisp of a king who suffered from this speech defect. The king is variously identified on Internet sites as Alfonso X el Sabio or Felipe II: "Alguien me dijo una vez (no sé ni cuándo ni dónde) que todo empezó con Felipe II que era un rey muy simpático pero que el pobre ceceaba." ['Someone told me once (I don't know when or where) that everything began with Felipe II, who was a very nice king but who unfortunately lisped.'] The reign of Alfonso X ended several centuries before the phoneme /θ/ came into existence, while Felipe II was living (1556–98) at the time when the older /s̺/ was moving toward the interdental place of articulation.

In any case, the story is completely false. Chapter 7 shows that the phoneme /θ/ has a different origin from that of /s/ and that its medieval counterpart is not /s/ but /ts/ (and /dz/). Furthermore, the very fact that /s/ continues to exist in Peninsular Spanish is sufficient proof of the absurdity of the theory: a lisping king would have pronounced *la cena es deliciosa* as /la 'θe na eθ de li 'θjo θa/, a pronunciation sometimes heard in parts of Andalusia, rather than /la 'θe na es de li 'θjo sa/, as modern-day inhabitants of northern Spain do.

Since English also has the phoneme /θ/, and no one believes that English speakers lisp, one wonders why this phoneme is believed to be out of place in Spanish. The answer is that it is jarring in Peninsular Spanish because it appears in words in which English and American Spanish have alveolar /s/. In American Spanish, this is due to the generalized *seseo*. For English speakers, /θ/ is unexpected because it appears in Castilian words written *ci-* and *ce-*, whose English cognates are pronounced with /s/, such as *cease, cell, cement, cipher, circle, circuit, cite,* and *city,* which correspond respectively to the Castilian words *cesar, célula, cifra, círculo, circuito, citar,* and *ciudad.* All of these English words were borrowed from Old French, a language in which, like American Spanish, the products of Latin /ke/, /ki/, /kj/ and /tj/ all merge with /s/.

One interesting thing about this linguistic myth is what it shows about the popular conception of linguistic change. Prestige is correctly identified as the fundamental element in the process, but in a caricatured way: it is doubtful that a lisping king would consider it flattering for his subjects to imitate his speech defect.

nominal morphology, for example, we see the abandonment in the sixteenth century of the pronoun combinations *ge lo, ge la* in favor of *se lo, se la*, et cetera. The sixteenth century also marks the end of the practice of using the feminine allomorph *el* of the definite article before any vowel-initial feminine noun. Thus, beginning at this time, one no longer says *el espada* 'the sword', *el esquila* 'the cowbell', *el otra parte* 'the other part', but instead *la espada, la esquila, la otra parte*. Feminine *el* is now used only before feminine nouns with initial tonic /a/: *el arpa* 'the harp', *el hambre* 'the hunger', *el agua* 'the water', all of which remain feminine—as in *el agua bendita* 'the holy water', *las aguas subterráneas* 'the underground waters', and so on.

There is also an important adjustment in the system of second-person pronouns or, more broadly, forms of address. We saw in chapter 6 that by the end of the Middle Ages the following system was in use:

Late Medieval Castilian

	SINGULAR	PLURAL
familiar	*tu/uos*	*uosotros*
formal	*uuestra merced*	*uuestras mercedes*

What is striking here is the change in the functions of *uos*, which at the beginning of the Middle Ages performed practically all the functions on this table except for the one that it now performs as equivalent of Med. Cast. *tu*. In the function of familiar plural it is replaced by the grammaticalized compound *uos otros*, and in the function of formal singular and plural it yields to the equally grammaticalized *uuestra merced* and *uuestras mercedes*. In the transitional usage as familiar singular, *uos* becomes stigmatized and ends up losing even this new function in Peninsular Spanish, according to Penny (2002:138), between the sixteenth and eighteenth centuries. However, *uos*—now written *vos*—manages to remain viable in American varieties as a feature brought there by the first conquistadors and colonists. The use of *vos* instead of *tú* is now called the *voseo*, and the phenomenon is found in all Spanish-American countries except Puerto Rico and the Dominican Republic. The history and current status of the *voseo* are examined in detail in chapter 9.

During this same period, the forms *uuestra merced* and *uuestras mercedes* begin to suffer a series of abbreviations and deformations typical of grammaticalized forms, passing through *uuessa merçed* (1540), then *vuasted* (1617) and *vusted* (1619), until finally the form *usted* (1620) becomes dominant in the eighteenth century. Since *uuestra merced* originates as an honorific, it governs third-person verb forms, and its corresponding oblique pronouns and possessive adjectives (*lo, los, le, les, su, sus*) are also third person.[11] *Os*, the abbreviated form of *uos* that arises in the fifteenth century, is now the oblique form corresponding to *vosotros*.

Finally, it should be pointed out that even Mod. Sp. *vosotros* is discarded in favor of *ustedes* in large parts of the Spanish-speaking world. According to Calderón Campos and Medina Morales (2010:202), while the speakers in western Andalusia vacillate between *ustedes hacen* and *ustedes hacéis* 'you do', 'you make', in eastern Andalusia, the Canary Islands, and America only *ustedes hacen* is used.

For all these reasons, forms of address are very different in Spain and Spanish America. The Spanish American situation is extremely complex, such that it does not lend itself to a detailed schematic representation.

Modern Peninsular Spanish

	SINGULAR	PLURAL
familiar	*tú*	*vosotros*
formal	*usted*	*ustedes*

Modern American Spanish

	SINGULAR	PLURAL
familiar	*tú*/*vos*	*ustedes*
formal	*usted*	*ustedes*

In verbal morphology, a series of relatively small changes gradually give Spanish its modern form. The second-person plural end-

---

11. Notably, with the process of grammaticalization (here pronominalization), the component *merced* 'mercy' loses its status as a feminine noun, leaving *usted* free to agreee with its referent: *usted está cansado* (male), *usted está cansada* (female).

ings *-ades, -edes, -ides* change to *-áis, -éis, -ís* (that is, *hablades* > *habláis* 'you speak', etc.). The alternative endings of imperfect and conditional for the second and third conjugations, so frequent in the thirteenth century in second and third-person forms—as in *tenies, tenie, tendries, tendrie*—begin to lose prestige to the modern-day endings in the fourteenth century and are completely obsolete by the fifteenth. The medieval forms *so* 'I am' (< Lat. *sum*), *do* 'I give' (< *dō*), *estó* 'I am' (< *stō*), and *vo* 'I go' (< *vādō*) are expanded with a final palatal glide to produce *soy, doy, estoy,* and *voy*. Lloyd (1987:356–57) attributes the origin of this particle *-y* to the medieval adverb *y* 'there' (< *ibi*), which is present in the word *hay*, composed of *a* (< *habet*) + *y*. Dieter Wanner (2006) rejects this hypothesis for *soy, estoy,* et cetera, basing his conclusion on chronological data that show that *soy* (in which the meaning 'there' is not clearly present) is established first, through the thirteenth and fourteenth centuries, while *doy, estoy,* and *voy* are not frequent until the fifteenth or dominant until the sixteenth century. According to Wanner, the innovation *soy* should be attributed to analogical leveling with the final glide of the preterite form *fui*; once *soy* was generalized, the ending *-y* would have been extended by analogy to the other verbs.

Two of the more notable aspects of the verbal morphology of Medieval Castilian are the future subjunctive and the past perfect in *-ara /-iera*. Both forms continue to exist in Modern Spanish, if only in the most archaizing styles. The future subjunctive is replaced by the present subjunctive in most of its uses, as in adverbial clauses, with a loss of precision in the sequence of tenses:

> *E maguer que esto te digo quando yo entendiere* [Mod. Sp. *entienda*]
> *que es sazon non te dexare folgar* 'and although I tell you this,
> when I understand that it is time I will not let you rest'
> *& podras yr mas ayna o quisieres* [Mod. Sp. *quieras*] 'and you
> will soon be able to go wherever you want'

Also in indefinite adjectival clauses:

> *E con el qui no lidiare* [Mod. Sp. *lidie* or *pelee*] *que prez gana ell
> otro en la su lid* 'and with him who will not fight, the other
> gains honor in their battle'

In conditional sentences the future subjunctive is usually replaced by the present indicative:

> *Pero si lo fizieres* [Mod. Sp. *haces*] *digo te que mas tarde iras* 'but if you do it, I say that you will go later'
>
> *Si ell acusador prouare* [Mod. Sp. *prueba*] *que los cristianos fazen ninguna cosa que sea contra las lees romanas* 'if the accuser proves that the Christians do nothing against Roman laws'

The future subjunctive begins its long decline in the seventeenth century and today exists only as a linguistic relic in legal writing, certain fixed expressions (*sea como fuere* 'be that as it may') or in proverbs (*adonde fueres, haz como vieres* 'when in Rome do as the Romans do'); see Veiga 2006:136–67 for a complete study of the phenomenon.

We have seen several examples of the past perfect in *-ra* in our medieval texts:

> *Dixo les de como non le diera* [Mod. Sp. *había dado*] *el Rey mas de nueue dias de plazo* 'he told them how the king had not given him more than nine days'
>
> *Et mostroles lo quel el Rey enuiara* [Mod. Sp. *había enviado*] *dezir* 'and he showed them what the king had ordered to be told to him'

According to Veiga (2006:206), the first evidence of the change of the forms in *-ra* to subjunctive mood appears in the thirteenth century, and by the end of the fourteenth they are used exclusively as such. However, at the end of the eighteenth and beginning of the nineteenth centuries several authors of the Romantic movement resurrect *-ra* in its etymological sense—or even as an equivalent of the preterite—and this usage still persists, especially in literary and journalistic prose. The following examples are taken from twentieth-century authors.[12]

---

12. See Real Academia Española 1973:480 and Rojo and Veiga 1999:2924–27. The latter (2925) even documents the analogical transferral of the indicative sense to the subjunctive endings in *-se*, as in the sentence *el jugador que marcase* [= *había marcado, marcó*] *el gol de la victoria* 'the player who [had] made the winning goal'.

Al día siguiente el conserje entró en el salón y vio que aún estaba tal como él lo dejara. (Azorín) 'The next day the janitor entered the living room and saw that it was still just as he had left it.'

En sueños le fuera anunciado el retorno de San Gudián. (Valle-Inclán) 'The return of San Gudián had been announced to him in dreams.'

Dejar quisiera mi verso como deja el capitán su espada, famosa por la mano viril que la blandiera. (A. Machado) 'I would like to leave my verse as the captain leaves his sword, famous for the virile hand that had brandished it.'

Traía a la mente las perpetuas bodas de Camacho que atrás dejara. (Pardo Bazán) 'It brought to mind the perpetual wedding of Camacho that he had left behind.'

SYNTACTIC CHANGES. Some of the syntactic modifications that take place in Spanish during the Renaissance and Golden Age were discussed in chapter 6. During this period, for example, the grammaticalization of the auxiliary verb *auer/haber* is completed. This is perhaps most clearly seen in the future tense, which becomes completely synthetic during this period. In his study of the Castilian prose of the sixteenth century, Hayward Keniston (1937:438) finds thirty-four examples of the analytic construction (of the type *ser uos emos* for *le seremos* 'we will be for you'), of which twenty-one appear before 1550 and the rest before 1575. Thereafter the synthetic form is used exclusively.

Keniston (1937:9–12) also portrays the evolution of the direct object with "personal *a*" in this century. In general, he says, the essential parameters of the particle are already established by the sixteenth century, if indeed exceptions continue to be numerous:

el qual mató el Infante don Sancho 'who killed the Infante don Sancho'

andaban a buscar por todo el reino . . . un capitan Machin 'they looked all over the realm . . . for Captain Machín'

dejó la mujer, perdonó la suegra 'he left his wife, forgave his mother-in-law'

Penny (2002:116) maintains that the "personal *a*" becomes fully obligatory in the seventeenth century.

Also in chapter 6 it was noted that the passive reflexive has formed part of Castilian grammar since the origins of the Romance vernacular. Félix Sepúlveda Barrios's study (1988:111) of the passive voice in the Spanish of the seventeenth century reveals that by this date the passive reflexive is used with the same frequency and under the same conditions as it is in Modern Spanish, in which the passive reflexive and the passive with *ser* differ stylistically. In journalistic style the passive reflexive occurs 57.16 percent of the time, the passive with *ser* 33.73 percent, and the passive with *estar* 9.11 percent. Conversely, in the colloquial style of the theater, the domination of the passive reflexive is more pronounced: 73.77 percent (passive reflexive), 10.95 percent (passive with *ser*), 15.28 percent (passive with *estar*).

Finally, the current rules for the placement of clitic pronouns are gradually established. The gamut of criteria applied in Medieval Castilian (importance of the referent, grammatical person, distance between referent and pronoun) yield to the current system, in which clitic pronouns go before all verb forms except the imperative (*dámelo*), the infinitive (*dármelo*), and the gerund (*dándomelo*). Penny (2002:137) claims that the new system is imposed toward the end of the seventeenth century, but such forms continue to occur as stylistic archaisms even in the nineteenth, as in the following, taken from Benito Pérez Galdós's *Doña Perfecta* (1876):

> *el cual movíase al compás de la marcha* 'which moved with the rhythm of the march'
> *fijose en la desgarbada estatura* 'he noticed the ungainly stature'
> *un momento después señor y escudero hallábanse a espaldas de la barraca* 'a moment later knight and squire found themselves with their backs to the hovel'

Text Analysis

Un monte era de miembros eminentes
este (que, de Neptuno hijo fiero,
de un ojo ilustra el orbe de su frente,

émulo casi del mayor lucero)
Cíclope, a quien el pino más valiente,
bastón, le obedecía, tan ligero
y al grave peso junco tan delgado,
que un día era bastón y otro cayado.[13]
(Luis de Góngora, "Fábula de Polifemo y Galatea", lines 49–56)

The difficulty of this poem derives principally from the application of five techniques characteristic of Spanish Baroque poetry. (1) There is use of semantic Latinisms, in which the Spanish word adopts the etymological or Latin meaning. Thus *eminente* is used here in the physical sense of 'protruding' or 'prominent', the meaning of its Latin etymon *ēminēns*; *ilustrar* means 'to illuminate' like its etymon *illustrāre*; *grave* has the meaning of its etymon *gravis -e* 'heavy'. (2) Góngora introduces lexical Latinisms like *émulo* 'imitator', 'rival', a reflex of Lat. *aemulus* introduced into sixteenth-century Spanish. (3) The poet takes maximum liberties with word order, evident in phrases such as *de Neptuno hijo fiero* for *fiero hijo de Neptuno* 'fierce son of Neptune' and *bastón, le obedecía, tan ligero* for *bastón tan ligero, le obedecía* 'staff so light, obeyed him'. Readers are also confused by the long parenthesis that separates *este* 'this' and *Cíclope* 'Cyclops' and, in general, the length of the one sentence that makes up the whole poem. (4) There are numerous metaphors: Cyclops is a mountain, an eye is an orb, and the pine tree is a walking stick, reed, and shepherd's crook. (5) Góngora expresses himself in a vague and inexact way, changing the sense of some words and leaving others out. Cyclops, for whom the most valiant (thick) pine obeyed (served) as a light cane and upon (supporting) such a grave (heavy) weight (was like) a thin reed, (such that) one day it was a walking stick and the next a shepherd's crook.

13. Dámaso Alonso's translation of these verses, with minor emendations, is as follows: "Era como un monte de miembros salientes este cíclope feroz, hijo del dios Neptuno. En la frente, amplia como un orbe, brilla un solo ojo, que podría casi competir aun con el sol. El más alto y fuerte pino de la montaña lo manejaba como ligero bastón: y, si se apoyaba sobre él, cedía al enorme peso, cimbreándose como delgado junco de tal modo que, si un día era bastón, al otro ya estaba encorvado como un cayado." Taken from Lázaro Carreter and Tusón 1981:193.

Clearly, Spanish orthography represents pronunciation with considerable precision, especially when compared to English, which uses six different spellings to represent /s/ (*sap, psychology, pass, peace, scissors, fasten*) and eleven for /i/ (*beet, beat, we, receive, key, believe, amoeba, people, Caesar, Vaseline, lily*).

First, however, it must be clarified that Spanish orthography can in no way be called "phonetic", since many Spanish phonemes have allophones that are not reflected in the spelling. The phonemes /bdg/, for example, have fricative allophones that are not distinguished in writing: *baba* ['ba βa] 'drivel', *dada* ['da ða] 'given', *gago* ['ga ɣo] 'stuttering'. The phoneme /n/ has many allophones in preconsonantal position since in this context the nasal is **homorganic** with the following consonant (i.e., it automatically adopts its place of articulation): *un peso* [um 'pe so] 'a weight', *ando* ['an̪ do] 'I walk', *ancho* ['añ ʧo] 'wide', *anca* ['aŋ ka] 'haunch', et cetera.

This is not a problem, since allophones are predictable and under normal circumstances speakers are unaware of allophonic differences. Speakers are very conscious, on the other hand, of phonemic differences, which by definition distinguish meanings in minimal pairs such as *vale* 'it is worth'/ *dale* 'give to him', *tal* 'such' / *tan* 'so', *come* 'she/he eats'/ *corre* 's/he runs', and *mano* 'hand'/ *mono* 'monkey'.

A completely phonemic orthography would be a writing system in which each phoneme would correspond to only one letter, and each letter would correspond to only one phoneme. Analyzed on this criterion, Spanish orthography falls short in several ways.

On the one hand, there are phonemes represented by more than one letter, such as /b/ (*vaca* 'cow', *bala* 'bullet', *wáter* 'toilet'), /k/ (*cama* 'bed', *quiero* 'I want', *kilo* 'kilo'), /r/ (*rey* 'king', *carro* 'cart'), /x/ (*gime* 'she/he whines', *jefe* 'boss', *México* 'Mexico'), /θ/ (*cero* 'zero' and *alza* 'rise'), and /s/ (*soy* 'I am', *taxi* 'taxi', and in dialects lacking /θ/, *cero* and *alza*). In *yeísta* dialects, /ʝ/ is written as in *yeso* 'gypsum' and *llamo* 'I call'.

On the other hand, there are letters that correspond to more than one phoneme, including *c* (*cama* /'ka ma/ 'bed', *cero* /'θe ro/ or /'se

> A LINGUISTIC MYTH *(continued)*
>
> ro/ 'zero'), g (*gato* /'g̠a to/ 'cat', *gime* /'xi me/, or /'hi me/ 'she/he whines'), w (*wáter* /'b̠a ter/ 'toilet', *whisky* /'wis ki/ 'whisky').
>
> Additional complications: Some phonemes are written with digraphs, that is, with two letters: /ʧ/ (*leche* 'milk'), /ʎ/ or /ɟ/ (*calle* 'street'), /r/ (*carro* 'cart'). Aside from its presence in the digraph *ch*, the letter *h* is silent (*honor*).

Questions

1. Why is the Reconquest not completed in the thirteenth century when the Christian forces achieve military domination of the Peninsula?

2. Why is the year 1492 so important in the history of the Spanish language?

3. Comment on the following sentences, taken from act 21 of the *Celestina*, in terms of the linguistic tendencies they exemplify:

   e porque el incogitado dolor te dé más pena 'and so that the inconceivable pain may cause you more suffering'
   muchos mucho de ti dijeron 'many people said a lot about you'
   por medio de tus brasas pasé 'I passed through your embers'

4. Identify some of the most important dates in the history of the Royal Academy's *Diccionario*.

5. Apply, in chronological order, the twenty-nine phonological changes presented in this book to the following words, in such a way as to illustrate their phonological evolution between Latin and Modern Spanish:

aliu > ajo	*dīcit > dice*	*puteu > pozo*
facit > faze	*romanicē > romance*	*apicula > abeja*
satiōne > sazón	*auricula > oreja*	*malitia > maleza*
clausa > llosa	*martiu > marzo*	*tensu > tieso*
meliōre > mejor	*uncia > onza*	*corticia > corteza*

vermiculu > bermejo   *decimu > diezmo*   *anniculu > añejo*
lumbrīce > lombriz   *taxāre > tajar*   *condūxī > conduje*
pausāre > posar

5. Using the information provided in this chapter, complete the explanation of the phenomena illustrated by the following sentences in chapter 6.

   a. *Et gradecieron gelo mucho los senados.*
   b. *Et dixo les de como non le diera el Rey mas de nueue dias.*
   c. *Ascondudas so ell agua.*
   d. *Non auedes uos otros por que temer.*
   e. *En ell armario de los libros fallaras* [future tense] *lo que demandas.*
   f. *A manera de los que an uençuda alguna batalla.*
   g *Ser uos emos uasallos leales.*
   h. *E ellos mostraron le los libros de la eglesia.*
   i. *& el tenielos cercados dell otra part.*
   j. *Dixol que por desacuerdo se perdien las cosas.*

History of the Spanish Lexicon

8

Up to this point we have focused on the phonological, morphological, and syntactic history of Spanish, but the language's vocabulary—also called the lexicon—has a history as well. Like the other components, the lexicon is involved in a permanent and implacable state of change, which operates according to the same principles and mechanisms that determine phonological and morphological change. After a given factor (e.g., linguistic contact, speaker creativity, linguistic error) motivates the creation of a new word, it enters into competition with traditional equivalents, if there are any. If it is accepted as a marker of a specific social group, it may be diffused to other groups as well until it is accepted (or not) as an element of the common lexicon.

The first section of this chapter is an examination of the different ways in which words have come to form part of the Spanish vocabulary. We shall see that there are essentially three categories of words: those that have passed directly from spoken Latin to Castilian (called popular or popularly transmitted words), those that have been adopted from other languages (borrowings or loanwords), and those that were created through the internal mechanisms of the language. This last category includes not only the products of the various types of word formation (derivation, compounding, etc.) but also the results of semantic change, a phenomenon whereby a signifier adds an additional signified or meaning. The second section is a brief discussion of **etymology**, a discipline whose objective is to identify the origins of words, while the final section is a sketch of the principal stages through which the Spanish lexicon has passed during its two millennia of existence.

Sources of Words in Spanish

POPULARLY TRANSMITTED WORDS. This category comprises words that existed in the spoken Latin that forms the foundation of Spanish and were transmitted from generation to generation down to the present. This includes almost all the most frequent words in the language, as can be shown by an analysis of the frequency lists established in Davies 2006, which shows that ninety-nine of the one hundred most frequent words were popularly transmitted (exception: the preposition *hasta*, a borrowing form Arabic).

Significantly, not all popularly transmitted words are of native Latin origin. Since the lexicon of a language, like all other components, is subject to a continual process of transformation, the popular lexicon must be defined as beginning at some more or less arbitrary point. In the case of Castilian, this arbitrary point can be situated perhaps in the fifth or sixth century AD, given that all words present in the lexicon beginning at this time undergo all the phonological changes that transform Latin into Castilian, while words that enter later do not. When we define the popular lexicon as the set of words existent in the language by this fifth- or sixth-century set point, whatever their origin, we include various categories of non-Latin elements, including pre-Roman elements in Iberian Latin such as Celtic, whence *carro* 'cart', *cerveza* 'beer', *camino* 'road', and *braga* 'pants', and early Germanic *sopa* 'soup', *banco* 'bench', *harpa* 'harp', *tregua* 'truce', *guerra* 'war', and *blanco* 'white'. Later on we will see that a considerable number of Hellenisms present in Latin from an early date were also transmitted popularly, including *baño* 'bath', *cesta* 'basket', *cuchara* 'spoon', and *cuerda* 'cord, rope'. Words like these suggest the need to create a special category called perhaps "popular words of non-Latin origin". On the other hand, we exclude from the popular vocabulary Visigothic borrowings presumably absorbed in the seventh century such as *Alfonso* and *ganso* 'goose', whose /ns/ cluster does not reduce to /s/ as dictated by change 10. Also excluded are Arabic words, all absorbed after 711, such as *álgebra*, whose intertonic /e/ is retained, and *guitarra*, whose intervocalic /t/ does not undergo lenition.

BORROWINGS. The terms **borrowing** and **loanword** suggest some positive action on the part of the language whose word is adopted by another, when in reality the language that "lends" the word does nothing. A borrowing is actually the "absorption" or "adoption" of a word from another language without its cooperation or permission.

A loanword is incorporated into a language through some kind of linguistic contact, either oral (conversation, bilingualism) or written (reading), between two languages or two varieties of the same language (regional or chronological). A word that exists in the vocabulary of one language passes to the vocabulary of the other, duly adapted to the phonological and morphological patterns of the new language (without which the word continues to be foreign). Borrowings are usually classified according to whether they are popular or learned, where the latter, pronounced *learnèd* (/'lɜ‑ nɪd/), means 'adopted from classical Latin or Greek'.

Learned Latin borrowings, or Latinisms, exemplify the absorption of words from a chronologically different variety of the same language. Given the long tradition of using Latin in writing, it is not surprising that when writing in Romance becomes common, its vocabulary is supplemented with some of the Latin words that scribes have been using all along. Gloria Clavería Nadal (2006) notes that already in the works of Alfonso X there is a considerable number of Latinisms (some of which are of Hellenic origin) in lexical fields such as medicine (*esperma* 'sperm', *estupor* 'stupor'), geology (*esmeril* 'emery', *ónice* 'onyx'), and zoology (*onagro* 'onager', *orca*). There are also nouns pertaining to rhetoric and science (*oposición* 'opposition', *exposición* 'exposition', *estipulación* 'stipulation', *operación* 'operation', *experimento* 'experiment'), together with adjectives of various meanings (*eclesiástico* 'ecclesiastic', *escolástico* 'scholastic', *estival* 'pertaining to the summer', *estoico* 'stoic', *ordinario* 'ordinary'). Above I mentioned the important role that Juan de Mena plays in enriching the Spanish lexicon with Latinisms, which include the following: *último* 'last', *subsidio* 'gift', *ilícito* 'illicit', *inoto* (Mod. Sp. *ignoto*) 'unknown', *nauta* 'sailor', *nítido* 'brilliant', *intelecto* 'intellect', *túrbido* (Mod. Sp. *turbio*) 'turbid', *sumulacra* (Mod. Sp. *simulacro*) 'simulacrum', *sacro* 'sacred', and *nefando* 'very ugly', besides *diáfano* 'diaphanous' and *jerarquía* 'hierarchy', Latin Hellenisms. In the Renaissance and Baroque periods (seventeenth century), the influx of Latinisms continues to accelerate, and Latin continues to be an important source of new words down to the present day, though Latinisms now commonly pass through an intermediary language before reaching Spanish, as in the following examples, taken from Lorenzo 1966, which make their way into Spanish through English: *actuario* 'actuary', *corporación* 'corporation', *hábitat* 'habitat', *interferencia* 'interference', *junior* 'junior', *procrastinar* 'to procrastinate', *quórum* 'quorum', *recesión* 'recession', and *tándem* 'tandem'.

The phenomenon of **etymological doublets** is especially interesting. These occur when a single Latin word is transmitted into the vernacular twice, once through popular and once through learned channels. One normally finds in these cases that the popularly transmitted word has a concrete meaning, while the learned counterpart has a more abstract sense, as shown by the following examples:

LATIN WORD	POPULAR REFLEX	LEARNED REFLEX
articulus	*artejo* 'knuckle'	*artículo* 'article'
calidus	*caldo* 'broth'	*cálido* 'warm'
cathedra	*cadera* 'hip'	*cátedra* 'academic chair'
collocāre	*colgar* 'to hang'	*colocar* 'to place'
dēlicātus	*delgado* 'slender'	*delicado* 'delicate'
frīgidus	*frío* 'cold'	*frígido* 'frigid'
lēgālis	*leal* 'loyal'	*legal* 'legal'
lītigāre	*lidiar* 'to fight'	*litigar* 'to litigate'
operārī	*obrar* 'to act'	*operar* 'to operate'
strictus	*estrecho* 'narrow'	*estricto* 'strict'

The adoption of Latinisms into the lexicon of Spanish is part of a more general process often referred to as **relatinization**. According to Steven Dworkin (2005), Latinisms were prized for their clarity and precision in the expression of abstract concepts, and in rare cases they may even end up replacing Romance words considered to be less expressive, such as *pálido* for *descolorido* 'pallid' or *ejército* for *hueste* 'army'. In another work (2012:181), Dworkin explains that relatinization also affects phonology, since the influx of Latinisms causes the reintroduction of long-lost consonant clusters and a large increase in the number of proparoxytonic words (*cálido*, *cátedra*, *frígido*). Relatinization also occurs in derivative morphology in the introduction of Latin affixes (suffixes and prefixes), as in *equi-distante* 'equidistant', *gris-áceo* 'grayish'. In contrast, its effects on syntax—exemplified by the hyperbaton—are transitory.

Many foreign languages have contributed loanwords to the lexicon of Spanish, in different quantities and in diverse semantic fields, according to the intensity and the character of contact between its speakers and those of Spanish or the linguistic ancestors of Spanish. In many cases this contact has been direct. In an earlier chapter, reference was made to the lexical contributions made by peoples who participated directly in the history of the Iberian Peninsula, like the Celts, Basques, Visigoths, Muslims, and Mozarabs. Naturally, the other languages that developed on the Peninsula, such as Galician-Portuguese and Catalan, have also had an effect on the vocabulary. Given the importance of maritime life in Galicia and Catalonia, it is not surprising that they have made a considerable contribution to the Castilian maritime vocabulary: consider the Portuguese loanwords *almeja* 'clam', *balde* 'bucket', *carabela* 'caravel', *chubasco* 'heavy shower', *mejillón* 'mussel', *tanque* 'tank', and the Catalan loanwords *buque* 'ship', *esquife* 'light boat', *galera* 'galley', *golfo* 'gulf', *muelle* 'pier', *timonel* 'helmsman'.[1] Once the conquest of America begins, there is contact with the Amerindian languages, from which Spanish absorbs names of objects, plants, and animals not known in Spain, like *canoa* 'canoe', *maguey*, and *iguana* (from Araucanian); *chocolate, tomate,* and *ocelote* 'ocelot' (from Nahuatl); *condor, papa* 'potato', and *llama* (from Quechua); *mandioca* 'cassava' and *jaguar* (from Guaraní). According to Rafael Lapesa (1981:562), contact with the languages of African slaves imported into America results in the introduction of words in semantic areas such as musical instruments (*bongó, conga, mambo, samba*), drinks (*funche, guarapo*), and plants and fruits (*banana, malanga*). In practice, it is rarely possible to identify the precise African language from which these loanwords are taken.

It should be pointed out that the foreign languages that have

1. Sources: Penny 2002 and Alvar et al. 1967.

affected the Spanish lexicon most heavily have done so not through direct contact with Spanish speakers but through the importation of their culture through the written word. This is the case with Italian, French, English, and Greek.

The high point of Italian influence corresponds to the most glorious period in this language's history, the Renaissance. The Italian culture of this period is so brilliant and versatile that its mark may be found in almost all the arts: literature (*novela* 'novel', *soneto* 'sonnet'), theater (*bufón* 'jester', *comediante* 'actor'), painting (*miniatura* 'miniature', *pintoresco* 'picturesque'), architecture (*balcón* 'balcony', *fachada* 'facade'), and music (*serenata* 'serenade', *soprano*). **Italianisms** are also common in other semantic fields, such as the military (*batallón* 'battalion', *emboscar* 'to ambush'), commerce (*bancarrota* 'bankruptcy', *crédito* 'credit', 'loan'), and society (*charlar* 'to chat', *cortejar* 'to court').

Though French has been contributing words to the Spanish vocabulary since the Middle Ages (as mentioned in chapter 3), its influence reaches its high point in the eighteenth century, when words from various semantic fields are absorbed, such as the military (*brigada* 'brigade', *cadete* 'cadet'), fashion (*bisutería* 'costume jewelry', *pantalón* 'pants'), and domestic life (*botella* 'bottle', *sofá* 'sofa'). The obsession with Gallic culture and terminology becomes so intense in the eighteenth century that it even motivates the following—admittedly short-lived—borrowings: *golpe de ojo* 'look' (Fr. *coup d'oeil*, Sp. *mirada*), *chimia* 'chemistry' (Fr. *chimie*, Sp. *química*), and *remarcable* 'remarkable' (Fr. *remarquable*, Sp. *notable*). Among twentieth-century **Gallicisms** or French loanwords we find an interesting group of Anglicisms that pass through French before reaching Spanish: *camping* 'camping', 'campsite', *parking* 'parking lot', *smoking* 'tuxedo', *vagón* 'coach'.

The current wave[2] of Anglicisms flowing into the Spanish lexi-

2. Juan Gómez Capuz (1996:1289) identifies three periods of Anglo-American influence: 1820–1910, via translations of English romantic works; 1910–39, when Anglicisms begin to rival Gallicisms; 1939 to present day, in an explosion of American Anglicisms fostered by technical advances, cinema, and the military and touristic presence of Americans in Spain.

con is concentrated in the facets of life most affected by the innovations of twentieth- and twenty-first-century Anglo-American culture: technology (*misil* 'missile', *radar*, *télex*), economics (*dumping*, *marketing*, *trust*), social life (*bikini*, *champú* 'shampoo', *cóctel* 'cocktail'), cultural life (*trailer*, *vídeo*, *best seller*), science (*quark*, *clon*), and sports (*golf*, *caddie -y*, *penalty -i*). The influence of English is also seen in semantic borrowing, as in the following: *agresivo* 'provoking, attacking' → 'dynamic' (Eng. *aggressive*), *crucial* 'in the form of a cross' → 'decisive' (Eng. *crucial*), *firma* 'signature' → 'business' (Eng. *firm*), *planta* 'plan' → 'factory' (Eng. *plant*), *sofisticado* 'unnatural' → 'very elaborate' (Eng. *sophisticated*).

Even though Greek has contributed a large number of words to the Spanish vocabulary, almost all of them have arrived through an intermediary language, until recently mostly Latin, then through various European languages in the twentieth and twenty-first centuries. Among the Hellenisms that are at the same time Latinisms, we can identify three principal strata. Due to the intimate contact between speakers of Latin and Greek during several centuries of the imperial era, Latin adopted many Hellenisms involving daily life that continue to be used in Spanish today, such as *baño* 'bath', *cesta* 'basket', *cuchara* 'spoon', and *cuerda* 'cord, rope'. These words, like the words of Celtic and Germanic origin cited above, should be considered to be part of the popular vocabulary. Later on, with the adoption of Christianity, many Hellenisms are absorbed in the area of ecclesiastical terminology, such as *bautismo* 'baptism', *Biblia* 'Bible', *blasfemar* 'to blaspheme'. The most important sphere of usage for Hellenisms, however, has always been scientific terminology. Already in the thirteenth century the Castilian vocabulary absorbs **Hellenic Latinisms** such as *anatomía* 'anatomy', *clima* 'climate', *cólera* 'cholera', and *órgano* 'organ'. The fifteenth century witnesses the adoption of *arteria* 'artery', *diarrea* 'diarrhea', *epilepsia* 'epilepsy', and *gangrena* 'gangrene'. Throughout the nineteenth and twentieth centuries, Hellenisms have continued to serve as the basic tool for the creation of scientific terminology, as in *anemia* 'anemia', *fonética* 'phonetics', *psiquiatría* 'psychiatry', and *sismo* 'earthquake', but such words tend to appear in all modern European languages at approximately the same time.

WORDS CREATED THROUGH THE INTERNAL MECHA-NISMS OF THE LANGUAGE. The most common types of **word formation** in Spanish are **derivation**, that is, the use of **prefixes** and **suffixes** to create new words, and **compounding**, in which a new word (called a **compound**) is coined by combining two or more preexisting words. Another important word-formation process is called **conversion**, defined as any change of grammatical class that is not achieved through suffixation or compounding. This includes cases of **nominalization** (*parecer* 'opinion', *pésame* 'condolence', *ancho* 'width'), **adjectivization** (*una idea monstruo* 'a monster idea', *comportamiento muy hombre* 'manly behavior'), **adverbialization** (*jugar limpio* 'to play clean', *hablar alto* 'to talk loud'), and **verbalization** (*concretar* 'to concretize', *llenar* 'to fill', *escamar* 'to scale'), in which conversion is achieved through the addition of a verbal inflexion.

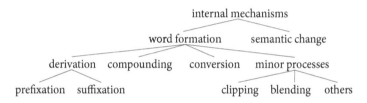

There are several additional but less important formative types, such as **acronymy**, which combines the initial letters of the words that serve as the usual name of something: *UNAM* 'Universidad Nacional Autónoma de México'; **clipping**, which involves abbreviating a word: *profe* for *profesor* 'professor', *cole* for *colegio* 'school'; and **blending**, the intentional intermingling of two words to produce a new one: *analfabestia*, a blend of *analfabeto* 'illiterate person' and *bestia* 'beast', 'idiot', and *chocolaterapia* 'therapy through eating chocolate' < *chocolate* and *terapia* 'therapy'. We might also bring up at this point the various playful processes through which new words are constantly being coined. Of special interest in this context are the **templates** (see sidebar) or patterns that are used in the formation of new playful words, such as **reduplication** (*bullebulle* 'person who cannot sit still', And. *lame-lame* 'brown-noser'), **apophonic reduplication** (*rifirrafe* 'scuffle', *ñiqueñaque* 'piece of junk'), and reduplication with consonantal variation (*cháncharras máncharras*

THE REDUPLICATIVE PLAYFUL TEMPLATE

The word *template* is used in industry to denote a pattern or gauge, such as a thin metal plate with a cut pattern, used as a guide in making something accurately. A common example of a template is the stencil, used to make letters or numbers with various materials, such as paper, cardboard, wood, or metal. What is crucial in a template is the fact that its products are all identical, no matter what the shape of the material from which they are cut.

When we apply the concept of template to word formation, we identify a mechanism of analogical change that has the effect of modifying words in such a way that they come into compliance with the parameters of the template.

Take the case of the reduplicative template, which has the form **X X**, designating words that consist of a repeated sequence. This form can be produced in several ways. The easiest is to reduplicate a sequence, as when the verb form *corre* 'she/he runs' is reduplicated in Cuban *correcorre* 'rush of people'. The word *chacha* 'babysitter' is produced by clipping the initial syllable of *muchacha* 'girl', 'babysitter'. The template motivates a vocalic change in the case of *lele*, an American variant of *lelo* 'silly', and a consonantal change in American Spanish *yaya* 'boo-boo', an infantile variant of *llaga* 'sore'. In sum, these changes appear random when considered separately, but viewed together they reveal the analogical effects of the reduplicative template.

For more information on playful words in Spanish, see Pharies 1986.

'excuse for not doing something', *a trochemoche* 'wildly'). Another playful category is **onomatopoeia**, or sound imitations. In Hispano-Romance the most interesting onomatopoeia is *quiquiriquí* 'cock-a-doodle-do', because it has served as a model (or template) for the formation of many more words, many of which are also onomatopoeias, like *tintirintín* 'sound of a bugle', Leon. *tuturuvía* 'golden oriole', and Navarrese *mamarramiáu* 'caterwauling', in all of which the quality of the vowels and consonants varies freely while the structure or template of *quiquiriquí* is maintained.

Prefixes³ are bound morphemes attached at the beginning of a base in order to form a derivative. Scholars do not agree on the question of the current inventory of authentic prefixes in Spanish. Some assert that the number is around forty, while others place this number between one and two hundred. Everyone includes popular prefixes such as those of *a-grupar* 'to group', *des-coser* 'to unstitch', *en-cabezar* 'to head up', *es-coger* 'to choose', *entre-comillar* 'to put in quotation marks', *so-cavar* 'to undermine', *sobre-pasar* 'to exceed', and *tras-nochar* 'to stay up all night', and also the learned equivalents of these, the prefixal Latinisms that appear in *ad-juntar* 'to join', *dis-traer* 'to distract', *in-titular* 'to entitle', *ex-carcelar* 'to release from jail', *inter-faz* 'interface', *sub-desarrollo* 'under-development', *super-conductor*, and *trans-porte* 'transport'. Everyone also recognizes the prefixal Hellenisms in words such as *a-fónico* 'having laryngitis', *anti-americano* 'anti-American', *dia-crónico* 'dia-chronic', and *epi-carpio* 'epicarp'. Nevertheless, some initial elements should not be considered genuine prefixes, such as morphemes that in Latin and Greek were not prefixes but initial components of nominal compounds, like those of *tele-scopio* 'telescope', *ferr-o-viario* 'pertaining to the railroad', *arist-o-cracia* 'aristocracy', and *bibli-o-grafía* 'bibliography'. Prefixes do not change the grammatical category of their stems—*des-coser* 'to unstitch', like *coser* 'to sew', is a verb—but they do affect their meanings. Among other things, they can indicate quantity (*bi-anual* 'biannual', *centi-litro* 'centiliter'), quality (*archi-duque* 'archduke', *neo-barroco* 'neobaroque'), position (*ante-cámara* 'antechamber', *endo-cardio* 'endocardium'), reflexivity (*auto-adhesivo* 'autoadhesive'), size (*mini-falda* 'miniskirt', *mega-voltio* 'megavolt'), intensity (*super-inteligente* 'superintelligent'), and contrary or opposite (*des-coser* 'to unstitch', *in-acción* 'inaction').

It is equally difficult to say exactly how many suffixes (i.e., bound morphemes attached at the end of stems) there are in Spanish, but they can be classified according to the same etymological categories that were employed above with the prefixes. Thus we have popular suffixes (as in *hall-azgo* 'finding', *diner-al* 'load of money', *roj-izo* 'reddish', *fall-ecer* 'to pass away'), learned Latin suffixes (*lider-*

---

3. Amply described in Varela and García 1999.

ato 'leadership', *gris-áceo* 'grayish', *port-átil* 'portable'), and learned Greek suffixes (*alcald-ía* 'mayoralty', *inc-aico* 'Incan', *polic-íaco* 'pertaining to the police'). Although they may appear to be suffixes, certain final elements actually reflect final components of compounds, either Latin (*lucí-fugo* 'light-avoiding', *magní-fico* 'magnificent', *caprí-pedo* 'goat-footed') or Greek (*antropó-fago* 'man-eating', *psiqu-iatra* 'psychiatrist', *tele-scopio* 'telescope'). Unlike prefixes, suffixes can alter the grammatical category of their bases: from the verb *hallar* 'to find', the noun *hall-azgo* 'finding' is derived; from the verb *perdurar* 'to last', the adjective *perdur-able* 'long-lasting'; from the adjective *español* 'Spanish', the verb *español-izar* 'to make Spanish'. In other cases, the addition of the suffix only changes the meaning of the stem: a *diner-al* is a lot of *dinero* 'money' (both nouns), an object that is *roj-izo* is somewhat *rojo* 'red' (both adjectives). Franz Rainer (1993) identifies some of the functions that may be performed by suffixes, among them intensity (*alt-ísimo* 'very tall', *gord-ote* 'plump'), disposition (*mujer-iego* 'womanizing', *brom-ista* 'given to playing practical jokes'), characteristic activity (*payas-ada* 'clowning around', *niñer-ía* 'childish act'), similarity (*sanchopanc-esco* 'like Sancho Panza', *sufij-oide* 'suffixlike element'), small size (*mes-ita* 'small table', *avion-eta* 'light aircraft'), passive possibility (*document-able, labrant-ío* 'arable'), name of an action (*hidrata-ción* 'hydration', *funciona-miento* 'functioning'), and name of the agent of an action (*boxea-dor* 'boxer', *sirv-iente* 'servant').

Compounding is not as frequent as derivation in the Spanish lexicon.[4] As was mentioned above, a compound is a word formed by the combination of two or more individual words. Spelling is not a determining factor in deciding whether a word is a compound. They are sometimes written together (*mediodía* 'noon', *alicaído* 'crestfallen', lit. 'with fallen wings'), sometimes with a hyphen (*actor-director*), and often without any unifying element (*coche cama* 'sleeper car'). What is essential in compounds is that their components form a semantic and syntactic unity and that they appear together frequently.

---

4. Spanish also has a system of learned compounding, using as constituents the elements of Latin and Greek compounds mentioned above, cf. *tele-scopio* 'telescope', which is composed of the Greek roots *tele-* 'far' and *scop-* 'to see'.

Compounds can be classified according to both their grammatical and their semantic structure. Applying the grammatical criterion, we find a large number of patterns, among which the following are most common:

Noun + adjective → noun (*arma* 'arm' + *blanco* 'white' → *arma blanca* 'any sharp instrument used as a weapon')

Adjective + noun → noun (*medio* 'half' + *naranja* 'orange' → *media naranja* 'other half, spouse')

Verb + noun → noun (*matar* 'to kill' + *moscas* 'flies' → *matamoscas* 'fly-swatter')

Noun + *i* + adjective → adjective (*ala* 'wing' + *caído* 'fallen' → *ali-caído* 'crestfallen')

Following the semantic criterion, three important categories can be identified. The first comprises **endocentric** compounds, where one of the components—the head—names the basic concept, and the other modifies it. A *coche cama* 'sleeper car', literally 'bed car', for example, is a car above all, but of a certain type, those that have beds inside. Its plural form is *coches cama*. In compounds of this type, the first component tends to be the head, although in other subcategories it can be in second place, as in *madreclavo*, literally 'mother-clove', a clove that has remained on the tree for two years. The second category, **binomial** compounds, is closely related to the first, since in this case both components can be interpreted as being heads. An *actor-director*, for example, plays two roles at the same time, those of actor and director, each of equal importance. In theory, if not in practice, the order of the constituents could be reversed without affecting the meaning. Binominal adjective compounds include the type (*hombre*) *sordomudo* 'deaf and dumb (man)', which implies the simultaneous presence of the two qualities, just as in (*sabor*) *agridulce* 'sweet and sour (taste)', (*dilema*) *ético-moral* 'ethical-moral (dilemma)', and (*economía*) *agrícola-ganadera* 'agriculture-livestock (economy)'. Here the constituents could also be inverted without semantic consequences, but pluralization is usually shown on the second constituent only: (*personas*) *sordomudas* 'deaf and dumb persons', *bebidas agridulces* 'sweet and sour drinks', *dilemas ético-morales* 'ethical moral dilemmas'. The third category is more productive in Spanish. These are the **exocentric** compounds, neither of whose elements performs the role of head. A *sacacorchos* 'corkscrew', for example, is an instrument and therefore can be understood neither as the action of taking out (*sacar* 'to take out') nor as a cork (*corcho*). Additional examples: *tocadiscos* 'record player' (lit. 'plays records'), *cuentagotas* 'dropper' (lit. 'counts drops'), *limpiabotas* 'shoeshine boy' (lit. 'cleans boots'). Among other exocentric categories are those exemplified by (*persona*) *sin techo* 'homeless person' (lit. 'without roof') and (*invertebrado*) *ciempiés* 'millipede' (lit. 'hundred feet').

SEMANTIC CHANGE. If a word or **linguistic sign** is defined as the combination of a **signifier** (form) and a **signified** (meaning), it is clear that the replacement of one signified by another, or the addition of a new signified, implies the creation of a new entity, that is, of a new complex of signifier and signified. This procedure does not constitute part of word formation proper but does have to be included in any discussion of the ways in which new words arise in the lexicon of a language.

In general, changes in meaning are due to the networks of associations that develop among the signifieds or meanings of a language. The great majority of semantic changes are due to an association based on the similarity of two meanings or on the contiguity of two meanings (that is, on the tendency of two meanings to be connected in some way in the real world).

Semantic change based on association by similarity of meanings is called **metaphor**. For example, *bicicletas* 'bicycles' is primarily a name for vehicles with two wheels, but because of the similarity of the form of these vehicles and that of a pair of glasses, a new word *bicicletas* 'glasses' arises metaphorically.

(Signifier)   *bicicletas*   *gafas*   *bicicletas*
                    | | ⌃
(Signified)   'bicycles'   'glasses' *through similarity* → 'bicycles' 'glasses'

The similarity of the two concepts associated metaphorically is always arbitrary or random. Here, for example, there is no connection in reality between bicycles and glasses.

Here are additional examples:

araña 'spider' → 'type of candelabra (shaped like a spider)'
dinamita 'dynamite' → 'explosive person or thing' (similar
    behavior)
falda 'skirt' → 'foothill' (similar form)
palillo 'toothpick' → 'skinny person' (similar form)
pelota 'ball' → 'head' (similar form)
bache 'pothole' → 'period of depression' (similar form)

Semantic change based on association by contiguity is called
metonymy. This type of association is based not on shared features
but on shared contexts. For example, a *corona* 'crown' is primarily a
hoop-shaped head adornment, but since kings have the custom of
wearing crowns as a symbol of their royal authority, the new word
crown 'royal authority' arises metonymically.

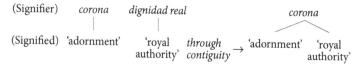

The great majority of metonymic associations are synecdoches, in
which the whole (here, royal authority) is designated by the name
of a part (here, the crown). For this reason, metonymic associations
are not arbitrary but based on some real connection between the
two concepts.

Here are additional examples:

sopa 'soup' → 'piece of bread that is dunked in a liquid' (due to
    the custom of eating bread and soup together)
autoridad 'authority' → 'a person who has authority' (because
    the authority resides in the person)
vidrio 'glass' → 'recipient for fluids' (because of the practice of
    making fluid recipients with glass)
pluma 'feather' → 'pen' (because feathers used to be used as
    pens)
cambio 'change' → 'transmission' (because a transmission is
    used to change gears)

A few semantic changes are motivated by similarity or contiguity of signifiers, such as when the word *América* acquires the meaning *Estados Unidos de América* through contiguity of signifiers and *dar un voltio* acquires the meaning of *dar una vuelta* through similarity of signifiers. This latter process also explains semantic borrowing, as when the word *registrar* 'to search' acquires the meaning 'to register (for a course)' from its English cognate. Ruiz Gurillo (2010) shows how grammaticalization, as well, proceeds through a series of metonymic associations, as when the phrase *desde luego*, originally meaning 'from then', acquires the meaning 'as a consequence' (since causes precede effects), and finally 'of course' (reinforcing the consequence), before becoming a mere discourse marker.

Etymology

Etymology is the study the origins of words. Of course, in many cases it is not possible to arrive at the real "origin" of a word, since as we know from our study of the genealogy of Spanish (chapter 2), many of the words of the Latin, Greek, or Celtic base can be traced back several millennia to the period of common Indo-European. It can be assumed that the words in this prehistoric language also had their own histories. For this reason it is customary among Spanish etymologists to limit the scope of their research. If they are studying a popularly transmitted word, they content themselves with identifying the Latin word that eventually produced this outcome and its date of first attestation in Castilian. In the case of borrowings, they try to identify the language it was borrowed from, the word that was borrowed, and the moment when it was introduced into Spanish, without necessarily pursuing the details of the history of the word in the contributing language. Where words were created internally, etymologists strive to identify the lexical elements of which the word is composed—**lexemes**, suffixes, prefixes—and the moment at which they were first combined. Once the origin or **etymon** of a word has been identified, etymologists try to follow its trajectory to the present.

In order to carry out etymological research, Spanish etymologists need to know the **historical grammar** of the language. By historical grammar is meant the history of its phonological and morphological development, that is, exactly what was presented in Chapters 5 through 7 of this book. Thus, when Chapter 5 traced the phonological evolution of Lat. *umbilīcu* to Sp. *ombligo* 'navel', it was making a contribution to its etymology. Similarly, when *vuestra merced* was identified in chapter 6 as the original form of the modern word *usted*, that was a contribution to its etymology. Since word formation is also considered to be part of a language's morphology, the present chapter's discussion of the origins of words such as *archiduque* 'archduke' (a prefixal derivative), *liderato* 'leadership' (a suffixal derivative), and *cuentagotas* 'dropper' (a compound) was etymological.

Besides knowing historical grammar, etymologists have to be acquainted with the vocabularies of the languages with which Spanish has been in contact, either directly or culturally, in order to be able to identify the sources of loanwords,—for example, to know that *fachada* 'facade' is from Italian and that *alcalde* 'mayor' is from Arabic. They must also have extensive knowledge of semantic change, because, as we have just seen, meanings tend to change with time. Finally, etymologists must know a lot about the earlier stages of a language because, logically, the oldest form and meaning of a word tend to reflect more faithfully the form and meaning of the etymon, since they have undergone fewer phonological and semantic changes. For example, when studying the etymology of Sp. *tamaño* 'size', it is preferable to begin with the medieval variant *tamanno* 'so big', as this meaning reflects more closely that of the Latin etymon *tam magnus* 'so big'.

The most respected authority in questions of Spanish etymology is the *Diccionario crítico etimológico castellano e hispánico* by Joan Corominas (with the collaboration of José Antonio Pascual), published in six volumes between 1980 and 1991. Faced with this monumental work, one might be tempted to conclude that everything is known in Spanish etymology, but this is not the case. On the one hand, Corominas is sometimes wrong, especially in his treatment of playful words, which he often and inadvisably attributes to onomatopoeic imitation. For example, he attributes *títere* 'puppet' to "an imitation of the high-pitched sound *ti-ti* that the puppeteer gives to his puppets" (5:510). According to Pharies 1985, *títere* is in reality an elaboration on a Gascon or Provençal loanword *tite* 'doll', an abbreviated version of *petite* 'little one', a name that little girls typically give to their dolls, toys very similar to puppets. On the other hand, not even the immense number of words studied by Corominas accounts for the total vocabulary of Modern Spanish in all its registers and dialects. His dictionary does not include, for example, *lendakari, lehendakari* 'president of the autonomous government of the Basque provinces', an extremely frequent borrowing in Spanish after 1978, and it is also less than inclusive of words from slang and the lower registers of the language, such as *gachí* 'good-looking woman' (a borrowing from Romany, the language of the Gypsies), *pitopausia* 'loss of sexual ability in men due to aging' (a blend of *pito* 'dick' and *menopausia* 'menopause'), and *paganini* 'person who has to pay the expenses of others' (a play on words based on the synonymous slang word *pagano*, originally 'pagan'—and the name of the Italian musician).[5] A quick glance into any modern dictionary of dialect or slang vocabulary will suffice to convince potential etymologists that there is still a lot of work left to do in Spanish etymology.

In addition, it should be emphasized that besides studying the origins of lexemes (lexical bases of words), etymology investigates the histories of other types of morphemes, including suffixes and prefixes. The most extensive study of suffixal origins is the *Diccionario etimológico de los sufijos españoles* (Pharies 2002). This book shows that the methods involved in the study of suffixal origins differ little from those used to study word origins, and that suffixal origins can be equally interesting. We already considered, in chapter 6, the origins of the suffix -*mente,* which changes from a word to a suffix through a process of grammaticalization. Another fascinating case is that of the suffix -*ura,* which is used to form names of qualities from the corresponding adjectives, as in *dulzura* 'sweetness' (from *dulce* 'sweet') and *blancura* 'whiteness' (from *blanco* 'white'). The suffix owes its origin to a mistaken analysis (also called "reanalysis") of certain Latin nouns ending in -*tūra* that are derived from verbs (*mixtūra* 'action of mixing' < *miscēre* 'to mix'). When in Medieval Castilian words such

5. Examples from León 1980.

as *derechura* 'doctrine' and *estrechura* 'narrow place' lose their association with their etyma *dīrec-tūra* and *estric-tūra*, they are associated instead with the corresponding adjectives *derecho* 'right' (< *dīrectu*) and *estrecho* 'narrow' (< *strictu*) and are consequently reanalyzed as *derech-ura* and *estrech-ura*, resulting in the creation of a new suffix *-ura*. This serves as a model for a whole series of derivations on stems that are not verbal, as in *alt-ura* 'high place' (< *alto* 'high') and *loc-ura* 'crazy act' (< *loco* 'crazy').[6] Later on, derivatives ending in *-ura* cease to denote things having a certain quality and begin to denote the quality itself: *altura* 'highness', *locura* 'craziness'.

Stages in the History of the Spanish Lexicon

The evolution of the vocabulary of a language is a reflection of the cultural history of the people who use it, because a vocabulary has to adapt continually to the historical circumstances and conceptual needs of each era. If a people finds itself invaded and dominated by another, for example, it is probable that their language—and especially their vocabulary—will reflect contact with the language of the invaders. Examples of this type of adjustment are innumerable, but two cases are especially notable. One of these, English, absorbed so many French words after the Norman invasion of 1066 that they grew to constitute a lexical stratum in their own right. Another is Basque, whose contact with Latin and its continuations over more than two millennia has resulted in a vocabulary estimated to be 75 percent of Latin or Romance origin. Sometimes the language of the invader may also change in these situations. Consider in this respect the case of American Spanish, which has adopted and continues to adopt words from indigenous American languages that are considered apt to describe elements of American life.

Other circumstances that can bring about important lexical changes are cultural and technological revolutions. A good example of the former is the Renaissance, a cultural movement that triggered a profound transformation in the economic, political, social, philosophical, religious, and aesthetic values of medieval civilization. We

---

6. This explanation was proposed by Pattison (1975:56–70).

saw in chapter 7 that in Spain this movement led to a transformation of the Spanish lexicon through the introduction of thousands of Latin and Greek loanwords. Among technological revolutions, none compares with the one that we are currently experiencing, which is forcing the language to adapt to advances that are being made in a wide variety of fields, especially scientific, as in the following words, from the field of medicine: *empalme genético* 'genetic splicing', *clon* 'clone', *hipoglucemia* 'hypoglycemia', *liposucción* 'liposuction', *mamografía* 'mammography', *desfibrilar* 'to defibrillate', *progesterona* 'progesterone', *anorexia* 'anorexia', *antioxidante* 'antioxidant'; or these, from computer science: *bit*, *caché* 'cache', *escáner* 'scanner', *web*, *megabyte*, *internet*.

The language that is now known as Spanish is the continuation of the variety of Latin that the Romans brought to the Iberian Peninsula more than two millennia ago. It is probable that the evolution of Iberian Latin followed that of the Latin of Rome during the initial centuries, with the inevitable variability caused by the distance between the capital and the province. We may assume that the sophistication of the vocabulary inherited from Latin began to decline in parallel with that of postimperial Roman civilization, a process that continued and accelerated as a consequence of the Visigothic and Muslim invasions. However, after this long period of decadence, the language and its vocabulary finally begin to recover their vitality in the thirteenth century, when for the first time the vernacular is considered to be a linguistic vehicle worthy of being used for written communication. The tendency of the learned poets of the beginning of this century is to enrich the vocabulary of Castilian with the Latin words that they are using on a daily basis in other writings. This is the first of several waves of learned borrowings that have continued almost unabated to the present day.

The Renaissance begins in Italy toward the middle of the fourteenth century, and one century later it begins to affect Castilian through writers such as Juan de Mena, who more than any of his contemporaries endeavors to spice up his poetry with the Latinisms he needs for its classical themes. This tendency continues for several centuries, leading on the one hand to the brilliant literature of the Golden Age but also, on the other, to the dead end represented by the Spanish Baroque. We see in the poetry of Góngora the zenith of the obscurantist tendency, which transforms Castilian into a language practically incomprehensible even to its own speakers.

When the Bourbons try to introduce the Enlightenment, with its ideals of tolerance and reason, into eighteenth-century Spain, they run into the traditionalism of the Spanish people and the opposition of the Catholic Church. From this time forward, the great linguistic challenge facing Spanish culture is to modernize its language, transforming it into a linguistic tool capable of adapting to the scientific and technological revolutions on the horizon. The new Royal Academy might have been expected to undertake this task, but as Manuel Alvar Ezquerra points out (2002:273), "with respect to the nomenclature of the sciences, arts, and professions, the Corporation insists that they do not form part of the common language, and that their place is in specialized works".[7] The Academy announced at one point its desire to dedicate a separate work to the lexical contributions of these fields, but these intentions were never translated into action. As a result, this task—so crucial in the project of making Spanish an important international language—has been left to others.[8]

....

Questions

1. To what word-formational processes can the emergence of the following words be attributed?

   cine 'movie theater'
   boquiabierto 'open-mouthed'
   estadounidense 'American'
   mili 'military service'
   Cub. *correcorre* 'mob of people'
   parabrisas 'windshield'

---

7. "en cuanto a la nomenclatura de las ciencias, artes y profesiones, la Corporación insiste en que no forman parte de la lengua común, y su lugar son las obras especializadas".

8. In 1983 the Real Academia de Ciencias Exactas, Físicas y Naturales published a *Vocabulario científico y técnico*, now in its third edition (1996).

interacción 'interaction'
nutrición 'nutrition'
OTAN (*Organización del Tratado del Atlántico del Norte*) 'North
    Atlantic Treaty Organization'
hora punta 'rush hour'
tiquismiquis 'fussiness'
antecámara 'antechamber'
analfabestia 'illiterate person'
dentista 'dentist'
burrocracia 'stubborn bureaucracy'
ringorrango 'flourish in handwriting'
mexicano-brasileño 'Mexican-Brazilian'
cucurucú 'Colombian bird similar to the owl'

2. Are the following semantic changes due to metaphoric or metonymic association? (Examples from León 1980.)

baile 'action of dancing' → (in bank slang) 'error that consists of
    inverting two numbers'
bañera 'bathtub' → 'torture consisting of holding someone's
    head under water until they almost drown'
barriga 'belly' → 'pregnancy'
biblia 'Bible' → 'book of cigarette paper'
bicho 'little bug' → 'dose of LSD'
bistec 'piece of beef' → 'tongue'
blanca 'white' (f. adj.) → 'cocaine'
brutal 'brutal' → 'huge'
buitre 'vulture' → 'selfish' (adj.)
buzón 'mailbox' → 'large mouth'
tanque 'tank for liquids' → 'woman's purse'
belleza 'beauty' → 'beautiful person or thing'
paliza 'beating' → 'annoying or boring talk or conversation'
terraza 'terrace' → 'head'
plumífero 'having feathers' → 'writer'
picapica ('person or thing that stings') → 'ticket inspector on
    public transport'
pastel 'filled cake' → 'excessively ornate building'

3. Without consulting an etymological dictionary, identify the origins of the following slang words from León 1980:

bodi 'body'
cabezón 'fifty-peseta coin with an image of Franco'
cabroncete 'jerk'
californiano 'type of LSD'
comehostias 'overly pious person'
gandulitis 'laziness'
grogui (in boxing) 'groggy'
metepatas 'person who often sticks his foot in his mouth or commits faux pas'
michelines 'love handles'
mieditis aguditis 'a lot of fear'
míster 'soccer coach'
narizotas 'person with a huge nose'
necro 'autopsy'
orsay (in soccer) 'off-sides'
penene (for *profesor no numerario*) 'lecturer'
picapica 'ticket inspector on public transport'
plumífero 'writer'
puercada 'indecent act'
¡rediez! 'darn!'
ultra 'ultraconservative'
ridículo 'ridiculousness'

Varieties of Spanish

9

The terms *variety* and *dialect* are used to refer to linguistic modalities of restricted extension or use. Normally they refer to geographic varieties, as when one speaks of the Mexican dialect or, more specifically, of the Mexican dialect of Chihuahua, known as *chihuahuense*. Dialects can also be social in nature. Within *chihuahuense*, for example, we can differentiate among several social dialects, like that of the working class, or even that of working-class women between twenty-five and forty years of age.[1] In popular use the term *dialect* usually involves a negative connotation of "nonstandard", but in technical usage this restriction is eliminated, so that it is appropriate, for example, to speak of the dialect spoken by the upper-class inhabitants of Madrid, whose speech, along with that of others, is standard by definition.

Some linguists prefer the term *variety* to speak of linguistic forms that differ little among themselves, reserving *dialect* for forms that manifest more marked differences, as in the morphology. Not everyone makes this distinction, however, and since it turns out to be practically impossible to define the boundary between "not very different" and "markedly different", the two terms will be considered synonymous here.

The various meanings of the term *dialectology* naturally reflect those of *dialect*. Traditional dialectology studies the geographic varieties of a language, normally comparing them with the standard,

---

1. The matter is actually even more complex, since there are also "registers" or contextual levels in a language. A person's linguistic production varies according to whether he or she is speaking or writing, and also according to the rank of his or her interlocutors, the formality of the context in which the speech act is produced, etc.

which is not conceived of as a dialect. Social dialectology (also called sociolinguistics), on the other hand, has as its object the elucidation of the linguistic correlates of social variables such as gender, age, socioeconomic group, ethnic group, education, profession, and attitudes, in any variety whatsoever, including the standard.

It must be emphasized that Spanish dialectology is not the same as Hispano-Romance dialectology. Local varieties in Spain such as Asturian, Leonese, and Aragonese are typically called dialects, but from a historical perspective they are dialects not of Spanish but of the same primitive Hispano-Romance of which Castilian is itself a dialect, before it began the political and demographic ascendancy that culminated in its transformation into the national language, worthy of the name *Spanish*. This group of genetically cognate dialects, often called historical or **constitutive**, according to Pilar García Mouton (1994:9), are now disappearing (with the exception of Castilian), especially in urban areas, where they may subsist only as a local accent. Thus, when we speak of Spanish dialectology, we are referring exclusively to **consecutive** dialects, those that have developed within or from Castilian.

Varieties of Spanish in the Two Castiles

In the technical sense, the most important dialect of Peninsular Spanish is the standard, identified as the linguistic form used in speaking and writing by educated people in such Castilian cities as Valladolid, Burgos, and Salamanca. Everything that has been included in this book up to this point refers to this dialect. It should be mentioned, however, that Castilian is not monolithic, in the sense that in both Old and New Castile linguistic phenomena may be found that are considered aberrant.[2] To a certain extent, these are features of a social rather than a geographic variety, spoken by relatively uneducated rural populations. We know that this variety— often called **popular Spanish**—is ancient, since its peculiarities are found not only in the Castilian regions but in practically every

2. Here I draw on Hernández Alonso 1996 and Moreno Fernández 1996.

corner of the Spanish-speaking world, where they were originally brought by Castilian conquistadors and colonists.

Among the clearly archaic phonological features of popular Spanish are (1) simplification of consonant clusters (*dotor* for *doctor* and *ato* for *apto* 'apt'), (2) use of verb forms *comistes* (for *comiste* 'you ate') and *hablastes* (for *hablaste* 'you spoke'), which may be analogical with other second-person verb forms ending in -*s* (*comes, hablas*) or derive from obsolete forms corresponding to *vos*, (3) neutralization of the vowels *i/e* and *o/u* in unstressed initial position (*sigún* for *según* 'according to', *nenguno* for *ninguno* 'none', *pulicía* for *policía* 'police', *orbanizar* for *urbanizar* 'to urbanize'), (4) alternation of /b/ and /g/ before /w/ (*güeno* for *bueno, buele* for *güele* 'huele', *buevo* for *güevo* 'huevo') or before /u/ (*abuja* for *aguja, abujero* for *agujero*), and (5) the confusion of /r/ and /l/ in **implosive** (i.e., syllable-final) position, which is attested in primitive Hispano-Romance (Lloyd 1987:348): *arcarde* 'alcalde' (1246), *comel* 'comer' (1521), *alçobispo* 'arçobispo' (1576). The following are not archaic but still widespread: (6) **monophthongization** of diphthongs (*trenta* for *treinta* 'thirty', *pos* for *pues* 'well', *anque* for *aunque* 'although'), (7) loss of intervocalic /r/ in certain set phrases (*mía que eres tonto* for *mira que eres tonto* 'you're being really silly', *me paece* for *me parece* 'it seems to me'), and (8) reduction of /mbj/ > /mj/ (*tamién* for *también* 'also'). Add to these, in morphology, (9) the survival of archaic verb forms such as *truje* for *traje* 'I brought', *vide* for *vi* 'I saw', and analogical forms like *haiga* for *haya* 'she/he may have', *vaiga* for *vaya* 'she/he may go', *háyamos* for *hayamos* 'we may have', *andé* for *anduve* 'I walked', *juegar* for *jugar* 'to play', and *traíba* for *traía* 'she/he was bringing'. In syntax, we observe (10) use of the conditional in the protasis of conditional sentences (*si yo tendría tiempo* for *si yo tuviera tiempo* 'if I had time'), (11) use of *caer* and *quedar* in a transitive sense (*la quedó sola con los niños* for *la dejó sola con los niños* 'she/he left her alone with the children'), (12) *dequeísmo* (*pienso de que* for *pienso que* 'I think that') and *queísmo* (*me alegro que* for *me alegro de que* 'I'm glad that'),[3] and (13) inversion of the standard order of clitic pronouns (*te se cayó*

3. See Jiménez and Rodríguez Tovar 2012.

el vaso for *se te cayó el vaso* 'you dropped the glass'). Among the phenomena that are typical of Old Castile but that have not been adopted elsewhere are (14) the impersonal *leísmo*, that, the use of *le* to refer to animals and things (*el azadón le he dejado allí* for *el azadón lo he dejado allí* 'I left the hoe there', Med. Cast. *yo puedo destruir este templo e refazer le en tres días* for *yo puedo destruir este templo e refazer lo en tres días* 'I can destroy this temple and rebuild it in three days'), and (15) *laísmo* (*ya la escribí una carta a mi tía* for *ya le escribí una carta a mi tía* 'I already wrote my aunt a letter'). While many Spanish dialects (16) neutralize the first of two consonants in a cluster, only in the Castilian regions are /kt/, /pt/, and /kθ/ neutralized respectively as /θt/, /θt/, and /θ/, as in *perfectamente* /peɾ'feθ ta 'men te/ 'perfectly', *apto* /'aθ to/ 'apt', and *dirección* /di ɾe 'θjon/ 'direction'.

Andalusian

The first dialect that develops from Castilian is Andalusian. Andalusia—generally identified as the territory south of the Sierra Morena (see map 8)—is reconquered in two stages. Western Andalusia falls into the hands of the Castilians as part of the wave of victories that follow the decisive battle of Las Navas de Tolosa in 1212. In this period all the important western cities are taken, including Córdoba (1236), Jaén (1246), Seville (1248), Cádiz (1265), and Jerez (1265).[4] For reasons explained in chapter 7 (e.g., the slow pace of repopulation, Castilian political instability), the campaign to take eastern Andalusia is not initiated until two centuries later, when the Castilian armies under the Reyes Católicos take, in a succession of rapid victories, Ronda (1485), Loja (1486), Málaga (1487), Almería (1489), and Granada (1492).

The different dates of reconquest and repopulation of the two halves of the region have linguistic consequences. While it is true that all of Andalusia shares certain phonetic features, such as the aspiration of /s/ and the confusion of /ɾ/ and /l/, the eastern part of the region does not manifest many of the phenomena discussed

---

4. The principal source of information in this entire section is Narbona, Cano, and Morillo 2003.

below and thereby preserves a more Castilian character. Antonio Narbona, Rafael Cano, and Ramón Morillo (2003) trace the boundaries of many of these phenomena in a series of maps, which indicate, for example, that the northeast third of the region continues to distinguish not only between /s/ and /θ/ (155) but also between *vosotros* and *ustedes* (236), and that in Almería and Jaén the initial consonant of the word *jota* continues to be velar (202). On the other hand, one of the features typical of eastern Andalusian speech not found in Castilian is the so-called *desdoblamiento de vocales* (171), a term that refers to the opening of vowels in the environment of aspirated implosive or syllable-final /s/ (/mo 'no to no/ 'monotonous' [sg.], /mɔ 'nɔ tɔ nɔʰ/ 'monotonous' [pl.], /'bo βo/ 'foolish' [sg.], /'bɔ βɔʰ/ 'foolish' [pl.]).

One might ask why Andalusian ends up differentiating itself so thoroughly from its northern neighbor as to merit being recognized as a separate variety. We saw in chapter 2 that the combination of dispersion in space and the passing of time are sufficient to initiate the process whereby varieties are eventually formed. In view of this principle, it is clear that the lines of communication between recently conquered Andalusia and the Castilian cultural centers were few and weak, perhaps because of the geographic barrier that the Sierra Morena represented, perhaps because of the political indifference with which Castile regarded the south for a long time.[5] Another factor is the inevitable process of koineization that accompanied the process of repopulation. The recently conquered Andalusian regions became the home of colonists migrating not only from Castile but also from Leon, Galicia, and Portugal (in the west), Navarre and Catalonia (in the east), and even foreign lands (there are indications of the presence of German, English, Flemish, and Genovese settlers). Koineization implies, above all, a process of simplification of complex and variable linguistic structures, with a loss of phonological and morphological distinctions.[6]

5. Antonio Alatorre (1989:241) speaks of the "disdain of the two Castiles for Andalusia" ("desdén de las dos Castillas por Andalucía"), referring specifically to the linguistic factor.

6. Penny (1992:251) characterizes the results of the meeting of two linguistic modalities as follows: "What happens is the production of abundant linguistic variants,

The possibility that the formation of the Andalusian dialect took place due to the influence of Arabic and Mozarabic is not to be taken seriously. There was actually very little linguistic contact between the speakers of Arabic and the Castilian conquerors, since the two groups were inveterate enemies. In most of the cities taken by the Castilians in the thirteenth century, orders were issued to immediately expel the Arabic-speaking inhabitants, most of whom fled to Granada.

It might seem more reasonable to attribute the distinctive features of Andalusian to the influence of the Mozarabic dialect, but in actuality the conditions under which this dialect might have influenced local Castilian were also lacking. According to Narbona, Cano, and Morillo (2003:46), Mozarabic—always closely associated with Christianity—ceases to flourish in 1055 with the arrival of the Almoravids, a group of fundamentalist Muslims who order the expulsion of all Christians. The situation intensifies in 1147 in the south after the advent of the even more fanatical Almohads, who undertook the extermination of the few Christians still left in the area. Another factor that contributes to the decline of Mozarabic is the military action of the Christian kingdoms. As Lapesa (1981:189) affirms, "The Mozarabic dialects disappeared as the Christian kingdoms conquered the southern regions. Those decadent forms of speech could not compete with those brought by the conquerors, more vigorous and evolved. The absorption started with the conquest of Toledo (1085)."[7] Thus the differentiation of Andalusian cannot be due to the influence of Mozarabic, because this dialect was no longer spoken in the region at the time that the Andalusian dialect was forming.

Another essential factor in the history of Andalusian is the

---

in the speech of everyone, a situation that is later resolved through the selection of certain variants and the abandonment of others, leaving a dialect that differs from all those that contributed to its formation." ("Lo que ocurre es la producción de abundantes variantes lingüísticas, en el habla de todos, situación que luego se resuelve con la selección de ciertas variantes y el abandono de otras, quedando un dialecto que difiere de todos los que han contribuido a su formación.")

7. "Los dialectos mozárabes desaparecieron conforme los reinos cristianos fueron reconquistando las regiones del Sur. Aquellas hablas decadentes no pudieron competir con las que llevaban los conquistadores, más vivas y evolucionadas. La absorción se inició desde la toma de Toledo (1085)."

chronological question: At what point in history did the Castilian of Andalusia begin to be different from that of Castile? And at what point do these differences become so clear as to justify considering Andalusian as a separate variety?

To ask when the Andalusian dialect arose is the same as asking when each of its distinctive features appeared. Now the most noticeable Andalusian features, especially in the variety's western region, are principally a series of phonological features, such as the so-called **seseo** and **ceceo**, the local articulations of /s/, the **aspiration** of implosive /s/, the **glottal** articulation of the Castilian velar fricative, and *yeísmo*. In terms of grammar, the most salient feature is the loss of the pronoun *vosotros* in favor of the more recently coined *ustedes*.

The above-mentioned phenomena result from a series of changes that occurred independently of Castilian, each with its own **chronology** and limited in its applicability to different parts of the Andalusian speech area.

The independence of Andalusian phonological evolution is most evident in the sibilants, in terms of both distribution and articulation.[8] Regarding distribution, Penny (2002:102; see also Lloyd 1987:336–42) observes that in the greater part of Andalusia, the medieval sibilants /ts/ and /s/ (apical [s̩]), on the one hand, and /dz/ and /z/ (apical [z̩]), on the other, merged early on in the respective outcomes /s̩/ and /z̩/, both dorsodental. Notably, after devoicing, the four original sibilant phonemes were reduced to one only, /s̩/. This matter is complicated by the fact that this new phoneme was not pronounced the same in the entire region. According to Narbona, Cano, and Morillo (2003:72), from the fifteenth to the seventeenth centuries there was vacillation between two articulations of /s̩/, and this lack of consistency in the evolution of the sibilants is still reflected in contemporary Andalusian. Alonso Zamora Vicente (1970:301–8) notes that in almost the entire western part of Andalusia (except for the city of Seville), the sibilant in use tends to be flat and coronal, intermediate between /s̩/ and /θ/. This phenomenon is

---

8. Here I use the following phonetic symbols: [s̩] unvoiced apico-alveolar fricative, [z̩] voiced apico-alveolar fricative, [s̩] unvoiced dorsodental fricative, [z̩] voiced dorsodental fricative.

called *ceceo* (neutralization of /s/ and /θ/ in favor of the latter), and the regions are called *ceceantes*. In Seville and the northeastern part of Andalusia around Cordoba, the corresponding sibilant can be described as predorsal convex, similar to the /s/ of most Spanish-American varieties. This usage is called *seseo* (neutralization of /s/ and /θ/ in favor of the former), and the areas are called *seseantes*.

Regarding the phoneme /ʃ/ that resulted from the devoicing of /ʒ/, there is evidence (spellings like *hentil* for *gentil* 'kind' and *mehor* for *mejor* 'better') already in the first half of the sixteenth century suggesting that in western Andalusia its final product is the unvoliced glottal fricative /h/ rather than velar /x/.

Another phenomenon for which we have a beginning date in Andalusia is *yeísmo*. Although there are indications of an even earlier origin, the evidence does not become systematic until the eighteenth century. According to Narbona, Cano, and Morillo (2003:91), *yeísmo* is associated with Andalusian beginning in this century, even though it is not generally in use in the region, and it appears independently in Extremadura and La Mancha.

It is not possible to assign a beginning date for several phonetic phenomena that characterize varieties of Modern Andalusian. I have already mentioned, in this respect, the aspiration and elision of implosive /s/. Another example is the confusion of /ɾ / and /l/—generally in favor of the former, as illustrated in Juan Valera's untranslatable witticism *Sordao, barcón y mardita sea tu arma se escriben toas con ele* 'Soldier, balcony, and damn your soul are all written with *l*'. It is even harder to trace the history of phenomena such as the weakening of [ʧ] to [ʃ] in Cádiz and Seville, among other places (['ko ʃe] for *coche* 'cart', 'car'), the assimilation of consonant clusters with a geminate result ([a 'βjet ta] por *abierta*), the velarization of certain implosive consonants ([aŋ ti 'sek ti ko] for *antiséptico* 'antiseptic') and of word-final nasals (['a βlaŋ] for *hablan* 'they speak'), besides the so-called *jejeo* (see Rodríguez Prieto 2008), that is, the tendency to aspirate initial or intervocalic /s/ ([he 'ɲoɾ] for *señor*, [pe 'he ta] for *peseta*), heard in many parts of the region.

Regarding the use of *ustedes* and *vosotros*, since the former does not become frequent until the eighteenth century, this is a fairly late adjustment. While in eastern Andalusia the distribution of the two personal pronouns tends to match the Castilian arrangement, in the west *ustedes* replaces *vosotros* completely. However, verbal and pronominal forms continue to vary in the current speech of the region: one hears, besides *ustedes se van* 'you are going', also *ustedes se vais* and *ustedes os vais*.

Sample of Andalusian Spanish. An Andalusian mayor talks about healthcare in his community.

> *Pero sí es verdad que en el año ochenta y dos en el año ochenta había médicos que dormían en nuestro pueblo y que tenían una existencia, había en el pueblo una existencia más cercana. Una existencia en la que tú llamabas a cualquier hora y a ti te atendían porque estaban aquí en nuestro pueblo los médicos viviendo conviviendo con nosotros y también tenían unos días, cada médico, de urgencia y nos atendían. Eso ha evolucionado hacia el sistema de salud más moderno pero más alejado, hacia el sistema de salud que están fuera del ámbito de nuestro pueblo y que tardan, como mínimo, treinta minutos como mínimo en llegar si le coge la ambulancia en Estepa.*[9]

Canary Island Spanish

The Canary Islands have been known since antiquity, including by the Romans. Pliny the Elder speaks of an expedition to the island undertaken by King Juba of Mauretania.[10] The islands then disap-

9. From a video at http://www.youtube.com/watch?v=eEs500HArd8, beginning at 2:16. The relevant portion of this video is also available on the author's page at the University of Florida website. Translation: But it is true that in the year 82, in the year 80 there were doctors who slept in our town and who had their existence here, a more proximate existence. An existence in which you called at any time and they saw you because here in our town there were doctors living, coexisting with us and also each doctor had days on call and they saw us. That has evolved into the more modern but more remote health system, toward a health system where they are outside the sphere of our town and take at least thirty minutes at least to arrive if the ambulance picks them up in Estepa.

10. See www.laopinion.es/2c/2010/02/22/juba-ii-informe-islas-canarias/273117. html (consulted April 7, 2014).

pear from history, until they are rediscovered in the thirteenth century by a Genovese fleet. A papal document of 1433 grants rights to the islands to the Portuguese, but in 1436 this decision is reversed to grant rights to the Spanish Crown, a change recognized by the Portuguese in 1479.

When the islands are rediscovered, they are inhabited by an indigenous tribe called the Guanches, of probable Berber origin. The Guanches are not numerous (fewer than four thousand), and they live in caves, but in spite of their primitive culture they are able to resist the conquering forces for almost a century, between 1402, when the Spaniards disembark in Lanzarote, and 1496, when Tenerife, the largest of the seven islands, is conquered. Subsequently, there is a relatively brief period of immigration until 1520, during which colonists, especially from Spain and Portugal, arrive to join the indigenous inhabitants who have survived the defensive struggle. Until the end of the sixteenth century, the sugar industry is an important economic base, and the islands also become an obligatory stopping point on the shipping route to the Americas: Christopher Columbus himself restocks in the Canary Islands before crossing the Atlantic. However, the sugar industry fails, as do later the wine industry and the production of cochineal, a red dye derived from insects. For this reason, toward the end of the nineteenth century there is a period of massive emigration, first to Cuba and later to Venezuela. Nowadays the Canary Island economy is based on tourism and the banana industry.

According to Manuel Alvar (1996:329), Canary Island Spanish, like all Canary Island cultural manifestations, follows the model of Seville, the city that plays the greatest role in the conquest and later settlement of the islands. It is not surprising, therefore, that the local Spanish shares almost all of Seville's linguistic features, like the use of the *seseo*, the use of /h/ for /x/, *yeísmo*, aspiration of implosive /s/, velarization of final /n/, and in general the weakening of consonants in syllable-final position as well as the preference for *ustedes* over *vosotros*. Given the virtual identity between the linguistic features of the speech of the Canary Islands and Seville, I forgo the customary sample in this section.

Canary Island morphology is characterized by its popular nature, with phenomena such as the following: *siéntensen* for *siéntense* 'sit down', *no los da* for *nos lo da* 'she/he gives it to us', *llevastes* for *llevaste* 'you brought', *vénganos* for *vengamos* 'we may come', *habemos* for *hemos* 'we have', *cualo* for *cual* 'which'. Its syntactic eccentricities are equally popular: *me le acerco* for *me acerco a él* 'I go near him', *para tú entender* for *para que tú entiendas* 'so that you may understand', *hay más de cinco años* for *hace más de cinco años* 'over five years ago', *más nadie* for *nadie más* 'no one else', and *siempre no* for *no siempre* 'not always'.

American Spanish

On October 12, 1492, a small fleet captained by Christopher Columbus, in search of a direct seagoing route to India, disembarks on the Bahamian island of San Salvador. From there Columbus travels to Cuba and then to the island of Santo Domingo, now shared between Haiti and the Dominican Republic. Since Columbus thinks he is in India, he calls the inhabitants of these islands Indians. Between 1493 and 1504, he makes three additional voyages, during which he also "discovers" the eastern coast of Central America as well as the territories that today constitute Puerto Rico, Trinidad, and Venezuela.

After the unification of the kingdoms of Castile and Aragon (1479) and the completion of the Reconquest (1492) carried out by the Reyes Católicos, the new peninsular power is in a position to begin a new phase of expansion and conquest. One of the challenges of the Spanish monarchy's foreign policy is the competition with Portugal (until that time the principal Atlantic naval power) for the domination of the African trade in gold, slaves, and spices. The Portuguese Crown, concentrating its efforts on establishing a commercial route to India by circumnavigating Africa, has no interest in Columbus's transatlantic project, which is why he asks the Reyes Católicos to sponsor his search for a western route to India. The success of his transatlantic expeditions converts Spain into the greatest power in Europe.

The early stages of the conquest and colonization of the new

Spanish territories are especially bloody.[11] In 1519 Hernán Cortés, arriving on the Yucatán Peninsula with a force of only five hundred soldiers, undertakes an invasion of the Aztec Empire that culminates in the taking of its capital, Tenochtitlán, in November of the same year. After the death of the Aztec king Montezuma (Sp. *Moctezuma*), an uprising temporarily obliges the Spaniards to retreat, but when they return in 1521, they take the new king—Cuauhtémoc, a cousin of Montezuma—into custody, raze Tenochtitlán, and establish Mexico City upon its ruins. Francisco Pizarro carries out an analogous role in South America. Having accompanied Vasco Núñez de Balboa in 1513 when the latter discovered the Pacific Ocean, Pizarro receives in 1531 a directive from the king to conquer the Incan Empire, based in Peru. In 1532 he defeats the army of the emperor Atahualpa with a force of only one hundred incomparably better equipped soldiers, with cannons, swords, and horses. Atahualpa pays a large ransom to buy his liberty, but he is murdered nevertheless, and all Incan resistance ends a short time thereafter.

It is estimated that at the moment the Spaniards arrive in America there are approximately forty million indigenous people in the Americas, and that by the seventeenth century this number has been reduced to only four million.[12] This drastic reduction is due primarily to the introduction into the New World of several infectious diseases like diphtheria, measles, and especially smallpox. Not a few indigenous people die, however, from the abuse they receive from the Spaniards, who see them as a cheap labor force. In Venezuela, for example, according to John Lipski (1994:346–47), "Indians were pressed into slavery to gather the pearls. . . . Following the exploitation of pearls, exportation of Indian slaves to other Caribbean colonies became the principal economic basis of the Spanish colonies in Venezuela. The native population was quickly reduced; many died

11. According to Alatorre (1989:213), the Spanish conquistador Pedrarias Dávila legalizes the killing of Indians in 1514 with the so-called *requirimiento*, according to which any slaughter of Indians is justified if they do not instantly accept the Holy Trinity and the rights of the Spanish king.

12. Volker Noll (2001:57) estimates that the population of Mexico is reduced from 12–25 million inhabitants to only one million in the hundred years following the arrival of the Spaniards.

resisting capture." With the discovery of an enormous amount of silver in Potosí, Peru (337), "thousands of Indians were pressed into slavery to fill Spanish galleons with gold and silver". In Mexico (296) and elsewhere, the indigenous people are forced into de facto slavery under a system known as *encomienda*, according to which a group or village of Indians is obliged to work for an individual merely in exchange for his instructing them in the Catholic religion.

Nowadays the population of Spanish America can be divided into four principal groups: (1) the indigenous peoples, (2) the **creoles** or descendants of Spanish colonists, (3) the mestizos, descendants of unions between Spanish men and indigenous women, and (4) people of African heritage. These form three linguistic groups. The creoles, the Afro-Americans, and almost all the mestizos are monolingual speakers of Spanish. Among the indigenous peoples, some remain monolingual in their indigenous languages, while others are bilingual with Spanish. In spite of the existence of the indigenous languages, Spanish is the official language (or one of the official languages) of all the countries of Spanish America, and it enjoys the full prestige normally accorded to languages of government, commerce, and culture.

It is not surprising that American Spanish varieties differ from Modern Peninsular Castilian and that they differ among themselves, given the time that has transpired since the introduction of the language, the spatial separation between the speakers of the language on both sides of the Atlantic, and the particular circumstances that characterize colonization in each region, thus determining the outcome of the local process of koineization. Perhaps it is more surprising that differences are not greater than they are, given that for a time it was feared that under these conditions the language might lose its integrity. These fears have proved to be unfounded, since the speakers of the different varieties of Spanish, including those in Spain, continue to communicate with each other without appreciable difficulty.

The complexity of the dialectal structure of American Spanish resists classification. Lipski (1994) passes in review the various theories that have been proposed to explain the internal divisions of American Spanish, based either on external factors such as the influence of indigenous languages and the relative chronology of settlements, or on internal factors such as phonetic, morphological,

and lexical features. He comes to the conclusion that the only criterion of global applicability is the one that differentiates lowland dialects, those spoken in lands near the sea or on islands, from highland
dialects, those spoken in interior regions. Lowland varieties tend
to have a stable vowel system and a variable consonantal system,
with modifications that may be generally applicable (/h/ for /x/) but
normally only affect allophones in implosive or final position (aspiration of /s/, confusion of /ɾ/ and /l/, velarization of /n/ and other
consonants). Highland varieties, conversely, are characterized by a
stable consonantal system and an unstable or weak vocalic system,
such that vowels may be reduced in various ways, such as in duration, **voicing**, or quality (reduction or centralization to **schwa** [ə]),
duration, or sonority. Vowels may even be subject to elision.

The origins of the highlands-lowlands dichotomy are usually
sought in patterns of contact and colonization between Spain and
Spanish America. It is generally considered that lowland speech
fairly closely reflects the Andalusian variety of Spanish because of
Andalusian dominance in maritime traffic and commerce, which
guarantees intense and lasting contact between Andalusians and
Americans living in coastal areas or islands. In contrast, Andalusian influence is less intense in the highlands. The speech of these
regions, often seats of colonial government (as are Bogotá, Mexico
City, Quito, and La Paz), is more affected by the Castilian spoken by
the bureaucrats, politicians, soldiers, and businessmen who admin-
ister and supply goods to the capitals. However, the absence from
highland speech of several markedly Castilian features, such as /θ/
and *vosotros*, indicates that Castilian influence is not definitive here.
For this reason, the varieties of this area are generally considered
to be the product of local koineization processes involving all the
varieties brought by settlers — especially Castilian and Andalusian —
without a clear domination of either in local linguistic evolution.

The resemblance between American Spanish and some varieties
of Andalusian is quite noticeable. In particular, the presence of the
seseo and the replacement of *vosotros* (with its corresponding clitic
pronoun *os* and possessive adjective *vuestro*) by *ustedes* (with *los, sus*)
are striking. For this reason, the argument has long been made that
Andalusian served as the basis for the genesis of American Spanish. These arguments support what is usually called the **Andalusian**

theory of the origin of American Spanish. Now, the importance of Andalusian in the history of American Spanish is incontrovertible, but the manner in which this theory has traditionally been formulated is far from adequate. In particular, it has been claimed that the clearly Andalusian linguistic traits in "Antillean" Spanish—the term used for the American Spanish of the sixteenth century—are due to a supposed domination of Andalusian over other varietites during this period, such that all colonists arriving after this date were supposedly obliged to adapt their speech to this base. Lipski (1996:63–71) adduces two principal arguments against this supposition. First, he points out that the changes shared by Spanish varieties on both sides of the Atlantic after the sixteenth century are so numerous and substantial that it is impossible to attribute them to parallel evolution. These changes include, in phonology, the fundamental shift in the sibilant system and, in morphology, the complete transformation of forms of address. Second, Lipski cites statistics that indicate that immigration into America from the seventeenth to the nineteenth centuries was so heavy that it would easily have overwhelmed the speakers of the supposed Antillean variety.

In view of these arguments, Ramírez Luengo (2007:25) proposes the following global explanation for the differences among the varieties of American Spanish:

> Thus, one can speak of different koinés distributed among the various colonized areas, which will undergo new modifications in subsequent historical moments for reasons such as, for example, the arrival (or not) of new groups of settlers, the more or less close ties with the Viceroyal Courts and with Spain, or the presence—after independence—of immigrants from various European countries, all of which produces new processes of koineization and, on the basis of these, the birth of the various Spanish American varieties.[13]

---

13. "Se puede hablar, por tanto, de diferentes koinés repartidas por las distintas áreas de colonización, que sufrirán nuevas modificaciones en épocas posteriores por motivos como, por ejemplo, la llegada o no de nuevos contingentes poblacionales, la relación más o menos estrecha con las Cortes Virreinales y con España, o la presencia—ya en época independiente—de inmigrantes de diversos países europeos, todo lo cual produce nuevos procesos de koineización y, a partir de ellos, el nacimiento de las distintas variedades americanas actuales."

DEMOGRAPHY OF THE SPANISH LANGUAGE

The demography of a language constitutes part of its history. It includes where the language has been taken, in what countries it has become established as the official language, and in what countries it competes with other languages. In the table below, the population of each country reflects data taken from nationsonline.org in February 2014. The percentages and the lists of additional languages are from Noll 2001, Dietrich and Geckeler 1990, and pewresearch.org (for the United States). Spanish is an official language in all of these countries except the United States. Spanish is also spoken in Equatorial Guinea, but only as a second language.

COUNTRY	POPULATION MILLIONS	PERCENTAGE SPANISH-SPEAKING	OTHER LANGUAGES
Argentina	40.1	99.7	Quechua, Guaraní
Bolivia	10.4	87.7	Quechua, Aymara, Guaraní
Chile	17.4	89.7	Mapuche, Quechua, Aymara
Colombia	47	99.0	Chibcha, Arawak, Caribe, others
Costa Rica	4.3	97.5	Chibcha, English
Cuba	11.2	100	
Dominican Republic	9.4	98	Haitian
Ecuador	14.5	93	Quechua, Chibcha, Jíbaro
El Salvador	6.2	99.0	Pipil, Nahuatl
Guatemala	14.7	64.7	21 Quiché-Maya languages
Honduras	8.4	98.2	Miskito
Mexico	112.3	98.5	Nahuatl, Maya
Nicaragua	6.1	87.4	Miskito, Sumo, English

DEMOGRAPHY OF THE SPANISH LANGUAGE *(continued)*

COUNTRY	POPULATION MILLIONS	PERCENTAGE SPANISH-SPEAKING	OTHER LANGUAGES
Panama	3.4	76.6	Chibcha, Chocó, English
Paraguay	6.4	55.1	Guaraní (90%)
Peru	30.1	79.8	Quechua, Aymara
Puerto Rico	3.7	98.2	English
Spain	46.1	99.1	Catalan, Basque, Galician
United States	37.6	11.8	English
Uruguay	3.3	100	
Venezuela	27.1	96.9	Wayúu, Warao, Pemón

Four Representative Varieties of American Spanish

This section will provide an idea of the diversity and character of American Spanish, through descriptions of four representative varieties. The selection was made from among the many varieties spoken in Spanish American countries (including the United States), most of which exhibit a certain degree of internal linguistic diversity. In Argentina, for example, it is customary to distinguish between the River Plate variety as such—spoken in Buenos Aires and the southern coast—and the varieties spoken in several marginal areas whose history and particular circumstances have produced traits markedly different from those of the national standard. The extreme west of Argentina, for example, was colonized from Chile, for which reason its speech shares features with that of the neighboring country. In the border zones of the north, two more varieties can be identified, whose peculiarities are due in part to the presence of bilingualism with the indigenous languages spoken in each zone, Guaraní in the northeast, near Paraguay, and Quechua in the northwest, near Bolivia. The Spanish of Colombia shows a structure typical of the Andean countries: here the standard variety of the interior contrasts with the regional varieties of the coast—exhibiting typical lowland features—and those of the Amazon region, strongly marked by phenomena of **interlanguage** with an incompletely acquired Spanish functioning as a second language and showing heavy influence from the indigenous languages of the peoples who inhabit the region.

Of all these possible varieties, I present the four I consider to be most illustrative of the diversity of American Spanish: (1) the variety spoken in the River Plate region, called *Rioplatense*, (2) the variety spoken all along the Andean mountain range, (3) the variety characteristic of the Caribbean basin, and (4) the variety of Mexico and the southwestern United States. Below, each one of these varieties is analyzed in terms of its phonological, morphological, syntactic, and lexical characteristics.

RIOPLATENSE. This is the dialect spoken on both sides of the Río de la Plata, in particular in Buenos Aires (population in 2013: 15,625,000), where it is also called *Porteño*, and Montevideo (1,330,000),[14] the respective capital cities of Argentina and Uruguay. In terms of phonology, the most distinctive features of this variety are (1) the so-called ʒeísmo, (2) aspiration of implosive /s/, and (3) "circumflex" intonation.

The phenomenon called ʒeísmo represents a local further development of *yeísmo*, as a result of which the sound /j/ becomes /ʒ/ through a process known as *rehilamiento*, the production of a vibration at the place of articulation added to that of the vocal cords. As a result of this phenomenon, the phrase *yo me llamo Guillermo* 'my name is Guillermo', pronounced ['jo me 'ʎa mo ɣi 'ʎeɾ mo] in traditional Castilian dialects, and ['jo me 'ja mo ɣi 'jeɾ mo] in Andalusian and other *yeísta* varieties, is pronounced ['ʒo me 'ʒa mo ɣi 'ʒeɾ mo] by many Rioplatense speakers. It must be added, however,

---

14. Data from Ministerio de Economía of Buenos Aires Provincia, "Principales indicares socioeconómicos," n.d, www.ec.gba.gov.ar/Estadistica/datosbasicosenel4 .pdf, accessed February 15, 2014.

that *ʒeísmo* is now being replaced by another change in progress, the *ʃeísmo*, a phenomenon that consists in the devoicing of [ʒ] to [ʃ]. The most frequent pronunciation of our example in modern Rioplatense speech, therefore, is [ˈʃo me ˈʃa mo ɣi ˈʃer mo]. It is interesting to note that this series of changes recapitulates the evolution that [ʒ] undergoes in Medieval Castilian, when *ajo* [ˈa ʒo] 'garlic' changes to [ˈa ʃo] by change 26, "devoicing of voiced sibilants". One wonders whether in the next few centuries this variety will continue to repeat this ancient evolution of ancient [ʃ], in which case, just as [ˈa ʃo] changes to [ˈa xo] (change 28), [ˈʃo me ˈʃa mo ɣi ˈʃer mo] will become **[ˈxo me ˈxa mo ɣi ˈxer mo].

Regarding the aspiration of implosive /s/—mentioned above as a feature of Andalusian and lowlands American Spanish—if the River Plate's version of this phenomenon is notable for any reason, it is for its resistance to elision and aspiration before vowels. The phrase *estás aquí* 'you are here', which in Andalusian and other lowland varieties could be pronounced [e ˈta ha ˈki], with elision of the implosive /s/ and aspiration of the prevocalic /s/, tends to be pronounced [eh ˈta sa ˈki] in Rioplatense.

Lipski (1994:170) calls River Plate intonation **circumflex**, comparing the typical melodic curve of the variety, which rises significantly before falling at the end, to the visual form of the circumflex accent (^). This intonation is attributed to the influence of Italian, a language brought to Argentina by large numbers of Italian immigrants at the end of the nineteenth century. Between the arrival of these Italians and their complete linguistic assimilation, a Spanish-Italian hybrid language called Cocoliche arose in Buenos Aires, of which the circumflex intonation is possibly a holdover.

In terms of morphology, the most notable feature of the River Plate variety is the *voseo*, the use of *vos* instead of *tú* in the function of second-person singular familiar pronoun. Note, however, that the *voseo* has been incorporated into the language only partially. First, the corresponding object pronouns and the adjectives of possession are not related to *vos* or *vosotros* but to *tú*—as in *yo te veo a vos* 'I see you', *vos tenés tu propio dinero* 'you have your own money'. Second, *voseo* verb forms are used only in the imperative and present indicative; all remaining indicative tenses (*hablaste* 'you spoke', *comías* 'you were eating', *vivirás* 'you will live'), as well as all subjunctive tenses, are identical to those of the *tuteo*.[15]

The verbal forms of the present indicative (*vos hablás* 'you speak', *vos comés* 'you eat', *vos vivís* 'you live') and those of the imperative (*hablá* 'speak', *comé* 'eat', *viví* 'live') evolve from verb forms corresponding to medieval *uos* (modern *vosotros*), with the loss of /j/ from the former (*habláis* > *hablás*) and of /d/, in the latter (*hablad* > *hablá*).[16] According to Lapesa (1981:393), all of these forms originated in the Castilian of the sixteenth century: "*Amáis, tenéis, sois,* coexisted with *amás, tenés, sos,* which were soon considered vulgar and dropped, both in Spain and in the parts of America most influenced by the viceroyal courts, around 1560–70."[17]

Something that is not widely known outside of or even within Spanish America is that the *voseo* is part of the linguistic repertory of every Spanish American country except Puerto Rico and the Dominican Republic. This lack of knowledge is probably due to the sociolinguistic differences that characterize the use of the *voseo* in the different areas. In some countries, such as Chile and Peru, the *voseo* is limited to the lower classes. In some Central American states, the *voseo* is widely used but is considered less prestigious than the *tuteo*. In these countries, as well in those in which the *voseo* is even more widely accepted (Uruguay, Paraguay, Costa Rica, Nicaragua, Honduras, El Salvador, Guatemala), it is used in daily discourse, but the *tuteo* is used in dealing with foreigners and is taught in the schools

15. In the imperative, *vos* forms are limited to the affirmative: *tené* 'have', but *no tengas* 'don't have' (rather than *no tengás*). Admittedly, in some indicative tenses it is impossible to tell if a form corresponds to *tú* or to *vos*: *comías* 'you were eating' and *hablarías* 'you would speak' could be interpreted as variants of *comíais* and *hablaríais*. The future, on the other hand—*hablarás* 'you will speak', *comerás* 'you will eat'— clearly reflects *tú* rather than *vos*. In Central American dialects, it should be added, the *vos* forms of the subjunctive and negative imperative find more acceptance.

16. The relationship of these forms to the *vosotros* forms is emphasized by the fact that in a few American dialects the *voseo* forms are *habláis, coméis, vivís*.

17. "Coexistían *amáis, tenéis, sois,* con *amás, tenés, sos,* que pronto quedaron relegados por vulgares y desparecieron, tanto en España como en las zonas de América más influidas por las cortes virreinales, hacia 1560–70."

and universities. Only in Argentina is the *voseo* fully accepted as a form suitable for use by all social classes in all registers.

The lack of prestige associated with the *voseo* in most areas is a product of its history. I mentioned in chapter 7 that the pronoun *vos*—which originally expresses deference, like Modern Spanish *usted*—becomes a rival of *tú* as a pronoun of confidence and solidarity during the fifteenth century, just when emigration to America is beginning. Very soon, however, this use of *vos* becomes stigmatized, so that by the eighteenth century it ceases to be used in Spain. The American-Spanish speakers who use *vos* are undoubtedly made aware of the stigma associated with the *voseo* by Spanish immigrants after this date, but their reaction is not to abandon its use but to limit it to the most familiar registers. According to María Irene Moyna and Beatriz Ceballos (2008), the *voseo* is not attested in Argentina until the seventeenth century despite its presence since the beginning of colonization in the sixteenth century. The *tuteo* continues to serve as the written norm until the beginning of the nineteenth century, though the use of the *voseo* begins to increase toward the middle of that century, especially in rural areas. The change in linguistic equilibrium between the two pronouns may be attributable to declaration of independence in 1816 and a desire to differentiate linguistically from the mother country, and perhaps to the difficulty of the tripartite system (*vos*, *tú*, *usted*) for the many immigrants who are entering the country during this era. In the beginning, *vos* is used with the verb forms of the *tuteo*, but the *vos* conjugation wins out in the imperative and present indicative during the second half of the nineteenth century. Later on, the use of *vos* is freed from the stigma with which it has long been associated, in Argentina if not in Uruguay.

Nothing stands out as notable in the syntax of the River Plate variety, unlike other parts of Argentina, where interference from indigenous languages in the Spanish of bilinguals produces curiosities such as *lo quiere a su hija* for *quiere a su hija* 'she/he loves her/his daughter', an expression typical of Quechua bilinguals, in which the direct object is unnecessarily duplicated with a clitic pronoun, which also fails to agree with its antecedent. In Misiones, near the Brazilian border, one hears *tengo venido con ella* for *he venido con ella* 'I have come with her', where *tener* is used as an auxiliary verb, like Portuguese *ter*.

In the vocabulary of Argentina two words stand out: the vocative *che*, of unknown origin, and the farewell *chau*, a borrowing of Italian *ciao* 'goodbye'.

Sample of Rioplatense Spanish. An author from Buenos Aires discusses her novel.

> *Sí, en realidad, como vos decís Natu, la inmigración es uno de los temas que a mí me apasiona, sobre todo en lo que tiene que ver con ese transterraje. Es decir, cuando nosotros nos mudamos o nos vamos a vivir a otro lado, ¿qué es lo que llevamos con nosotros del lugar que nos crió o en el cual vivimos? ¿y qué es lo que no nos podemos llevar, ¿no? Yo viví el 2001 acá, y un poco, empecé a pensar la novela como, desde un costado irónico, digamos, porque todas estas familias que llegan alrededor de 1900 a Buenos Aires son las familias que después tienen nietos o bisnietos que terminan yéndose de vuelta a Europa en 2001.*[18]

ANDEAN SPANISH. The Andean mountain range extends from Cape Horn, on the southern tip of the South American continent, to Venezuela in the north, passing through Chile, Argentina, Bolivia, Peru, Ecuador, and Colombia. The Spanish spoken all along this mountain range features a series of phonetic and morphological traits that justify identifying an Andean variety of American Spanish.

18. Ana Ojeda, "Falso contacto / Nuevas voces de la narrative argentina," interview by Natu Poblet, *Dailymotion*, February 11, 2013, http://www.dailymotion.com /video/xxfbd5_ana-ojeda-falso-contacto-nuevas-voces-de-la-narrativa-argentina _creation, starting at 3:12. "Yes, really, as you say, Natu, immigration is one of the topics that interests me, especially as it involves changing locations. That is to say, when we move or go to live in a new place, what do we take with us from the place where we grew up or in which we live? And what can we not take? Right? I lived through 2001 here, and sort of started to think of the novel as, from an ironic point of view, let's say, because all these families that arrive in Buenos Aires around 1900 are the families that afterward have grandchildren or great-grandchildren who end up back in Europe in 2001."

The phonetic traits of Andean Spanish are typical of the highlands, in the sense that they feature a strong or conservative consonant system and a weak vocalic system. The conservatism of the consonantal system is manifested in the preservation of the phonological distinction between /j/ and /ʎ/ (though the latter is realized as /ʒ/ in the area of Quito), in the apico-alveolar articulation ([s̺]) of /s/ in many isolated areas (Antioquia, Colombia; Cuzco and Puno, Peru; the high plateau of Bolivia), and in the stability of this phoneme in implosive position. On the other hand, the treatment of /ɾ/ and /r/ is far from conservative. The former retains its tap articulation in intervocalic position (*para* ['pa ɾa] 'for'), but in final position it may undergo **assibilation** (*comer* [ko 'meř] 'to eat') or be made **retroflex** ([ko 'meɹ]). An unvoiced variant is also found in the cluster /tʃ/ (as in *tren* 'train') is similar to that of English *train*, though not retroflex.[19] Additionally, the trill /r/ may also be assibilated (*carro* ['ka řo] 'cart').

The unstressed vowels of Andean Spanish are subject to a variety of weakening processes. First, they can be shortened—*estos amantes* ['es tᵒ sᵃ 'man̪ tᵉs] 'these lovers'—or even elided, especially in contact with /s/: ['est sa 'man̪ts]. Second, they can undergo changes in quality or timbre. It is common, for example, for unstressed /a/ to be reduced to schwa: *las sábanas* [ləs 'sa bə nəs] 'the sheets'. In the Spanish of bilinguals who also speak Quechua—a language spoken nowadays by seven or eight million indigenous people all along the mountain range—a reduction in the vowel inventory can be observed, such that the five vowels of Spanish (/ieaou/) are reduced to the three of Quechua (/iau/). Our example would thus be pronounced as ['is tu sa 'man̪ tis] in these regions. Speakers of standard Spanish in the region disparagingly refer to this phenomenon as *motosidad*.[20]

I have already mentioned the importance of the *voseo* in this region, but the conditions of its use in some Andean countries should be examined in more detail (always with reference to Lipski 1994).

19. Pilar García Mouton (1994:30) points out that this same articulation is heard nowadays in varieties of Riojan and on the banks of the Ebro.

20. See Cerrón-Palomino 2003.

In Chile, for example, *voseo* verb forms, traditional among the peasant and worker classes, have become fashionable among middle-class young people. The actual pronoun *vos*, however, is rarely heard among these speakers, making this a kind of "crypto-*voseo*". In Bolivia, the use of *vos* is generalized in the highlands, but it often combines with *tuteo* verb forms: *vos tienes* 'you have', *vos quieres* 'you want'. In Peru, the *tuteo* is so strongly rooted in the cities that many Peruvians are not aware of the existence of the *voseo* among indigenous peoples in many parts of the country. In the Andean regions of Venezuela, the *voseo* is used only with children and persons considered to be socially inferior. Díaz Collazos (2015) reports that in all of Colombia the *ustedeo*—the use of *usted* with intimate friends and family members (in addition to its deferential function)—competes with the *tuteo*. However, in the western highlands, the most common familiar pronoun is *vos*, while in the rest of the country the *voseo* is considered to be practically extinct or at least unknown to scholarship.

The most interesting syntactic phenomena found in the Andean region can be classified according to whether they are typical of the respective standards of each area or of the interlanguages of indigenous bilinguals. In the standard Spanish of Peru, for example, the use of the present perfect for the preterite (also characteristic of Peninsular Spanish) is common, as in *ha muerto el año pasado* for *murió el año pasado* 'she/he died last year'. In Peruvian and also Ecuadoran Spanish, it is customary to use the present subjunctive after a perfective verb in sentences such as *quería que lo hagamos* for *quería que lo hiciéramos* 'she/he wanted us to do it'. In Venezuela, Colombia, and Ecuador (as well as Brazilian Portuguese), a change in progress called **intensive** *ser* is attested in sentences such as *ese señor vino es a caballo* 'that man came on horseback' and *yo vivo es en Caracas* 'I live in Caracas', an apparent result of the omission of relative adverbials: *(como) ese señor vino es a caballo* '(how) that man came is on horseback', *(donde) yo vivo es en Caracas* '(where) I live is in Caracas'.

Syntactic divergences in the speech of indigenous bilinguals are numerous. Here I will mention only those that involve the use of clitic pronouns. In the entire region it is customary to unnecessarily duplicate direct objects with clitic pronouns: *tú la tienes la dirección* for *tú tienes la dirección* 'you have the address', often with lack of agreement: *tú lo tienes la dirección*. Conversely, the clitic is occasionally omitted where it is obligatory in standard Spanish, as before an object moved to the left (*a la chica he visto ayer* for *a la chica la he visto ayer* 'I saw the girl yesterday') or when two clitics are needed: (*¿El dinero? A mi mamá le di* for *se lo di* 'The money? I gave it to my mother').

Regarding the lexicon, the Andean region is known for its adoption of numerous loanwords from indigenous languages, especially Quechua. Among the best-known Quechuan borrowings are *cancha* 'flat area', *chacra* 'small farm', *guacho* 'orphan', *poroto* 'bean', and *zapallo* 'gourd'. One also finds innumerable local peculiarities, such as the Peruvian use of *de repente* 'suddenly' in the sense 'maybe' and the Colombian interjection *¡listo!*, which fulfills the same function as *¡vale!* in Spain and *¡bueno!* in other parts of the Spanish-speaking world.

Sample of Andean Spanish. A professor talks about his academic unit.

> *La Facultad de Ciencias Médicas de la Universidad de Cuenca con una historia de más de cien años ha contribuido al desarrollo de la medicina de la enfermería y de las diferentes carreras de tecnología en el austro y en el país. Uno de los aspectos esenciales que ha trascendido ha sido justamente el haber participado activamente en la elaboración de propuestas para mejorar la calidad de vida y para asimismo a través de la investigación poner a los niveles de adhesión política las evidencias científicas necesarias que permitan elaborar política pública.*[21]

21. Arturo Quizhpe, "Facultad de Ciencias Médicas de la Universidad de Cuenca, 2012," http://www.youtube.com/watch?v=uMAwLH9PyBQ, starting at 0:41. The relevant portion of this video is also available on the author's page at the University of Florida website. 'The College of Medicine of the University of Cuenca, with a history of more than one hundred years, has contributed to the development of medicine, nursing, and diverse technological careers in the south and in the country. One of the essential aspects that has emerged has been precisely having participated actively in the elaboration of proposals to improve the quality of life and also, through research, to provide to the levels of political support the scientific information needed for the elaboration of public policy.'

CARIBBEAN SPANISH. This category includes the Spanish-speaking countries of Cuba, Puerto Rico, the Dominican Republic, and Panama, besides the coastal areas of Venezuela and Colombia. The other Central American countries on the Caribbean Sea (Costa Rica, Honduras, Guatemala, and to a lesser degree, Nicaragua) have a quite different linguistic profile.

The varieties of Spanish spoken in the Caribbean basin are paradigmatic of lowland Spanish. They are characterized by a vowel system whose stability contrasts starkly with the variability of their consonantal system. As we shall see in the next section, the features involved are largely the same ones we saw in Andalusian and Canary Island Spanish.

There is a long list of consonantal phonemes that suffer some weakening process in Caribbean Spanish. The lateral palatal /ʎ/ is replaced by /j/ (*yeísmo*). The velar fricative /x/ yields to the glottal aspiration of /h/. The alveolar trill /r/ is sometimes devoiced, producing /r̥/. The fricatives [β], [ð], [ɣ] (corresponding to the stops /b/, /d/, /g/) lose tension to the point of disappearing in many cases: *Cuba* ['ku ᵝa] (where the superscript indicates extreme weakness) or ['ku a], *Navidades* [na i 'a eh] 'Christmas'. Even /ptk/ are voiced in some contexts: *la policía* [la βo li 'si a] 'the police', *se trabaja* [se ðɾa 'βa ha] 'one works', *gramática* [gɾa 'ma ði ɣa] 'grammar'. The most striking of the weakening phenomena is certainly the aspiration and elision of implosive and prevocalic /s/: ['e to 'βa ko] 'these Basques', *estás aquí* [eh 'ta ha 'ki] 'you are here'. In the Caribbean, as in other varieties in which /s/ is aspirated, this feature has evolved into a sociolinguistic marker. That is, the speakers are aware that aspiration is "wrong", and they make an effort to pronounce the sibilant in formal and learned registers. Inevitably, the more educated speakers manage to do this with greater frequency than do the less educated, but in any case the phenomenon can only be measured statistically, because the frequency of use of [s], [h], and elision is not predictable in any given utterance: Caribbean speakers are perfectly capable of saying [eh 'ta ha 'ki] one moment and [es 'ta sa 'ki] five minutes later.

The sibilant /s/ is not the only one that undergoes weakening in implosive position. There is a tendency to velarize the consonant /p/

in this position, as in *septiembre* [sek 'tjem bɾe] 'September' and *apto* ['ak to] 'apt', and generally any word-final /n/ is velarized: *nación* [na 'sjoŋ] 'nation', *bien* [bjeŋ] 'well'. Particularly interesting is the series of phenomena that affect implosive /ɾ/ and /l/. While in Andalusian the tendency is to convert /l/ to /ɾ/, in Puerto Rican and eastern Cuban the tendency is the opposite: *viene tarde* ['bje ne 'taḷ de] 'she/he is coming late'. In Havana and the western part of Cuba, in contrast, a different Andalusian option is usually chosen, that of eliding the **liquid** and geminating the following consonant, pronouncing it as a stop: ['bje ne 'tad de]. In different parts of the Dominican Republic one hears not only these two variants but also the following: ['bje ne 'tah ðe] (aspiration), ['bje ne 'taŋ de] (nasalization and velarization), and ['bje ne 'taj ðe] (glide-formation, in the northern region of Cibao).

In its morphosyntactic component, the Caribbean area is notable for its faithfulness to the *tuteo* (except in eastern Cuba; see Blanco Botta 1982), as well as for certain syntactic peculiarities. Especially striking, for example, is the noninversion of subject pronouns and verbs in sentences such as *¿cómo tú te llamas?* for *¿cómo te llamas tú?* 'what is your name?' and *¿qué tú quieres?* for *¿qué quieres tú?* 'what do you want?' The use of pronoun subjects in infinitive phrases is also generalized, especially with *para*: *para yo creer eso* 'for me to believe that', where other varieties would prefer *para creer eso, yo* or *para que yo crea eso*. On the other hand, only in the Dominican Republic does one find the use of *ello* in the place of null subjects in existential expressions like the following: *ello hay maíz* for *hay maíz* 'there is corn', *ello es fácil llegar* for *es fácil llegar* 'it's easy to get there'.

The vocabulary of Caribbean Spanish shows, more than the other varieties, the effects of the linguistic contact between Spanish and the million and a half slaves transported from Africa to America by the nineteenth century. With few exceptions, these loanwords denote aspects of African culture that were preserved in spite of the oppression suffered by this part of the population. The Dominican vocabulary, for example, contains Afro-Hispanic words in the semantic fields of music (*mangulina* 'type of popular music'), food (*mofongo* 'dish made of meat and banana'), and spirituality (*fucú* 'evil spirit').

Another notable aspect of the Caribbean vocabulary is the large number of Anglicisms that have been incorporated by some varieties. While the flood of Anglicisms to Cuba itself was slowed by the revolution of 1959, it has become ever stronger in the Spanish spoken by the large community of Cuban exiles who live in south Florida. Roberto Fernández (1983) portrays the role played by Anglicisms in this variety, differentiating among the following categories: (1) semantic borrowings, in which a foreign word affects the meaning of a Spanish word: *actualmente* for *en realidad* (through the influence of Eng. *actually*), *carpeta* for *alfombra* (*carpet*), *aplicar* for *solicitar* (*to apply*); (2) phrasal calques (literally translated): *cambiar de mente* for *cambiar de opinion* (*to change one's mind*), *no te dolerá preguntar* for *no pierdes nada por preguntar* (*it won't hurt you to ask*), *llamar patrás* for *devolver la llamada* (*to call back*); (3) hybrid phrases: *estar lei* for *llegar tarde* (*to be late*), *coger un tan* for *broncearse* (*to get a tan*), *tener fon* for *divertirse* (*to have fun*); and (4) hybrid verbs coined with the verbal suffix *-ear*: *chopear* for *ir de compras* (*to shop*), *foldear* for *doblar* (*to fold*), *taipear* for *escribir a máquina* (*to type*). Many of these same examples would serve for Puerto Rican, a variety that is exposed to the influence of English through its political ties to the United States and the constant demographic shifts between the island and the continent, especially New York. Washington Lloréns (1968) cites the following English loanwords in Puerto Rican Spanish: *atachable* for *conectable* (*attachable*), *blanco* for *espacio vacío en un formulario* (*blank*), *blof* for *engaño* (*bluff*), and *hit* for *éxito* (*hit*).

Sample of Caribbean Spanish. A Cuban talks about his situation in Cuba.

> *Son carteles para nada gubernamentales, antigubernamentales, sino carteles que dicen vivan los niños cubanos, porque en esta área se organizan los fines de semana eventos y actividades para niños. Y bueno, los invito a pasar. Aquí podrán ver la biblioteca independiente que tenemos. En este lugar pequeño que ustedes ven, se dan talleres y se hacen actividades con niños infantiles, como verá aquí cuadernos*

que son de de las clases que se le imparten a los niños que vienen.
Clases de temas de inglés . . .[22]

THE SPANISH OF MEXICO AND THE SOUTHWESTERN UNITED STATES. With its more than 110 million inhabitants and almost two million square kilometers of territory, Mexico is far from being dialectally homogenous. Lipski (1994:278–83) distinguishes among four principal areas: central, northwestern, Yucatán, and central coasts (Veracruz/Tabasco and Acapulco). The coastal and Yucatán varieties exhibit some typical lowland features, such as aspiration of implosive /s/ and the replacement of /x/ by /h/. In the northwest, one frequently encounters the *jejeo* (*sí, señor* [ˈxi xe ˈɲor] 'yes, sir'). The central dialect, however, spoken in the capital and therefore of greatest prestige, is typical of highland varieties.

Given this fact, it is interesting to compare the standard Mexican variety with that of another large region of American highlands, namely, the Andean region. Among the many features shared by the two varieties are the velar articulation of /x/, the frequent if not completely uniform assibilation of /r/ and implosive /ɾ/, **vowel reduction**—especially in contact with /s/—and the preservation of implosive /s/, to such a degree that other Spanish speakers sometimes refer to Mexico as *un mar de eses* 'a sea of *s*'s'. Of course the two speech types do differ in other respects. In central Mexico, for example, one finds *yeísmo*, alveolar articulation of final /n/, and *tuteo*, whereas in the Andean region there is distinction between /j/ and /ʎ/, velarization of final /n/, and widespread *voseo*.

Even more than the Caribbean variety, Mexican Spanish grammar is fairly close to the international standard, though it does

---

22. See *La esperanza de Cuba*, November 2011, http://www.youtube.com/watch?v=jqKxuuHzvpM, from 2:20. The relevant portion of this video is also available on the author's page at the University of Florida website. 'They are posters that are not at all governmental, antigovernmental, but just posters that say "long live Cuban children", because in this area events and activities for children are organized during the weekends. And so I invite you to come in. Here you will see the independent library that we have. In this small place that you see, there are workshops and activities for children, like you see here notebooks that are for the classes that are taught to the children that come. Classes on topics like English . . .'

According to www.pewresearch.org, in 2010 Hispanics formed the most numerous ethnic minority in the country, with 50,477,594 people (16.35% of the total).

The Hispanic population is found in almost all parts of the country, but for historical and geographical reasons it is concentrated mostly in three regions, each one with its own demographic and dialectal character. In south Florida, for example, the Hispanic population has a markedly Cuban character, given the successive groups of Cuban exiles that have been settling there since 1959. The city of New York has traditionally been the preferred destination of Puerto Ricans, who, as US citizens, have the right to live in the United States. Finally, the Hispanic population in the southwestern part of the country is composed mostly of people of Mexican heritage, although immigration from Central America is becoming increasingly important. According to 2010 census data (http://www.infoplease.com/us /statistics/us-population-hispanic.html), 34,798,258 or 11.2 percent of the total of Hispanic immigrants in the United States are of Mexican origin, while 4,623,716 (1.49%) are Puerto Rican, 1,785,547 (0.57%) are Cuban, and 12,270,073 (3.97%) are from other countries.

The dialect features of the three regions are, to a great extent, identical to those of the countries of origin. That is to say, the speech of Cubans and Puerto Ricans residing in the United States exhibits the typical features of the Caribbean dialect area, while that of US Mexicans is very similar to Mexican speech.

Not all American Hispanics speak Spanish, however: of the 50.4 million, only 37.1 million, or 74.6 percent, claim to be able to speak the language. Because of the process of ethnic and linguistic assimilation that traditionally occurs in the United States, the survival of Spanish depends to a large extent on the constant arrival of new immigrants. A study on the retention of the Spanish language (Veltman 1988:44–45) arrives at the conclusion that Spanish-speaking immigrants quickly change to English: 70 percent of the immigrants who arrive at the age of ten or less, and 40 percent of those who arrive between the ages of ten and fourteen, end up abandoning Spanish completely.

Besides the Hispanics who do not speak Spanish and those who

> **SPANISH IN THE UNITED STATES** *(continued)*
>
> have not yet learned English, there is a considerable number of bilinguals, whose ability to express themselves in the two languages varies widely. Frequently the Spanish of these bilinguals is characterized by linguistic features attributable to English interference, in pronunciation (e.g., use of the English retroflex [ɹ] for the Spanish tap [ɾ]), syntax (*mi blusa es blanco* for *mi blusa es blanca* 'my blouse is white', *amor es ciego* for *el amor es ciego* 'love is blind', *cerca a la familia* for *cerca de la familia* 'near the family'), and lexicon (*los están busing para otra escuela* for *los transportan a otra escuela en autobús* 'they are busing them to another school'). Another common phenomenon is **code-switching** (*yo sé, porque I went to the hospital* 'I know, because . . .'). For more information on this phenomenon, see Varela Cuéllar 1988.
>
> Despite the pace of language shift in these populations, the Spanish language is not losing but gaining in prestige in the United States. There are several television channels that broadcast to Spanish speakers, advertising makes use of Spanish with increasing frequency, and in stores and governmental offices labels and signs addressing this part of the population have become omnipresent. At this point it seems inevitable that the Spanish language will eventually become the second national language of the United States.

share some peculiarities with other American and European varieties. Company Company (2006) cites, among others, constructions like *ya se los dije* (for *ya se lo dije* 'I already said it to him/her/them'), *habemos muchos que no lo sabemos* (for *somos muchos que no lo sabemos* 'there are a lot of us who don't know'), *recién lo vi* (for *lo acabo de ver* 'I just saw him/it'), besides a greater use of the preterite vis-à-vis the present perfect. Important divergences are found in Chiapas, where there is widespread bilingualism with Maya. Lipski's (1994:284–85) examples of clitic use are similar to those cited for Andean bilinguals, like the use of redundant *lo* without agreement (*¿ya lo anunciaste la boda?* for *¿ya anunciaste la boda?* 'did you already announce the wedding?') and the omission of clitics (*¿Son baratas estas tus manzanas? Son,* for *Lo son* 'Are your apples cheap? Yes, they are').

There is no dearth of words internationally recognized as typical of Mexico, such as *cuate* 'friend', *chaparro* and *chamaco* 'boy', *güero* 'blond', and several interjections ending in a grammatically empty particle *-le* like *ándale*, *híjole*, and *úpale*, used respectively to express agreement, surprise, and effort upon lifting something or someone. Several Mexicanisms have been exported together with its cuisine, like *taco*, *burrito*, and *tamal*. This latter example is a loanword from Nahuatl in Spanish, as are many others such as *coyote*, *ocelote* 'ocelot', *aguacate* 'avocado', *tomate* 'tomato', *chocolate*, and *chicle* 'chewing gum'.

Large parts of the southwestern United States belong originally to Spain and then to Mexico after its independence from Spain in 1821. Texas wins its independence from Mexico in 1836 and exists as a sovereign nation for nine years before becoming an American state in 1845. Upset by this new affiliation, the Mexicans attack American forces in 1846, thereby starting a war that ends in 1847 with Mexico's capitulation and loss, in 1848, of considerable territory—California, New Mexico, and the rest of western North America.

Americans take possession of these territories and hastily install their own institutions and citizens. However, Spanish continues to be spoken in these areas, and in a certain sense it could be said that Mexico is now reconquering the American Southwest, but by demographic rather than military means. Already in 2010 Hispanics constitute 47 percent of the population of New Mexico, 38.2 percent in Texas and California, 30.2 percent in Arizona, and 21 percent in Colorado,[23] and the tendency is rising.

Sample of Mexican Spanish. A Mexican author talks about one of his works.

> *Yo me sentí muy honrado que nos invitaron eh . . . porque . . . supongo que el hecho de estar contemplado, ¿no? en un proyecto de este tipo implica que mi trabajo narrativo tiene alguna resonancia. Tenía un cuento que, breve, que "Carne Natal" se llama, que además era, es, un cuento de ciencia ficción como muy, como muy alejado en su con-*

---

23. US Census Bureau, "State and County QuickFacts: New Mexico," July 2014, http://quickfacts.census.gov/qfd/states/35000.html.

*texto . . . todo en el espacio profundo durante miles de años. Entonces
me parecía que era una idea como lo suficientemente extraña como
para provocar alguna reacción en alguien que, bueno, de entrada no
tenía ningún contacto previo con, o suponía yo, con este tipo de histo-
rias, de lecturas.*[24]

....

Questions

1. Explain the different uses of the term *dialect*. Distinguish
   between geographic or regional dialectology and social dialectology.
2. What is "popular Spanish"? Where is it spoken? List five linguistic traits associated with this variety.
3. What factors explain the formation of a variety deriving from
   Castilian in the southern part of the Iberian Peninsula?
4. Regarding the highlands-lowlands dichotomy in Spanish
   American dialectology, explain why such a dichotomy exists
   and how the two varieties differ from each other.
5. List the various periods in the history of Spanish in which a
   process of koineization has intervened.
6. Define the following terms: *yeísmo, ſeísmo, ʒeísmo, ceceo, seseo,
   voseo,* implosive /s/, *leísmo, laísmo, desdoblamiento de vocales.*
7. Explain the history of the diverse forms of address that are
   found in American varieties of Spanish.
8. For each one of the dialect samples, list the linguistic traits that
   contribute to the identification of the varieties represented.

24. See Bernardo Fernández, interview, 2013, https://vimeo.com/63763513, starting at 0:18. The relevant portion of this video is also available on the author's page
at the University of Florida website. 'I felt very honored that they invited us . . . because . . . I suppose the fact of being thought of, you know, in a project of this type
implies that my narrative work has some resonance. I had a story that, short, that was
titled "Carne natal," which besides was a science fiction story like really, really far
away in its setting . . . all in deep space during thousands of years. So it seemed like
an idea that was strange enough to provoke a reaction in someone who, well, to begin
with did not have previous contact with, or I supposed, with this kind of stories, of
readings.'

Make a detailed phonetic transcription of the passages that illustrate dialectal traits.

9. Taking into account the phonological changes between Latin and Medieval Castilian (chapter 5), between Medieval Castilian and Modern Spanish (chapter 7), and the many changes that characterize the current varieties of the language, identify the changes that have been repeated in the history of the language.

Rudiments of Spanish Phonetics and Phonology

Classification of Sounds in Terms of Articulation

The systems of identification for vowels and consonants are different.

A vowel is a sound that is produced when air passes through the mouth (or nose) with no audible obstruction except for the vibration of the vocal cords. A consonant is a sound whose production depends on the obstruction of the air from the lungs by one of the speech organs, generally the tongue, touching or contacting another part of the mouth. The glides /j/ and /w/ are generally recognized as having both vocalic and consonantal traits, which explains their participation in so-called diphthongs—sets of two different vocalic elements pronounced in a single syllable. The glide /j/ contrasts with the consonant /j/ of *yo* /jo/, which is frequently strengthened, as in *yo* [dʒo]. In theory one could make an analogous distinction between glide and consonantal /w/.

Vowels owe their different quality or timbre to the position of the tongue in the mouth, although other factors may intervene as well, such as the form of the lips (rounded or not) and nasality.

Spanish distinguishes among five vowels, according to the following chart, whose terms *high/mid/low* and *front/central/back* refer to the position of the tongue in the mouth on the vertical and horizontal axes respectively. In Spanish, front vowels are unrounded and back vowels are rounded.

	FRONT	CENTRAL	BACK
high	i		u
mid	e		o
low		a	

In the articulatory identification of vowels, it is customary to name the vowel's place first on the horizontal axis, then on the vertical.

(NB: Speech sounds are written in brackets to differentiate them from letters, which are written in italics.)

[i] high front vowel
[u] high back vowel
[e] mid front vowel
[o] mid back vowel
[a] low central vowel

In order to identify a consonant in articulatory terms, it is necessary to specify three parameters: (1) its mode of articulation, (2) its place of articulation, and (3) its sonority. The term *mode of articulation* refers to the way in which the air from the lungs is obstructed.

If it is completely obstructed, the sound is called a stop ([p t k b d g]).

If it is obstructed by friction, it is called a fricative ([f θ s x j]

If it is fully obstructed, then released by friction, it is called an affricate ([ʧ]).

If it is obstructed by having to exit around the tongue, it is called a lateral ([l]).

If it is obstructed by a flap or vibration of the tongue (or the uvula) it is called a tap ([ɾ]) or trill ([r]).

If it is obstructed by being routed through the nose, it is called a nasal ([n m ɲ]).

The term *place of articulation* refers to the place where the obstruction of the air occurs. In most consonants, the obstruction is due to the action of the tongue, which touches or approaches other parts of the mouth.

If the tongue touches or approaches the velum, the consonant is called velar ([g k x]).

If the tongue touches or approaches the palate, the consonant is called palatal ([j λ ɲ ʧ]).

If the tongue touches or approaches the alveolar ridge, the consonant is called alveolar ([n s l ɾ r]).

If the tongue touches or approaches the teeth, the consonant is called dental ([d t]).

If the tongue is placed between the upper and lower incisors, the consonant is called interdental ([θ]).

In some cases, the tongue is not involved in the obstruction of the air.

> If the air is obstructed by contact between or proximity of the lips, the consonant is called bilabial ([b p m]).
> If the air is obstructed by contact between the lower lip and the upper incisors, the consonant is called labiodental ([f]).
> If the air is obstructed in the glottis (i.e., the space between the vocal cords), the consonant is called glottal ([h]).[1]

The term *sonority* refers to the presence or absence of vibration of the vocal cords during the articulation of a sound. Consonants articulated without the vibration of the vocal cords are called *unvoiced* ([k x s t θ p f h ʧ]), and those whose articulation is accompanied by this vibration are called *voiced* ([g j λ n m ɲ l ɾ r d b]).

According to this classification, the following chart of the consonantal inventory of Spanish can be constructed.

Place of Articulation

Mode of Articulation	Bilabial	Labiodental	Interdental	Dental	Alveolar	Palatal	Velar	Glottal
stop								
unvoiced	p			t			k	
voiced	b			d			g	
fricative								
unvoiced		f	θ		s		x	h
voiced						j		
africate								
(unvoiced)						ʧ		
lateral (voiced)					l			
tap, trill (voiced)					ɾ r			
nasal (voiced)	m				n	ɲ		

1. The consonant [w] is usually identified as a voiced labiovelar fricative, because its articulation involves both the tongue, which approaches the velum, and the lips, which are rounded.

The consonants are identified as follows:

[p] unvoiced bilabial stop   [h] unvoiced glottal fricative
[t] unvoiced dental stop   [j] voiced palatal fricative
[k] unvoiced velar stop   [ʧ] unvoiced palatal affricate
[b] voiced bilabial stop   [l] voiced alveolar lateral
[d] voiced dental stop   [ɾ] voiced alveolar tap
[g] voiced velar stop   [r] voiced alveolar trill
[f] unvoiced labiodental fricative   [m] voiced bilabial nasal
[θ] unvoiced interdental fricative   [n] voiced alveolar nasal
[s] unvoiced alveolar fricative   [ɲ] voiced palatal nasal
[x] unvoiced velar fricative

Phonemes and Allophones

In practice, the inventory of Spanish sounds includes more sounds than those depicted above, because some sounds vary according to the phonetic context in which they occur. For example, in the phrase *con sal* 'with salt', *con* is pronounced with a final alveolar nasal ([kon 'sal]), but in *con queso* 'with cheese', the nasal is velar ([koŋ 'ke so]). In *hasta* 'until' the alveolar fricative is unvoiced (['as ta]), but some speakers pronounce this sound in *mismo* 'same' as a voiced fricative (['míz mo]).

For this reason it is necessary to distinguish in phonology between phonemes and allophones. A phoneme, which is indicated by front slashes (for example, /n/ or /s/), is a sound or group of sounds that in a given language serves to distinguish one word from another. We know that /n/ and /s/ are different phonemes because they serve to distinguish among pairs of words that differ in only one sound, such as *ni/si* and *en/es*. On the other hand, [s] / [z] and [n] / [ŋ] do not constitute different phonemes, because ['mis mo] and ['miz mo] mean the same thing, as do [kon] and [koŋ]. We say, therefore, that [s] and [z] are allophones of the phoneme /s/, and that [n] and [ŋ] are allophones of the phoneme /n/. Allophones are indicated by brackets. Now it becomes clear why it is necessary to identify the phonemes of each language individually: in English, /s/ and /z/ constitute different phonemes, since *sue* /su:/ does not mean the same as *zoo* /zuː/; /n/ and /ŋ/ are different phonemes too, since *sin* /sɪn/ is not the same as *sing* /sɪŋ/. The two languages have the four sounds in common but organize them differently.

Phonological Processes

Language sounds undergo a large variety of changes, both in the normal course of speech and over time. These changes are known as *phonological processes*. Vowels, for example, can change place of articulation on either the horizontal or the vertical axis, as when, historically, the Latin short high vowel /i/ becomes the Romance mid vowel /e/. Consonants can change in terms of mode or place of articulation, or sonority; consider the phoneme /k/ of Lat. *centum* /ˈken tum/ 'one hundred' > Med. Cast. /ˈtsjen/ > Mod. Sp. /ˈθjen/ or /sjen/ (a double change, of both mode and place of articulation), /f/ of lat. *farina* /fa ˈri na/ 'flour' > /ha ˈri na/ (change of place of articulation) and /ʒ/ of Med. Cast. *hijo* /ˈhi ʒo/ 'son' > sixteenth-century Cast. /ˈi ʃo/ (change in sonority). Our survey of the history of Spanish phonology contains examples of many additional processes, including **spirantization**, metaphony, epenthesis, metathesis, merger, and split.

Glossary of Linguistic Terms

ablative: [case] that expresses generally the withdrawal or separation of something; in Latin, it includes the functions of accompaniment, place of an action, and means or instrument by which an action is carried out

accusative: [case] that corresponds to the direct object of a verb and to indications of direction

accusative and infinitive construction: Latin syntactic construction in which the subject of a subordinate clause appears in accusative case and the verb in the infinitive

acronymy: word-formation type that combines the initial letters of each of the words that normally constitute the designation of something to form a new word

adjectivization: word-formation type, a subcategory of conversion, whereby a word is made adjectival without undergoing derivation or compounding

adverbialization: word-formation type, a subcategory of conversion, whereby a word is made adverbial without undergoing derivation or compounding

affix: a morpheme, a prefix or a suffix, added to a base in order to derive a new word

affricate: [consonant] whose mode of articulation combines occlusion and friction

agglutination: phenomenon by which two or more morphemes become fused into a single unit, while largely retaining their original form

allomorph: variant of a morpheme

allophone: variant of a phoneme

alveolar: [consonant] articulated by placing the tongue against the alveolar ridge

Americanism: word or linguistic feature typical of American Spanish

analogical: [change] in which the form of a word is affected by the form of another word or group of words

analogy: modification of words in order to adapt them to a more frequent or normal pattern in the language

analytic: 1. [language] that uses independent words to express syntactic relations; 2. [linguistic construction] that uses independent words to express a semantic content

Andalusian theory: hypothesis according to which the Andalusian variety of Spanish served as the basis for the formation of American Spanish

Anglicism: loanword adopted from English

anthroponym: proper name of a person

apheresis: loss of a sound at the beginning of a word

apical: [consonant] articulated with the tip of the tongue

apocope: loss of a sound at the end of a word

apophonic: showing variation in the tonic vowel of lexemes

Arabism: loanword adopted from Arabic

archaism: word or linguistic feature characteristic of a past era

aspiration: transformation of a sound into [h]

assibilation: introduction of a sibilant or hissing element into a sound

assimilation: process whereby a sound becomes more like a neighboring sound

atonic: unstressed

back: [vowel] articulated with the tongue in a relatively posterior position

bilabial: [consonant] articulated through the approximation or contact of both lips

bilingualism: habitual use of two languages in a speech community

binomial: [compound] of the endocentric type, in which both elements have the function of head

blending: word-formation type in which two words are intentionally intermingled to produce a new word

borrowing: 1. loanword, a word adopted from another language; 2. the process of absorbing a word from another language

calque: loan translation, i.e., the borrowing of the meaning but not the form of a foreign word or phrase

case: grammatical function of a word, usually as indicated by an inflection

case ending: nominal inflection denoting case at the end of a word

case system: morphological system based on the use of inflections to signal grammatical functions

castellano drecho: a regularized form of Medieval Castilian created at the court of Alfonso X el Sabio

Castilian: 1. dialect of the region of Castile; 2. national language of Spain

causal: [subordinate clause] that refers to the cause of the action expressed by the main clause

ceceo: merger of the phonemes /s/ and /θ/ in favor of the latter

central: [vowel] articulated with the tongue in a neutral position on the horizontal axis

centralization: change in the articulation of a vowel toward a central point on the horizontal axis

change in progress: a linguistic change that is currently diffusing through a language

chronology: order in which events happen in time

circumflex: [intonation] of River Plate Spanish supposedly affected by the speech of Italian immigrants

clipping: word-formation type in which part of the phonetic substance of a word is elided

clitic: [pronoun] that is linked with a verb

closed syllable: syllable that ends in a consonant

Cocoliche: Spanish-Italian interlanguage spoken by Italian immigrants before their complete assimilation to the culture of Buenos Aires

code-switching: alternation between two languages in a single utterance

cognate: word that is etymologically (i.e., genetically) related to another

comparative method: systematic comparison of languages in search of similar linguistic features

complement: word or phrase that depends syntactically on another in a sentence

compound: word produced through compounding

compound tense: tense formed by the combination of an auxiliary verb and another verbal element

compounding: word-formation type in which two words are combined to form a new word

concessive: [subordinate clause] that expresses an objection or difficulty for the accomplishment of the action of the main clause

conjugation: 1. the set of all forms of a verb; 2. the group to which a verb belongs according to its infinitive ending

consecutive: 1. [dialect] that was formed on the basis of Castilian; 2. [subordinate clause] that expresses the consequence of the action expressed in the main clause

consonant: a speech sound produced by the full or partial interruption of the air in speech

constitutive: [dialect or language] formed on the basis of Proto-Hispano-Romance

conversion: a type of word-formation whereby the grammatical class of a word is changed without recourse to suffixation or compounding—that is, though nominalization, adjectivation, adverbialization, verbalization

creole: 1. hybrid language developed on the basis of a dominant and a secondary language, used by a speech community as a native language; 2. Spanish American born of or descended from Spanish parents or ancestors

dative: [case] that corresponds to the function of indirect object

deaffrication: process whereby a consonant loses its affricate mode of articulation

declension: 1. the set of all the forms of a nominal element; 2. group or class to which a nominal element belongs, according to its inflectional endings

dental: [consonant] articulated with the tongue contacting the upper incisors

depalatalization: process whereby a consonant loses its palatal place of articulation

dequeísmo: use of *de que* for *que*

derivation: 1. historical evolution of a language or word; 2. word formation through the use of prefixes and suffixes

desdoblamiento de vocales: phenomenon whereby the aspiration of implosive /s/ in a word provokes the opening of its vowels

develarization: process whereby a consonant loses its velar place of articulation

devoicing: process whereby a sound becomes unvoiced, so that the vocal cords no longer vibrate when it is pronounced

diachronic: [linguistic discipline] that studies the evolution of languages over time

dialect: regional or social variety of a language

dialectology: study of the regional and social varieties of a language

diaphasic: [linguistic difference] conditioned by the diversity of registers or styles with which a language can be spoken.

diastratic: [linguistic difference] conditioned by the diverse social status of the speakers of a language

diatopic: [linguistic difference] conditioned by the diverse geographical origins of speakers

diglossia: type of bilingualism in which two languages or two forms of the same language are used in different contexts in a single linguistic community

diphthong: a set of two different vocalic elements pronounced in a single syllable

diphthongization: process whereby a diphthong is produced

dissimilation: process whereby one of two similar or identical sounds in a word is modified in order to become less like the other

dorsal: [consonant] articulated with the blade of the tongue

dorsodental: [consonant] produced by placing the tip of the tongue against the lower incisors

endocentric: [compound word], one of whose components designates the basic concept of the word, while the other modifies it

epenthesis: addition of a sound in the interior of a word

etymological doublet: a set of two words with the same etymological origin, one the product of learned, the other of popular transmission

etymology: 1. origin of a word; 2. study of the origin of words

etymon: root or word from which another word derives

exocentric: [compound word], neither of whose components designates the basic concept of the word

final: [subordinating clause] that expresses the end or goal of the action of the main clause

fricative: [consonant] whose mode of articulation involves friction between articulators

front: [vowel] articulated with the tongue relatively forward in the mouth

fusion: the melding of two linguistic elements into one

Gallicism: word or linguistic structure adopted from French

geminate: a doubled consonant sound

gender: in Castilian, grammatical category that classifies nouns as feminine or masculine

genealogical tree: chart in the form of a tree, with a trunk and branches, used to represent the relationships among the members of a language family

genitive: [case] that corresponds to the function of possession or pertinence

glide: speech-sound that has both vocalic and consonantal characteristics

glottal: [sound] articulated in the glottis, between the vocal cords

grammaticalization: process whereby a word loses its lexical meaning and assumes a purely grammatical function

Hellenic Latinism: Greek loanword transmitted as a learned borrowing into Romance through Latin

Hellenism: loanword adopted from Greek

hiatus: sequence of two vowels belonging to two different syllables

high: [vowel] articulated with the tongue relatively near the palate

historical grammar: study of the phonological and morphological history of a language

homorganic: [consonant] that shares its place of articulation with a contiguous consonant

hyperbaton: artificial alteration of normal word order in a sentence

imparisyllabic: [Latin noun] whose nominative and vocative forms have, in singular, a different number of syllables than the other cases

implosive: [consonant] occurring in syllable-final position

Ibero-Latin: variety of Latin spoken on the Iberian Peninsula

Indo-European: 1. pertaining to the Proto-Indo-European language or its speakers; 2. the Proto-Indo-European language

inflection: 1. nonlexical morpheme (especially an ending) used to signal grammatical categories such as gender, case, number, person, tense, voice, mood, or aspect; 2. the use of nonlexical morphemes (especially endings) to indicate grammatical categories

innovation: in linguistic usage, a new variant that enters into competition with its preexisting equivalents

intensive *ser*: grammatical construction found in some Spanish varieties, characterized by the omission of an adverbial relative

interdental: [consonant] articulated with the tongue placed between the upper and lower incisors

interlanguage: hybrid linguistic variety typical of persons who are learning a new language, or whose acquisition of this language has fossilized

intertonic: atonic, neither initial nor final

intervocalic: [consonant] occurring between vowels

Italianism: loanword adopted from Italian

jejeo: tendency to aspirate initial or intervocalic /s/

koineization: process whereby complex and variable linguistic structures are simplified through rapid and intensive mixing of linguistic varieties or dialects

labiodental: [consonant] articulated by bringing the upper incisors into contact with the lower lip

labiovelar: [consonant] whose articulation combines rounded lips and a posterior tongue position

laísmo: use of the pronoun *la* as feminine indirect object complement, in place of *le*

language family: a set of languages that are genetically related

language isolate: language that belongs to no known language family

language shift: process whereby a language is gradually replaced by another

lateral: [consonant] in whose articulation air escapes to the sides of the tongue

Latinism: learned borrowing adopted from Latin

Latinization: the shift to Latin from other languages spoken in the territories conquered by the Romans

learned: [loanword] adopted from classical Latin or Greek

leísmo: use of the pronoun *le* as masculine direct object complement, in place of *lo*, usually when referring to persons

lenition: process of articulatory weakening that affects consonants

leveling: process whereby the forms of a paradigm become more regular through mutual influence

lexeme: minimal lexical unit, apart from any inflections with which it may combine

lexical: pertaining to the lexicon

lexicon: vocabulary of a language

linguistic sign: lexical unit composed of a signifier and a signified

liquid: mode of articulation of /l ɾ r/

loanword: borrowing, a word adopted from another language

low: [vowel] pronounced with the tongue at a maximum distance from the palate

marked: notable due to being less common or usual

merger: fusion of two phonemes into one, with the loss of one phoneme and its phonemic oppositions

metaphony: process whereby the quality of a vowel is modified due to the influence of a nearby vowel

metaphor: designation of a thing by the name of another, similar thing

metathesis: change of the location of a sound in the interior of a word

metonymy: designation of a thing by the name of another thing with which it is connected in reality

mid: [vowel] articulated with the tongue in a neutral position on the vertical axis

minimal pair: a set of two words with different meanings whose form differs in only one phoneme

mode of articulation: the way in which the articulators interrupt the air to produce a given sound

monolingualism: habitual use of a single language in a speech community

monophthongization: process whereby a diphthong or triphthong is changed into a monophthong

morpheme: minimal unit of meaning

morphology: study of the form of words in a language, including inflection and word formation

morphological: pertaining to morphology

morphosyntax: joint study of morphology and syntax

motosidad: tendency, in the bilingual indigenous population of the Andean area, to reduce the five Spanish vowels to three (/iau/).

Mozarab: Christian inhabitant of Muslim Spain

Mozarabic: Ibero-Romance language of the Christian inhabitants of Muslim Spain

nasal: [sound] in whose articulation all or part of the air exits through the nose

neologism: newly coined and as yet not generally accepted word or expression

nominal: pertaining to nouns, pronouns, adjectives, and articles

nominalization: word-formation type, a subcategory of conversion, whereby a word is made into a noun without undergoing derivation or compounding

nominative: [case] that corresponds to the function of subject

noun: 1. word that may function as subject or object of a verb; 2. [subordinate clause] that performs the function of subject or object of the action expressed in the main clause

oblique: [case] that signals any function other than nominative or vocative

occlusive: [consonant] whose mode of articulation involves a complete obstruction of the air from the lungs, also called *stop*

onomatopoeia: word whose sounds imitate the sound or noise that it denotes

open syllable: syllable that ends in a vowel

orthography: the set of norms that govern the written representation of a language

oxytonic: [word] stressed on the final syllable

palatal: [sound] whose articulation involves the approximation of the dorsum of the tongue to the palate

palatalization: process whereby a sound becomes more palatal

paradigm: a set of forms that serve as a pattern in various kinds of inflection such as declensions and conjugations

paroxytonic: [word] stressed on the penultimate syllable

passive reflexive: syntactic structure in which the passive element is expressed impersonally by a reflexive construction

passive voice: syntactic construction whose subject designates the person or thing that is the object of the action

patronymic: [name] formed on the stem of the father's first name

personal *a*: the use of the preposition *a* before a personal or personified direct object

phoneme: minimal distinctive phonological unit

phonemic: pertaining to phonemes

phonetic: pertaining to linguistic sounds

phonological: pertaining to phonology

phonology: the study of the speech sounds of a language and the rules governing pronunciation

pidgin: a simplified interlanguage used by individuals in communities that do not share a language

place of articulation: place in the articulatory tract where the speech organs interrupt the air to produce a given sound

popular Spanish: social dialect typical of rural and less educated people throughout the Spanish-speaking world

popular transmission: type of transmission that takes place within a language through normal linguistic evolution

predorsal: [consonant] articulated with the front part of the dorsum of the tongue

prefix: morpheme that, attached at the beginning of another morpheme, forms a derivative

proparoxytonic: [word] stressed on the antepenultimate or third-from-the-last syllable

prothesis: addition of a sound, usually a vowel, at the beginning of a word

Proto-Hispano-Romance: unattested Ibero-Romance language from which Castilian, Astur-Leonese, and Navarro-Aragonese develop

Proto-Ibero-Romance: unattested Romance language that formed on the Iberian Peninsula, from which evolved Galician-Portuguese, Catalan, Mozarabic, and the Hispano-Romance languages and dialects

Proto-Indo-European: unattested language that existed approximately nine thousand years ago, from which the Indo-European languages evolved

Proto-language: a language for which there is no written evidence

Proto-Romance: unattested language that formed from spoken Latin and from which all Romance Languages developed

queísmo: use of *que* for *de que*

quesuismo: replacement of the forms of *cuyo* 'whose' by *que su* 'that his/her/its/their'

reanalysis: phenomenon characterized by a change in the interpretation of the morphological structure of a word

reduplication: exact or approximate repetition of all or part of a word

register: form or style of expression conditioned by the situation in which speakers find themselves

rehilamiento: vibration produced at the place of articulation of some consonants in addition to that of the vocal cords

relatinization: process whereby phonological, morphological, and lexical elements of Latin are introduced into Spanish

repopulation: process whereby a political entity removes the original inhabitants of conquered lands and populates them with its own colonists

retroflex: [consonant] whose articulation involves the tip of the tongue being curled upward and back

Romance languages: vernacular languages that developed as a result of the evolution of spoken Latin

Romanization: imposition of Roman civilization upon lands conquered by the Romans

schwa: the name customarily used to refer to the sound [ə]

ʃeísmo: variety of *yeísmo* in which [j] is replaced by [ʃ]

semantic: pertaining to the meanings of linguistic signs

semilearned: [word] transmitted through popular channels that nonetheless retains some features of its Latin counterpart

seseo: merger of the phonemes /s/ and /θ/ in favor of the former

sibilant: [fricative consonant] characterized by a hissing sound

signified: concept represented by the signifier of a linguistic sign

signifier: form of a linguistic sign that represents a signified

sociolinguistics: subfield of linguistics that examines language in its social context

spirantization: process whereby a consonant acquires a fricative mode of articulation

split: division of one phoneme into two

spoken Latin: "low" variety of the Latin language in the diglossia that developed in Latin-speaking areas

standard: variety of a language spoken and written by the most educated speakers, characterized by a fixed grammar, lexicon, and orthography

stop: [consonant] whose mode of articulation involves a complete obstruction of the air from the lungs, also called *occlusive*

subordination: relationship between clauses in a compound sentence, one of which (the subordinate clause) depends logically and grammatically on the other (the main clause)

suffix: morpheme that, attached at the end of another morpheme, forms a derivative

syllable: sound or set of sounds comprising a nucleus (normally a vowel) and, optionally, one or more consonants

synchronic: [linguistic discipline] that studies a language as it exists at a specific point in time

syncope: loss of one or more sounds in the interior of a word

syncretism: concentration of two or more grammatical functions in a single morpheme

syneresis: reduction into a single syllable, within a word, of vowels that would normally be pronounced separately

syntactic: pertaining to syntax

syntax: [study of the] rules for the formation of sentences in a language

synthetic: 1. [language] that uses inflection to express syntactic relations; 2. [linguistic construction] that utilizes inflections to express a semantic content

tap: [consonant] in whose articulation the tongue briefly touches another articulator

template: pattern through which words are created or modified by analogy

tonic: [sound or group of sounds] that are stressed in a word or phrase

toponym: proper name of a place

transmission: the passing of a linguistic element between successive stages of the same language

trill: [consonant] in whose articulation the tongue rapidly and repeatedly touches another articulator

tuteo: use of *tú* as the singular second-person familiar pronoun

unvoiced: [sound] articulated without the vibration of the vocal cords

ustedeo: the use of *usted* as singular second-person familiar pronoun

uvular: [consonant] articulated with the uvula

variant: linguistic form that differs from another that is considered the norm

variety: dialect, i.e., form of a language characteristic of a specific region or social group

velar: [sound] whose articulation involves an approximation or contact between the back part of the tongue and the velum

verbal: pertaining to verbs

verbalization: word-formation type, a subcategory of conversion, whereby a word is made into a verb without undergoing derivation or compounding

vocative: [case] used to address or invoke a person

voiced: [sound] whose articulation involves the vibration of the vocal cords

voicing: process whereby an unvoiced sound begins to be articulated with vibration of the vocal cords

voseo: use of *vos* as singular second-person familiar pronoun

vowel: linguistic sound that is produced without a narrowing or closing of the speech organs, generally accompanied by vibration of the vocal cords

vowel reduction: process whereby a vowel is weakened by centralization, devoicing, reduction in duration, or elision

word formation: set of procedures for the creation of new words through the internal resources of a language, especially prefixation, suffixation, and compounding

yeísmo: merger of /j/ and /ʎ/ in favor of the former

yod: name that is customarily given to the sound [j]

ʒeísmo: variety of *yeísmo* in which [j] is replaced by [ʒ]

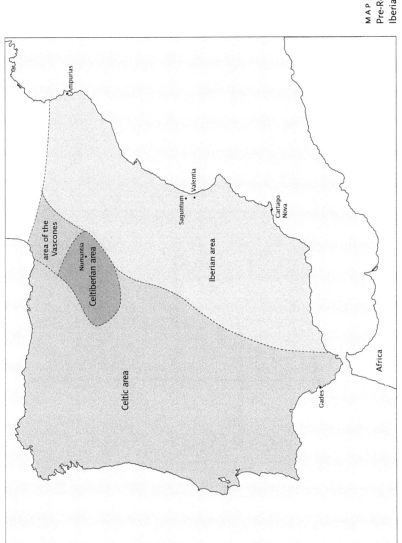

MAP 1.
Pre-Roman
Iberia

Ampurias

Valentia

Saguntum

Cartago
Nova

area of the
Vascones

Numantia
Celtiberian area

Iberian area

Celtic area

Gades

Africa

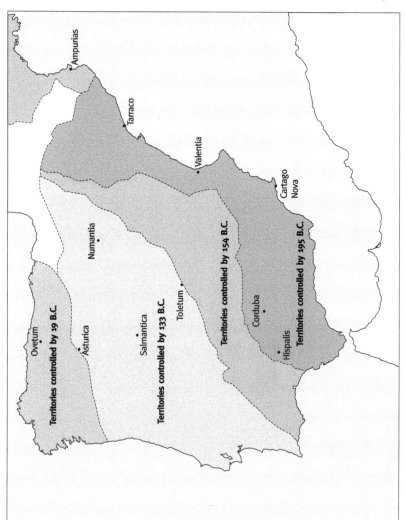

MAP 2.
Conquest of
Iberia

Ampurias

Tarraco

Valentia

Cartago
Nova

Numantia

Territories controlled by 154 B.C.

Toletum

Corduba

Territories controlled by 195 B.C.

Hispalis

Ovetum

Territories controlled by 19 B.C.

Asturica

Salmantica

Territories controlled by 133 B.C.

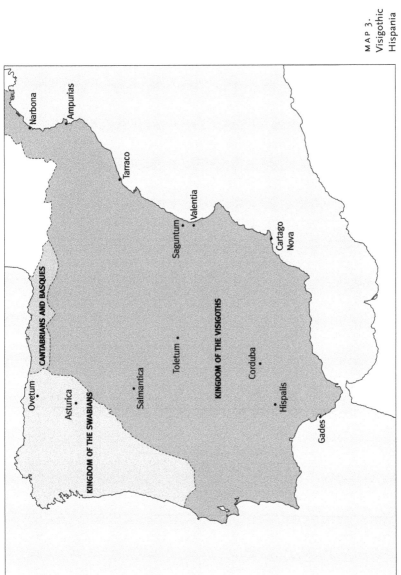

MAP 3.
Visigothic
Hispania

Narbona

Ampurias

Tarraco

Valentia

Saguntum

Cartago
Nova

CANTABRIANS AND BASQUES

Ovetum

Asturica

Salmantica

Toletum

KINGDOM OF THE VISIGOTHS

Corduba

Hispalis

KINGDOM OF THE SWABIANS

Gades

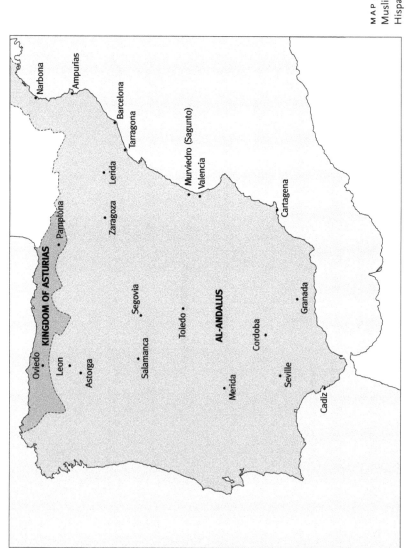

MAP 4.
Muslim
Hispania

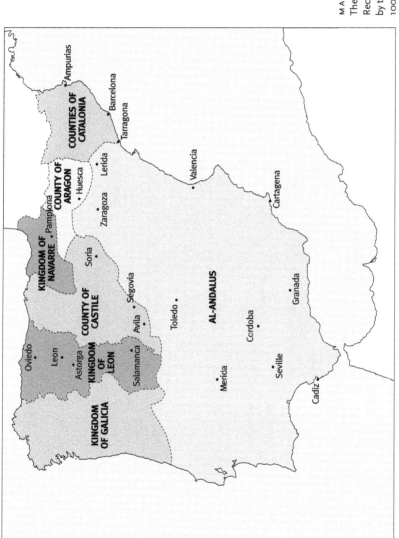

MAP 5.
The
Reconquest
by the Year
1000

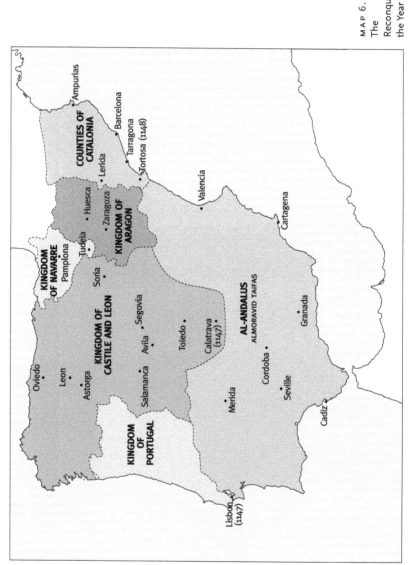

MAP 6.
The
Reconquest by
the Year 1150

KINGDOM OF NAVARRE

COUNTIES OF CATALONIA

Ampurias

Barcelona

Tarragona

Tortosa (1148)

Lerida

Huesca

Zaragoza

KINGDOM OF ARAGON

Valencia

Tudela

Pamplona

Cartagena

Soria

AL-ANDALUS
ALMORAVID TAIFAS

KINGDOM OF CASTILE AND LEON

Segovia

Granada

Avila

Toledo

Calatrava (1147)

Oviedo

Leon

Astorga

Salamanca

Cordoba

Merida

Seville

Cadiz

KINGDOM OF PORTUGAL

Lisbon (1147)

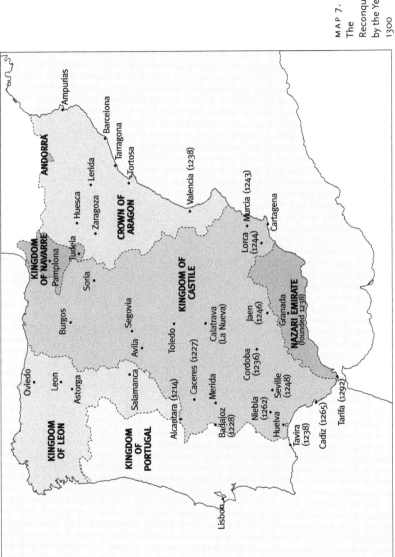

MAP 7.
The
Reconquest
by the Year
1300

KINGDOM OF LEON

KINGDOM OF PORTUGAL

Oviedo

Leon

Astorga

Salamanca

Lisbon

Alcantara (1214)

Caceres (1227)

Merida

Badajoz (1228)

Niebla (1262)

Huelva

Tavira (1238)

Cadiz (1265)

Tarifa (1292)

Burgos

Avila

Segovia

Toledo

Calatrava (La Nueva)

Cordoba (1236)

Seville (1248)

KINGDOM OF NAVARRE

Pamplona

Tudela

Soria

KINGDOM OF CASTILE

Jaen (1246)

Granada

NAZARI ÉMIRATE (founded 1238)

Lorca (1244)

Murcia (1243)

Cartagena

ANDORRA

Huesca

Zaragoza

Lerida

CROWN OF ARAGON

Valencia (1238)

Ampurias

Barcelona

Tarragona

Tortosa

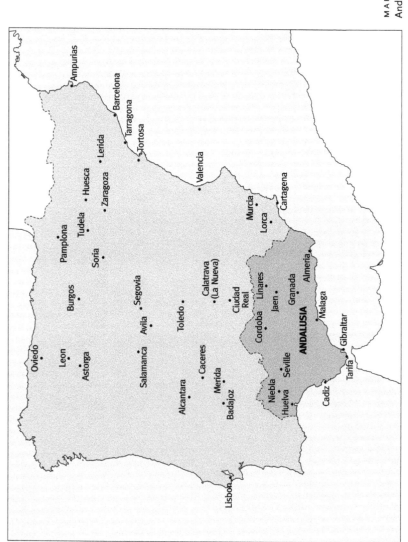

MAP 8.
Andalusia

Ampurias

Barcelona

Tarragona

Tortosa

Lerida

Valencia

Huesca

Zaragoza

Cartagena

Tudela

Murcia

Pamplona

Lorca

Soria

Calatrava
(La Nueva)

Almeria

Segovia

Linares

Granada

Burgos

Ciudad
Real

Jaen

Avila

Toledo

Cordoba

ANDALUSIA

Malaga

Oviedo

Gibraltar

Leon

Salamanca

Caceres

Seville

Tarifa

Astorga

Merida

Niebla

Alcantara

Badajoz

Huelva

Cadiz

Lisbon

MAP 9. Spanish America

Works Cited

Alatorre, Antonio. 1989. *Los 1001 años de la lengua española*. Mexico City: Tezontle.

Alborg, Juan Luis. 1972. *Historia de la literatura española: Edad Media y Renacimiento*. 2nd ed. Madrid: Gredos.

Allen, W. Sidney. 1978. *Vox Latina: The Pronunciation of Classical Latin*. 2nd ed. Cambridge: Cambridge University Press.

Alonso, Amado. 1942. *Castellano, español, idioma nacional: Historia espiritual de tres nombres*. 2nd ed. Buenos Aires: Losada.

Alonso de la Fuente, José Andrés. 2008. Review of Pharies 2007. *Linguistica Pragensia* 69:108–13.

Alvar, Manuel. 1996. "Canario." In *Manual de dialectología hispánica: El español de España*, edited by Manuel Alvar, 325–38. Barcelona: Ariel.

———, et al., eds. 1967. *Enciclopedia lingüística hispánica*, vol. 2, *Elementos constitutivos, fuentes*. Madrid: Consejo Superior de Investigaciones Científicas.

Alvar Ezquerra, Manuel. 2002. *De antiguos y nuevos diccionarios del español*. Madrid: Arco/Libros.

Arias, Andrés Enrique. 2006. "El cambio de *gelo* a *selo* desde la perspectiva de la teoría de la gramaticalización." In *Actas del VI Congreso Internacional de Historia de la Lengua Española*, edited by José Jesús de Bustos Tovar and José Luis Girón Alconchel, 1:305–16. Madrid: Arco.

Ariza, Manuel. 2004a. "El romance en Al-Ándalus." In *Historia de la lengua española*, edited by Rafael Cano, 207–35. Barcelona: Ariel.

———. 2004b. "El castellano primitivo: Los documentos." In *Historia de la lengua española*, edited by Rafael Cano, 309–24. Barcelona: Ariel.

Bahner, Werner. 1966. *La lingüística española del Siglo de Oro: Aportaciones a la conciencia lingüística de la España de los siglos XVI y XVII*. Madrid: Ciencia Nueva.

Barton, Simon. 2004. *A History of Spain*. New York: Palgrave Macmillan.

Bello, Andrés. [1847] 1951. *Gramática de la lengua castellana destinada al uso de los americanos*. Caracas: Ministerio de Educación.

Beltrán Lloris, Francisco. 2004. "El latín en la Hispania Romana: Una perspectiva histórica." In *Historia de la lengua española*, edited by Rafael Cano, 83–106. Barcelona: Ariel.

Blanco Botta, Ivonne. 1982. "El voseo en Cuba: Estudio socio-lingüístico de una zona de la isla." *Beiträge zur romanischen Philologie* 21:291–304.

Brumme, Jenny. 2003. "Historia de la reflexión sobre las lenguas románicas: Español." In *Romanische Sprachgeschichte*, edited by Gerhard Ernst et al., 1:265–79. Berlin: Walter de Gruyter.

Bustos Tovar, José Jesús de. 2004. "La escisión latín-romance: El nacimiento de las lenguas romances: el castellano." In *Historia de la lengua española*, edited by Rafael Cano, 259–90. Barcelona: Ariel.

Butt, John, and Carmen Benjamin. 1988. *A New Reference Grammar of Modern Spanish*. London: Edward Arnold.

Calderón Campos, Miguel, and Francisca Medina Morales. 2010. "Historia y situación actual de los pronombres de tratamiento en el español peninsular." In *Formas y fórmulas de tratamiento en el mundo hispánico*, edited by Martin Hummel, Bettina Kluge, and María Eugenia Vázquez Laslop, 195–222. Mexico City: Colegio de México.

Cano Aguilar, Rafael. 1992. *El español a través de los tiempos*. Madrid: Arco/Libros.

Caravedo, Rocío. 2003. "Principios del cambio lingüístico: Una contribución sincrónica a la lingüística histórica." *Revista de Filología Española* 83:39–62.

Cerrón-Palomino, Rodolfo. 2003. *Castellano andino: Aspectos sociolingüísticos, pedagógicos y gramaticales*. Lima: Pontificia Universidad Católica del Perú.

Clavería Nadal, Gloria. 2006. "Aspectos del cultismo en las obras alfonsíes." In *Actas del VI Congreso Internacional de Historia de la Lengua Española*, edited by José Jesús de Bustos Tovar and José Luis Girón Alconchel, 2:1355–69. Madrid: Arco.

Collins, Roger. 1999. *Early Medieval Europe, 300–1000*. 2nd ed. New York: St. Martin's.

Company Company, Concepción. 2006. "Aportaciones teóricas y descriptivas de la sintaxis histórica del español americano a la sintaxis histórica del español general." In *Actas del VI Congreso Internacional de Historia de la Lengua Española*, edited by José Jesús de Bustos Tovar and José Luis Girón Alconchel, 1:21–66. Madrid: Arco.

Comrie, Bernard, ed. 1990. *The World's Major Languages*. Oxford: Oxford University Press.

Corominas, Joan, with José A. Pascual. 1981–90. *Diccionario crítico etimológico castellano e hispánico*. 6 vols. Madrid: Gredos.

Corriente Córdoba, Federico. 1997. *Poesía dialectal árabe y romance en Alandalús*. Madrid: Gredos.

———. 2004. "El elemento árabe en la historia lingüística peninsular." In *Historia de la lengua española*, edited by Rafael Cano, 185–235. Barcelona: Ariel.

Davies, Mark. 2006. *A Frequency Dictionary of Spanish: Core Vocabulary for Learners*. New York: Routledge.

Díaz Collazos, Ana María. 2015. *Desarrollo sociolingüístico del voseo en la región andina de Colombia (1555–1976)*. Berlin: Mouton de Gruyter.

Dietrich, Wolf, and Horst Geckeler. 1990. *Einführung in die spanische Sprachwissenschaft: Ein Lehr- und Arbeitsbuch*. Berlin: Erich Schmidt.

Diez, Miguel, Francisco Morales, and Ángel Sabín. 1980. *Las lenguas de España*. 2nd ed. Madrid: Ministerio de Educación.

Dworkin, Steven. 2005. "La historia de la lengua y el cambio léxico." *Iberoromania* 62:59–70.

———. 2012. *A History of the Spanish Lexicon*. Oxford: Oxford University Press.

Echenique Elizondo, María Teresa. 2008. "Presencia romance en la documentación latina de los orígenes peninsulares." In *El primitivo romance hispánico*, edited by Beatriz Díez Calleja, 73–92. Burgos: Instituto Castellano y Leonés de la Lengua.

———. 2003. "Nivellement linguistique et standardisation en espagnol (castillan) médiéval." In *The Dawn of the Written Vernacular in Western Europe*, edited by Michèle Goyens and Werner Verbeke, 337–50. Louvain, Belgium: Leuven University Press.

———, and Juan Sánchez Méndez. 2005. *Las lenguas de un reino: Historia lingüística hispánica*. Madrid: Gredos.

Elcock, W. D. 1975. *The Romance Languages*. Revised by John N. Green. London: Faber and Faber.

Elvira, Javier. 2002. "Sobre el desarrollo de la pasiva refleja en español medieval." In *Actas del V Congreso Internacional de Historia de la Lengua Española*, edited by M. Teresa Echenique Elizondo et al., 1:597–607. Madrid: Gredos.

Fear, A. T. 2000. "Prehistoric and Roman Spain." In *Spain: A History*, edited by Raymond Carr, 11–38. Oxford: Oxford University Press.

Fernández, Roberto G. 1983. "English Loanwords in Miami Cuban Spanish." *American Speech* 58:13–19.

Fernández-Ordóñez, Inés. 2004. "Alfonso X el Sabio en la historia del español." In *Historia de la lengua española*, edited by Rafael Cano, 381–422. Barcelona: Ariel.

Fernández Trinidad, Marianela. 2010, "Variaciones fonéticas del yeísmo: Un estudio acústico en mujeres rioplatenses." *Estudios de fonética experimental* 19:263–92.

Flores Cervantes, Marcela. 2006. "Leísmo, laísmo y loísmo." In *Sintaxis histórica de la lengua española*, edited by Concepción Company Company, 1:671–749. Mexico City: Universidad Nacional Autónoma de México.

Galmés de Fuentes, Álvaro. 1983. *Dialectología mozárabe*. Madrid: Gredos.

Garcés Gómez, María Pilar. 2002. "Aspectos de la evolución del neutro en español." In *Actas del V Congreso Internacional de Historia de la Lengua Española*, edited by M. Teresa Echenique Elizondo et al., 1:621–31. Madrid: Gredos.

García de Cortázar, José Ángel. 2004. "Resistencia frente al Islam, reconquista y repoblación en los reinos hispanocristianos (años 711–1212)." In *Historia de la lengua española*, edited by Rafael Cano, 239–56. Barcelona: Ariel.

García Gómez, Emilio. 1975. *Las jarchas romances de la serie árabe en su marco*. Madrid: Alianza.

García Mouton, Pilar. 1994. *Lenguas y dialectos de España*. Madrid: Arco/Libros.

Gifford, D. J., and F. W. Hodcroft. 1966. *Textos lingüísticos del medioevo español*. 2nd ed. Oxford: Dolphin.

Gómez Capuz, Juan. 1996. "Tendencias en el estudio de las diversas etapas de la influencia angloamericana en español moderno (con especial atención al nivel léxico)." In *Actas del III Congreso Internacional de Historia de la Lengua Española*, edited by A. Alonso González et al., 2 vols., 2:1289–307. Madrid: Arco/Libros.

González Jiménez, Manuel. 2004. "El reino de Castilla durante el Siglo XIII." In *Historia de la lengua española*, edited by Rafael Cano, 357–79. Barcelona: Ariel.

Gray, R. D., and Q. D. Atkinson. 2003. "Language-Tree Divergence Times Support the Anatolian Theory of Indo-European Origin." *Nature* 426:435–39.

Harris, Martin. 1988. "The Romance Languages." In *The Romance Languages*, edited by Martin Harris and Nivel Vincent, 1–25. New York: Oxford University Press.

Harris-Northall, Ray. 1990. "The Spread of Sound Change: Another Look at Syncope in Spanish." *Romance Philology* 44:137–61.

———. 1999. "Official Use of the Vernacular in the Thirteenth Century: Medieval Spanish Language Policy?" In *Advances in Hispanic Linguistics: Papers from the Second Hispanic Linguistics Symposium*, edited by Javier Gutiérrez-Rexach and Fernando Martínez-Gil, 1:152–65. Somerville, MA: Cascadilla.

Hartman, Steven Lee. 1992. "Evolución lingüística interna." In *Lexikon der Romanistischen Linguistik*, edited by Günter Holtus et al., 6:1:428–40. Tübingen: Niemeyer.

Henriksen, Nicholas C. 2008. "A Reanalysis of Paradigmatic Variation in the Old Spanish Imperfect." *Studies in Hispanic and Lusophone Linguistics* 1:287–316.

Hernández Alonso, César. 1996. "Castilla la Vieja." In *Manual de dialectología hispánica: El español de España*, edited by Manuel Alvar, 197–212. Barcelona: Ariel.

Hilty, Gerold. 2006. "La gramaticalización de las conjunciones concesivas." In *Actas del VI Congreso Internacional de Historia de la Lengua Española*, edited by José Jesús de Bustos Tovar and José Luis Girón Alconchel, 3:3047–51. Madrid: Arco.

Jiménez, Ricardo María, and Antonio Rodríguez Tovar. 2012. "Novedades académicas sobre el queísmo." *Revista Cálamo FASPE* 59:10–16.

Kasten, Lloyd, John Nitti, and Wilhelmina Jonxis-Henkemans. 1997. *The Electronic Texts and Concordances of the Prose Works of Alfonso X, El Sabio.* CD-ROM. Madison, WI: Hispanic Seminary of Medieval Studies.

Keniston, Hayward. 1937. *The Syntax of Castilian Prose: The Sixteenth Century.* Chicago: University of Chicago Press.

Kulikowski, Michael. 2004. *Latin Roman Spain and Its Cities.* Baltimore: Johns Hopkins University Press.

Labov, William. 1994. *Principles of Linguistic Change*, vol. 1, *Internal Factors.* Oxford: Blackwell.

———. 2001. *Principles of Linguistic Change*, vol. 2, *Social Factors.* Oxford: Blackwell.

Laca, Brenda. 2006. "El objeto directo: La marcación preposicional." In *Sintaxis histórica de la lengua española*, edited by Concepción Company Company, 1:423–75. Mexico City: University Nacional Autónoma de México.

Ladero Quesada, Miguel-Angel. 2004. "Baja edad media: El entorno histórico." In *Historia de la lengua española*, edited by Rafael Cano, 507–32. Barcelona: Ariel.

Lapesa, Rafael. 1981. *Historia de la lengua española.* 9th ed. Madrid: Gredos.

Lázaro Carreter, Fernando. 1949. *Las ideas lingüísticas en España durante el siglo XVIII*. Barcelona: Crítica.

Lázaro Carreter, Fernando, and Vicente Tusón. 1981. *Literatura española 2*. Madrid: Anaya.

León, Víctor. 1980. *Diccionario de argot español*. Madrid: Alianza.

Lipski, John. 1996. *El español de América*. Madrid: Cátedra.

Lleal, Coloma. 1990. *La formación de las lenguas romances peninsulares*. Barcelona: Barcanova.

Lloréns, Washington. 1968. *El habla popular de Puerto Rico*. San Juan: Academia de Artes y Ciencias.

Lloyd, Paul M. 1987. *From Latin to Spanish*, vol. 1, *Historical Phonology and Morphology of the Spanish Language*. Philadelphia: American Philosophical Society.

Lorenzo, Emilio. 1966. *El español de hoy, lengua en ebullición*. Madrid: Gredos.

Luquet, Gilles. 1988. "Sobre la desaparición del futuro de subjuntivo en la lengua hablada de principios del siglo XVI." In *Actas del I Congreso Internacional de Historia de la Lengua Española*, edited by M. Ariza et al., 1:509–14. Madrid: Arco/Libros.

Malkiel, Yakov. 1959. "Toward a Reconsideration of the Old Spanish Imperfect in *-ía* ~ *-ié*." *Hispanic Review* 26:435–81.

Marín, Diego. 1969. *La civilización española*. Chicago: Holt, Rinehart, and Winston.

Miglio, Viola. 2009. [Reseña de Pharies 2007]. *eHumanistica* 12:355–61.

Mondéjar Cumpián, José. 2002. *Castellano y español: Dos nombres para una lengua, en su marco literario, ideológico y político*. Granada: Editorial Comares.

———. 2008. "El topónimo 'Andalucía,' raíz y derivación." In *Estudios de lengua española: Homenaje al profesor José María Chamorro*, edited by José María Becerra Hiraldo and Francisco Torres Montes, 247–58. Granada: Universidad de Granada.

Moreno Fernández, Francisco. 1996. "Castilla la Nueva." In *Manual de dialectología hispánica: El español de España*, edited by Manuel Alvar, 213–32. Barcelona: Ariel.

Moyna, María Irene, and Beatriz Ceballos. 2008. "Representaciones dramáticas de una variable lingüística: Tuteo y voseo en obras de teatro del Río de la Plata (1886–1911)." *Spanish in Context* 5, no. 1: 64–88.

Narbona, Antonio, Rafael Cano, and Ramón Morillo. 2003. *El español hablado en Andalucía*. Seville: Fundación José Manuel Lara.

Nieuwenhuijsen, Dorien. 2006. "Cambios en la colocación de los pronombres átonos." In *Sintaxis histórica de la lengua española*, edited by Concepción Company Company, 2:1339–1404. Mexico City: Universidad Nacional Autónoma de México.

Noll, Volker. 2001. *Das amerikanische Spanisch: Ein regionaler und historischer Überblick*. Tübingen: Niemeyer.

Paredes, Florentino, and Pedro Sánchez-Prieto Borja. 2008. "A Methodological Approach to the History of the Sociolinguistics of the Spanish Language." *International Journal of the Sociology of Language* 193/194:21–55.

Pattison, David Graham. 1975. *Early Spanish Suffixes: A Functional Study of the Principal Nominal Suffixes of Spanish up to 1300.* Oxford: Basil Blackwell.

Penny, Ralph J. 1992. "La innovación fonológica del judeoespañol." In *Actas del II Congreso Internacional de Historia de la Lengua Española*, edited by M. Ariza et al., 2:251–57. Madrid: Pabellón de España.

———. 1993. *Gramática histórica del español.* Barcelona: Ariel.

———. 2000. *Variation and Change in Spanish.* Cambridge: Cambridge University Press.

———. 2002. *A History of the Spanish Language.* 2nd ed. Cambridge: Cambridge University Press.

———. 2004. "Evolución lingüística en la baja edad media: Evoluciones en el plano fonético." In *Historia de la lengua española*, edited by Rafael Cano, 593–612. Barcelona: Ariel.

———. 2009. "La pertinencia de la dialectología y de la sociolingüística para la historia del español: Unidad y divergencia en el romance peninsular." In *Tendencias actuales en la investigación diacrónica de la lengua*, edited by Laura Romero Aguilera and Carolina Julià Luna, 45–60. Barcelona: Universitat de Barcelona.

Pérez Galdós, Benito. 1876. *Doña Perfecta.* Madrid: Noguera.

Pharies, David. 1985. "The Etymology of Spanish *títere* 'puppet.'" *Journal of Hispanic Philology* 10:61–70.

———. 1986. *Structure and Analogy in the Playful Lexicon of Spanish.* Tübingen: Niemeyer.

———. 1990. *The Origin and Development of the Ibero-Romance -nc-/-ng- Suffixes.* Tübingen: Niemeyer.

———. 2002. *Diccionario etimológico de los sufijos españoles.* Madrid: Gredos.

———. 2007. *Breve historia de la lengua española.* 1st ed. Chicago: University of Chicago Press.

Rainer, Franz. 1993. *Spanische Wortbildungslehre.* Tübingen: Niemeyer.

Ramírez Luengo, José Luis. 2007. *Breve historia del español de América.* Madrid: Arco.

Ramsey, M. Montrose. 1902. *A Spanish Grammar with Exercises.* New York: Holt.

Ranson, Diana. 2009. [Reseña de Pharies 2007]. *La Corónica* 37:208–13.

Real Academia Española. 1973. *Esbozo de una nueva gramática de la lengua española.* Madrid: Espasa-Calpe.

———. 2001. *Diccionario de la lengua española.* 22nd ed. Madrid: Espasa-Calpe.

Real Academia Española de Ciencias Exactas, Físicas y Naturales. 1996. *Vocabulario científico y técnico.* 3rd ed. Madrid: Espasa-Calpe.

Rini, Joel. 1992. *Motives for Linguistic Change in the Formation of the Spanish Object Pronouns.* Newark, DE: Juan de la Cuesta.

———. 2010. "When *h-* Went Silent: How Do We Know?" *Bulletin of Spanish Studies* 87:431–46.

Rodríguez Molina, Javier. 2008. [Reseña de Pharies 2007]. *Revista de Filología Española* 88:227–32.

Rodríguez Prieto, Juan Pablo. 2008. "Distribución geográfica del 'jejeo' en español y propuesta de reformulación y extensión del término." *Revista española de lingüística* 38:129–44.

Rojo, Guillermo, and Alexandre Veiga. 1999. "El tiempo verbal: Los tiempos simples." In *Gramática descriptiva de la lengua española*, 3 vols., edited by Ignacio Bosque and Violeta Demonte, 3:2867–934. Madrid: Espasa Calpe.

Ruiz Gurillo, Leonor. 2010. "Interrelaciones entre gramaticalización y fraseología en español." *Revista de Filologia Española* 90:173–94.

Sáez Rivera, Daniel. 2006. "*Vuestra merced > usted*: Nuevos datos y perspectivas." In *Actas del VI Congreso Internacional de Historia de la Lengua Española*, edited by José Jesús de Bustos Tovar and José Luis Girón Alconchel, 3.2899–911. Madrid: Arco.

Sánchez-Prieto Borja, Pedro. 2004. "La normalización del castellano escrito en el siglo XIII: Los caracteres de la lengua: grafías y fonemas." In *Historia de la lengua española*, edited by Rafael Cano, 423–48. Barcelona: Ariel.

Sepúlveda Barrios, Félix. 1988. *La voz pasiva en el español del siglo XVII: Contribución a su estudio.* Madrid: Gredos.

Sihler, Andrew L. 1995. *New Comparative Grammar of Greek and Latin.* New York: Oxford University Press.

Tuten, Donald N. 2003. *Koineization in Medieval Spanish.* Berlin: Mouton de Gruyter.

Varela, Soledad, and Josefa Martín García. 1999. "La prefijación." In *Gramática descriptiva de la lengua española*, 3 vols., edited by I. Bosque and V. Demonte, 3:4993–5040. Madrid: Espasa Calpe.

Varela Cuéllar, Beatriz. 1988. "El español en los Estados Unidos." In *Actas del Primer Congreso Internacional de Historia de la Lengua Española*, edited by M. Ariza et al., 2:1575–80. Madrid: Arco/Libros.

Veiga, Alexandre. 2006. "Las formas verbales subjuntivas: Su reorganización modo-temporal." In *Sintaxis histórica de la lengua española*, edited by Concepción Company Company, 1:95–240. Mexico City: Universidad Nacional Autónoma de México.

Veltman, Calvin. 1988. *The Future of the Spanish Language in the United States.* New York: Hispanic Policy Development Project.

Wanner, Dieter. 2006. "An Analogical Solution for Spanish *soy, doy, voy,* and *estoy*." *Probus* 18:267–308.

Wright, Roger. 2010. "Romance, latín, y otra vez romance en la Península Ibérica en el siglo XII." In *Modelos latinos en la Castilla medieval*, edited by Castillo Lluch, Mónica López Izquierdo, and Marta López Izquierdo, 25–42. Madrid: Iberoamericana.

Zamora Vicente, Alonso. 1970. *Dialectología española.* 2nd ed. Madrid: Gredos.

Index of Spanish Words Cited

Subject Index

Lightning Source UK Ltd.
Milton Keynes UK
UKHW010857130520
363106UK00003B/405